OUR LOST BORDER

ESSAYS ON LIFE AMID THE NARCO-VIOLENCE

Edited by
Sarah Cortez and Sergio Troncoso

Arte Público Press
Houston, Texas

Our Lost Border: Essays on Life amid the Narco-Violence is funded in part by grants from the city of Houston through the Houston Arts Alliance.

Recovering the past, creating the future

Arte Público Press
University of Houston
4902 Gulf Fwy, Bldg 19, Rm 100
Houston, Texas 77204-2004

Cover design by Mora Des!gn

Our Lost Border : Essays on Life amid the Narco-violence / edited by Sarah Cortez and Sergio Troncoso.
    p. cm.
English and Spanish.
ISBN 978-1-55885-752-0 (alk. paper)
    1. Mexican-American Border Region—Civilization. 2. Drug traffic—Mexican-American Border Region. 3. Violent crimes—Mexican-American Border Region. I. Cortez, Sarah. II. Troncoso, Sergio, 1961–
F787.O96 2013
972'.1—dc23
                                                2012043780
                                                CIP

♾ The paper used in this publication meets the requirements of the American National Standard for Information Sciences—Permanence of Paper for Printed Library Materials, ANSI Z39.48-1984.

13 14 15 16 17 18 19 20   10 9 8 7 6 5 4 3 2 1

TABLE OF CONTENTS

THE PERSONAL STORIES

FOREWORD

It's time for the United States to wake up. This work compiled by Sarah Cortez and Sergio Troncoso is on target, it is also timely, and, if one reads carefully, it's a clarion call for the United States and for us, as Americans, to consider the danger, the economic drain and, consequently, our future as an effective nation.

It's axiomatic that the United States is blamed for producing the firearms and, thus, accepts the responsibility for the casualties south of the border. What the reader will see is the other side of the coin: Mexico too is a drug-addicted country, and for years, the previous state and national governments, up until the presidency of Felipe Calderón, have been a party to the current problems.

How? Through bribery. Where? In the highest places of state and federal governments and down to local municipalities. A shameful record of the PRI, (*Partido Revolucionario Institucional*) whose politicians, in the main, tended to line their pockets and to turn their eyes away from the crookedness that surrounded them, and in which, too often, they participated actively.

Is it any wonder, then, that the general populace held the PRI in contempt? And how did the PRI maintain its hold on the political offices? First, second and always, through bribery. In this case, then, we can also place the general populace and particularly, the middle class.

The contributors to this valuable and eye-opening anthology are serious scholars, and, in the case of the Mexican nationals who have contributed to this work, they have placed their lives and the lives of their families in danger. This statement is not a frivolous one. The number of newspaper reporters who have been murdered and mutilated is in the hundreds and the carnage continues.

The Mexican press, with very, very few exceptions, does not publish the recurring incidents of violence among the cartels themselves as well as the fate of the unlucky bystanders who are shot, maimed and murdered.

No, it isn't a pleasant book to read, but it is an enlightening one.

How can a country put up with, tolerate and, at times directly and at others indirectly, contribute to crooked behavior? Take the following: one needs something, a visa to cross into the United States, the petitioner knows he will be required and expected to pay a 'mordida', a bite, to whomever is in charge. This has been going on for years, and it has become part of the culture; so endemic is it, that jokes about the mordida produce laughter and a nod from the listener who then contributes his encounter with a civil servant or some local, regional or federal civil servant in this or that matter.

A small thing, perhaps, but it is so pervasive that it becomes an acceptable part of the culture. When one political party ruled the nation for over 70 years and established, changed and also circumvented federal laws, it did what it darned well pleased. In this case, the crookedness worked from the top down and, as it continued, from the down up, as well.

And how can this be, how can this take place? Easily: through bribery, and, if this doesn't work effectively, through violence and this is where Mexico now stands.

Freedom of the press has a nice ring to it. But what if you, as a reporter, and your family, are threatened, or, as has happened too often, murdered because of what was written and printed? You quit your profession, or, say you're the editor, you are threatened, perhaps kidnapped for a sizeable fortune. The family pays the ransom, but there is no guarantee that the victim will be released; in too many cases when the ransom has been paid, the victim may have been murdered during the negotiation.

No, it isn't a happy book. It is, however, an important one.

The contributors speak and write with authority and are taking their lives in their own hands. How can this be? The answer, again: easily.

One will also read of abandoned houses, neighborhoods and, in some cases, of abandoned towns close to the border of the United States. One's home isn't a safeguard either. Why? Because, in too many instances, the local police has fled or, also in too many instances, the police has joined the cartels or, at the least, is in their pay.

That the above is happening within the proximity of millions of U.S. citizens is a sobering thought.

The writing is on target; it's personal, and this brings an immediacy to the reader. It's the type of book that the buyer will read more than once; it's a keeper, and, thus, worth many readings.

To repeat, this isn't a jeremiad, it's a clarion call to this country, to its citizens and to the state and federal governments as well.

Rolando Hinojosa-Smith

INTRODUCTION

What lies in between can so easily be forgotten or misunderstood, and so it has been with the U.S.-Mexico border. Yet the unique experience of living on the border between two languages, cultures and countries has been a life of possibilities, surprises and adaptations. What the recent drug violence has undermined—and even destroyed—is this constant dialogue between people, as well as their creation of a borderland easily navigable by those creative and intrepid enough to live in this in-between. *Our Lost Border: Essays on Life amid the Narco-Violence* was born of a vision to bear witness to how this violence has shattered life on the border, to remember the past, but also to point to the possibilities of a better future.

From Laredo and Nuevo Laredo, to El Paso and Ciudad Juárez, to San Diego and Tijuana, the 2000 miles of the borderlands are dotted by twin cities and towns, one on the north and another on the south. What these dots on a map do not reveal, however, are the close familial, cultural, economic and even political ties that have existed between *fronterizos*, those who make the border their home. The practical adaptation of doing international business locally and the linguistic wordplay of Spanglish are examples of how the borderlands have developed a unique 'third culture,' largely unacknowledged in the diatribes emanating from faraway national capitals.

The recent bloodbath between and among drug cartels is not the first time this fascinating human interplay between the United States and Mexico has been interrupted by violence. During the Mexican Revolution, thousands of bystanders escaped to the north, while eager onlookers stared at the battlefields from rooftops in neighboring American cities. Then, as now, the border was opportunity, adventure and possibility —a place where curiosity could be satisfied. Then, as now, the border life bifurcated by violence was the price silently paid by many *fronterizos* and easily dismissed by those who never understood what it meant to live on the border.

What the reader will discover in this anthology are essays about life on the Mexican-American border before and after the recent drug violence, from remembrances of a peaceful, if uneasy coexistence, to the painful disruptions and the abandoned possibilities. The siege of entire towns, students and elders caught amid the violence, entrepreneurs forced to make painful choices, the abandonment of a cherished home or ranch—these dramas are the human toll that points not only to the past and to contemporary events, but also to what the border can be when this darkness lifts.

The essays in this anthology are divided into two sections. The first entitled "The Tortured Landscape" features four writers, Lolita Bosch, Liliana V. Blum, Diego Osorno and María Socorro Tabuenca Córdoba, who have lived in Mexico and have experienced first-hand the complicated and tragic and almost incomprehensible results of the narco-violence generated by the drug cartels. The urgency of what their essays reveal forms an essential backdrop to the second section entitled "The Personal Stories." Here are presented essays focusing on the authors' own internal and external maneuverings, or those of family and friends, as the violence has progressed. The tone varies from José Skinner's black humor to Maria Cristina Cigarroa's pensive sadness to Sergio Troncoso's reflective hope. Several of the essays by Sarah Cortez, Richard Mora and Paul Pedroza also bring the reader into a considered intimacy with the author's own history—sometimes troubled, sometimes not—with the different identities required (or allowed) on the two sides of the border.

We believe that those who wish to understand the richness of the lives that could be lived on the border—before the current drug violence—will find the varied style and content of all the essays invaluable.

We conceived of this anthology as a way not to forget what we knew from experience to be true: the border was a living experience, at once both vital and energizing, sometimes full of thorny contradictions, sometimes replete with grace-filled opportunities. What the drug violence has accomplished, temporarily we hope, is to stop the easy and vibrant interaction that was common and the bi-cultural, bi-national way of life that opened up a unique space in this world. With these words, we hope to point to a future that will be as good as the past.

Sarah Cortez and Sergio Troncoso

THE TORTURED LANDSCAPE

LA FRONTERA MÁS ANCHA

Liliana V. Blum

Vivo desde hace años en Tampico, Tamaulipas, puerto famoso por sus jaibas y en donde la clase media aspira a ir de shopping a McAllen, Texas, a sólo seis horas por carretera. Tampico, conurbado con Madero y Altamira, zona más petrolera que turística, con su mar del Golfo oscuro y frío. Aquí está mi hogar, pero yo nací en Durango, cuna del revolucionario Doroteo Arango, mejor conocido como Pancho Villa. Recuerdo a mi abuela recontar cómo el "Centauro del Norte" de niña, la sentaba en sus rodillas cuando iba a visitar a mi bisabuelo, medio hermano de Villa, según dicen. Parientes cuestionables aparte, soy mexicana del norte, mujer norteña. Siendo México un país centralista como siempre lo ha sido, aun antes de que los españoles se apropiaran del territorio, no es de extrañar que al norte, tan lejos del centro (al que se le atribuyen adjetivos como culto y civilizado) se le asocie con lo bravo: el "México bárbaro". Pareciera, pues, que la violencia, mítica e histórica, real y actual, ha acompañado al norte de México desde siempre, así como la arena y los alacranes de sus desiertos.

1

La criminalidad por la que era conocida la frontera de México con Estados Unidos se limitaba, precisamente, a la franja limítrofe entre los *vecinos distantes*. Así que, hasta hace relativamente poco, yo podía decir que soy norteña, mas no fronteriza. Sin embargo, de un tiempo a la fecha, la frontera se ha desbordado, ensanchándose cientos de kilómetros, devorándonos. Lo que nos devora no es cualquier tipo de violencia; se trata, en específico, de la generada por los narcotraficantes. Me refiero a esos cuerpos decapitados, colgados de puentes, manos cercenadas, rostros desollados, cuerpos en trozos, genitales mutilados, mensajes. Pero también a lo que yo llamo la para-narcoviolencia: esto es, las otras actividades que afectan a la gente común y corriente, como un subproducto o derivado de la primera: secuestros, violaciones, robos, balas perdidas que a veces encuentran. Lo que antes estaba contenido en ciertas ciudades famosas por sus niveles de criminalidad, como Ciudad Juárez o Tijuana, en su momento, se ha expandido a partes insospechadas (al menos para muchos ciudadanos) del territorio nacional. Ahora, por ejemplo, las muertas de Juárez se han perdido en el mar de asesinatos impunes: cada ciudad lleva su propio conteo de cadáveres, pero nada más.

Pero con todo lo brutal de la evidencia, no incurramos en el error de pensar que se trata de algo reciente. Así como la tos del fumador no es más que un síntoma visible de unos pulmones ya muy dañados, lo que vemos ahora en México es el resultado de una sociedad que se ha venido pudriendo desde hace muchos años. La indiferencia, la corrupción, la pobreza, la negligencia, la ambición, la complicidad, la omisión, tanto de las autoridades como de la sociedad en general, se ha fermentado a lo largo de varias décadas en esta composta de gases hediondos, contaminantes e inflamables que es la narcoviolencia. Lo cierto es que el narcotráfico no es un fenómeno nuevo en el país, ni las acciones en su contra, ni la violencia generada en torno suyo. Tampoco la actitud cómplice y pasiva de la población y sus gobiernos que le ha permitido al narco crecer en tan monstruosas proporciones. Ante la complicidad y la impunidad, los asesinatos y los crímenes se volvieron, si no más brutales, más descarados, más explícitos. La violencia se convirtió, también, en el lenguaje que los cárteles de droga utilizan para comunicarse con sus rivales, con la sociedad civil y con el gobierno. La diferencia es que cobijados bajo el totalitarismo de los gobiernos priistas, se comunicaban a susurros: más discretos, más socavados. Ahora, sucede, se gritan de una esquina a otra del país, de un territorio a otro, a todo pulmón. De pronto, entonces, comienzan a escuchar este diálogo terrible quienes hasta entonces habían permanecido distraídos con otros ruidos de la vida cotidiana y política del país. Pero las palabras de sangre, el lenguaje de la violencia, siempre han estado aquí.

Podemos ubicar en el tiempo a la guerra en contra de las drogas en 1971, cuando Richard Nixon declaró a las drogas el enemigo número uno de América. El violento estado actual de México y el alto consumo de drogas tanto en Estados Unidos como en México (antes un país de producción y tránsito, pero ahora también importante consumidor), así como en Europa, nos indican que la guerra ha sido un rotundo fracaso. Muchos dirán que no se trata de nuestra guerra, sino la de nuestros vecinos del norte. Pero no podemos obviar que la frontera nos une, para bien y para mal: somos gemelos siameses, compartimos órganos vitales. Es imposible delimitar el problema, cercenarlo y dejar pasar. Sobre todo, porque México produce, pero también trafica drogas desde otros países, como Colombia, para introducirlas a territorio estadounidense, donde son consumidas con avidez; sobre todo, porque de Estados Unidos entran la mayoría de las armas que los cárteles de la droga utilizan para cometer todos sus crímenes. Llamémosle guerra, llamémosle lucha, esfuerzo, problema, situación, no importa: nos concierne a los dos países y nos concierne profundamente.

No es tan sencillo como apuntar un dedo y fincar culpabilidades en terceros, lavarnos las manos y seguir como si nada: ya lo hemos hecho durante muchas décadas y ahora es imposible obviar esta realidad. No es suficiente alegar que nuestros narcos existen para abastecer las demandas de jovencitos adictos norteamericanos. Ojalá fuera tan sencillo. Hay registros de que en los años treinta, en varios lugares del país, había establecimientos donde se podía fumar opio: en la Ciudad de México, en Ciudad Juárez, en Mexicali, en Tampico y en Tijuana, por ejemplo. En la siguiente década, la zona serrana en la que confluyen Sinaloa, Durango y Chihuahua (hoy llamados el Triángulo Dorado de la Droga) comenzó a dedicarse al cultivo de la mariguana y la amapola. La reputación de esos estados como tierra de narcos comenzó desde entonces.

Mi recuerdos de niñez en Durango están espolvoreados de eventos que eran parte del contexto, pero que años después descubro con cierto asombro. La gente armada en Durango era tan natural como los alacranes, las higueras y durazneros en los jardines, como los patos del parque Guadiana, como los sombreros y las botas. Un incidente de tráfico cualquiera, un choque, o simplemente unos insultos con el claxon de un vehículo a otro podían ser suficientes para que un hombre que se bajara a amenazar al otro con una pistola. Desde entonces, la ciudad les pertenecía, pero la hegemonía de ciertos cárteles en su región le daba al país una cierta paz. Sin embargo, las armas, la violencia, y los hombres violentos con armas, ya estaban allí. Mi padre cuenta que cuando yo todavía no nacía, tuvo que ir por cuestiones de trabajo en el Instituto Tecnológico de Durango, a uno de los municipios del estado. Iban en una camioneta cerrada del instituto, mi padre y un chofer, cuando los detuvieron unos hombres armados. Sintetizo: necesitaban transporte para llevar a unos heridos a un centro de salud. Ellos accedieron: no parecían tener otra opción. Al término del servicio, mi padre y el chofer fueron pagados, en dólares, generosamente. Eran aquellos "tiempos dorados" en los que, dice la gente, los narcotraficantes tenían valores. Yo no creo que sea necesariamente verdad; más bien, sus ganancias eran tan abundantes, que podían darse el lujo de convidar, a la Pablo Escobar. Tanta riqueza salpicaba a la población que se veía beneficiada directa o indirectamente, del narcotráfico. Por eso las personas estaban más dispuestas a mirar a otro lado, a encubrir o a colaborar alegremente. Aunque no queramos admitirlo, los narcos eran y han sido parte activa y palpable de nuestras comunidades. Y solían ser tan buenos, añoran los añorantes.

Esa gente que añora tanto se refiere a los narcos que llegaban a las agencias de vehículos y en lugar de robarse las camionetas, como ahora, podían comprar las que quisieran, al contado. A los que hacían fiestas e invitaban al pueblo entero, los narcos que llenaban las urnas de las iglesias y tenían contentos a los curas. Se refieren a los que llegaban a las tiendas de agroinsumos y no regateaban precios ni pedían créditos como los agricultores: compraban en abundancia y pagaban por delante. Los que podían regalarle bicicletas a todos los niños de un pueblo. Eran también los tiempos del narco-glamour: las pistolas con piedras preciosas, las mansiones con leones a la entrada, los viajes a Las Vegas, las chicas más hermosas, los tigres como mascotas, los vehículos de lujo, las cadenas y los relojes de oro, los jets privados. Por eso muchos niños y jóvenes aspiraban a esta vida: parecía muy buena. Era, de una manera triste y retorcida, el "sueño mexicano" de muchos.

Pero vuelvo atrás, cuando algunos peces grandes comenzaron a caer. En 1983, durante la campaña de "Renovación Moral" del entonces presidente Miguel de la Madrid, es capturado Arturo "el Negro" Durazo, jefe de tránsito y policía del Distrito Federal durante el gobierno de López Portillo. Se le fincó relación con el narcotráfico: la policía y el narco trabajaban juntos. Todavía hay quien se sorprende cuando se descubre, hoy por hoy, que corporaciones enteras de policías locales en los estados y municipios, trabajan para y reciben nómina, directamente del narco. Se olvida que esto era ya una tradición bien arraigada en nuestro país. En 1989 también se arrestó a Ángel Félix Gallardo, que controlaba el negocio de la cocaína en México; eso desató una competencia sangrienta para ocupar la silla vacía. En ese mismo año, el general Jesús Gutiérrez Rebollo detuvo a Amado Carrillo Fuentes, el "Señor de los Cielos". El premio para el general fue la dirección del Instituto Nacional para el Combate de las Drogas. Sin embargo, ocho años después, con el presidente Ernesto Zedillo, Rebollo fue acusado y encontrado culpable de estar vinculado con, oh sorpresa, otra vez, el Señor de los Cielos. Tampoco olvidemos a Joaquín Guzmán Loera, el "Chapo", capturado en 1993, y quien escapó de una prisión de máxima seguridad en 2001, durante el sexenio de Vicente Fox.

La presencia del narco y su violencia no es cosa nueva, entonces, pero sí la lucha frontal en su contra, a partir del sexenio de Felipe Calderón Hinojosa. Toda la fermentación de aquellos años atrapada en un frasco, llegó a destaparse al fin y cuando se hizo, fue de manera explosiva. La aparente tranquilidad, producto de las alianzas de los gobiernos con los cárteles, llegó a su fin. Con la aprehensión de importantes líderes de varios cárteles, los grupos comenzaron a dividirse y a involucrarse en sangrientas batallas internas por ocupar los puestos de poder de cada organización. Simultáneamente, los diferentes cárteles luchaban para arrebatarle a sus rivales las "plazas" o territorios, tanto de tránsito de drogas como de su consumo.

Habrá que admitir que en los últimos sexenios México se convirtió en un gran consumidor. Ya no se trataba sólo de producir drogas y llevarlas a otros países; México es también un nada despreciable mercado. Con todo y las intrigas de palacio y la ambición de ocupar los lugares privilegiados en la cadena alimenticia del narco, el negocio florecía.

Sin embargo, a raíz de la guerra del Estado Mexicano en contra de los cárteles, el narco mexicano se ve atacado desde varios frentes. Esta guerra, entonces, es el elemento que viene a desestabilizar la aparente paz del país y la causa por la que, para muchas personas, el único culpable de todas las muertes sea el presidente en turno. Por supuesto, los narcotraficantes no reaccionaron bien a la idea de un combate en su contra: durante sexenios habían operado con total libertad e impunidad. Habían pactado con los políticos, pagaban puntualmente su nómina a los policías, tenían bien comprados a los jueces. Y de pronto, esta guerra inesperada: tenían sus razones para no estar contentos. Por una parte, los numerosos y sistemáticos decomisos de drogas y dinero en efectivo han mermado considerablemente sus ingresos. Por otra, como dije antes, sostienen una lucha constante en contra de los otros cárteles y, al mismo tiempo, contra el gobierno federal. Una guerra con dos frentes simultáneos, ya se sabe, supone costos extraordinarios. Y eso supone también medidas extraordinarias para hacerse de los fondos. Los narcos han tenido que recortar sus gastos: la vida ostentosa tendría que ponerse en pausa para los grandes capos. Las camionetas lujosas ahora habría que robarlas, ya no comprarlas. Las pérdidas millonarias generadas por las drogas o el dinero decomisado habrían que reponerse de alguna forma. Han sido muy considerables. Baste consultar la página de la SEDENA (Secretaría de Defensa Nacional) para ver detalladamente la lista de todos los decomisos desde el inicio de la guerra contra las drogas. Ante tales circunstancias, los narcotraficantes se volvieron en contra de la sociedad, indefensa y vulnerable, y hasta hace tan poco, tan condescendiente o al menos, desinteresada.

Entonces llegaron los secuestros, los asesinatos de los secuestrados, los asaltos. Los secuestros que se manejan siempre por debajo del agua (es sabido que las autoridades locales colaboran directamente con los secuestradores). Por eso cuando las víctimas son asesinadas a pesar del pago de los rescates, no hay forma de enterarse, a menos que sea alguien cercano a uno. En Tampico, dos ex alcaldes, empresarios conocidos del puerto, fueron secuestrados y liberados con vida. La gente rica, temerosa y aterrorizada, comenzó a emigrar a Texas y desde allá controla sus negocios y sus ranchos. Todo esto ha sucedido dentro un contenido silencio social, entre murmullos, rumores. Sin embargo, no es hasta que se encuentran las fosas de San Fernando, por ejemplo, que las cosas empiezan a saltar a la vista de forma casi pornográfica: porque en las fosas no sólo hay migrantes centroamericanos, sino también gente de Tampico previamente secuestrada y por quien ya se habían pagado rescates. El ejército libera cotidianamente casas de "seguridad" donde decenas de personas están privadas de su libertad, en espera de que sus familiares paguen, sin saber que igual irán a parar a las fosas clandestinas. A un par de cuadras de mi casa, la Policía Federal capturó a una mujer perteneciente a la organización de los Zetas: era nada menos que la encargada de cobrar a los migrantes centroamericanos su "paso" por el estado de Tamaulipas. En otras palabras, era quien decidía la vida o la muerte de los migrantes, al más puro estilo de los nazis a la llegada de los trenes. Los asesinos, los monstruos, los torturadores, son nuestros vecinos. Aquí en nuestro Tampico.

Soy reiterativa en especificar mi ciudad porque, aunque se pueden hacer ciertas generalizaciones sobre la narcoviolencia, cada ciudad tiene sus peculiaridades que la vuelven única.

Mucho se ha escrito sobre este fenómeno de manera periodista, académica y presuntuosamente, sobre todo, desde lugares donde la violencia es equivalente a la del Medio Oriente y se mira lejana. Los capitalinos que desde sus televisiones ven las noticias, van al Zócalo a marchar y a exigir la "desmilitarización" del país y describen sin conocerla una realidad más acorde a la de la dictadura militar Argentina, que nada tiene que ver con lo que vive el norte. Se habla con ignorancia, con cientos de kilómetros de por medio y con la seguridad que da el no vivir acá. Porque es imposible entender esta realidad si no es, literalmente, a través de los sentidos. Es demasiado fácil juzgar desde lejos, y confundir a veces los odios partidistas y, tristemente, prostituirlos, usando a los muertos de esta violencia como carne de cañón en contra del enemigo político. Hay quien le atribuye cada uno de estos más de cuarenta mil muertos directamente al presidente. Los narcotraficantes, los sicarios, los verdaderos asesinos, no podrían estar más contentos con la ayuda mediática que les regalan los detractores del régimen. Sobre todo los que están muy lejos de estas balas y no tienen que tirarse al piso, cotidianamente, para evitarlas.

Tampico, junto con todo el estado de Tamaulipas, es el campo de batalla de dos cárteles principalmente. Como en una mala telenovela, se trata de una madre e hija que terminan odiándose. En una esquina tenemos al Cártel del Golfo y en otra, a Los Zetas. El primero dio a luz al segundo. A grandes rasgos y sin reparar en los numerosos nombres de hombres que murieron en pos del cetro, la historia va más o menos así. El Cártel del Golfo fue fundado como una banda criminal que hacía contrabando con whisky, durante su prohibición; lo introducían a los Estados Unidos a través de Matamoros. En los años setenta, bajo el mando de Juan Nepomuceno Guerra, esta organización logró infiltrarse en la política nacional: tuvo absoluto control de jefes de policía, directores de penales, y un estrecho y provechoso vínculo (para ambas partes) con políticos de Tamaulipas, principalmente. En los años noventa, tras asesinatos e intrigas internas del cártel, Juan García Ábrego asumió el mando hasta 1996. A su caída se desató una lucha por el poder del cártel y, varios asesinatos de aspirantes después, Osiel Cárdenas Guillén terminó como el líder del Cártel del Golfo.

Fue precisamente Osiel Cárdenas, en 1999, quien comenzó a reclutar al grupo de ex militares conocidos como Los Zetas, para que fueran su brazo armado. Estos militares habían desertado del Grupo Aeromóvil de Fuerzas Especiales y del Grupo Anfibio de Fuerzas Especiales, ambos del Ejército Mexicano y fundados en 1994 con motivo del levantamiento zapatista en Chiapas. Estaban entrenados por expertos de Estados Unidos, Francia e Israel en manejo de armas sofisticadas y contrainsurgencia. En 2003, Osiel Cárdenas Guillén fue detenido, pero desde el penal de máxima seguridad de la Palma, ubicado en Almoloya, continuaba ejerciendo su actividad como cabeza del cártel. El 7 de marzo de 2005, el gobierno mexicano concedió a Estados Unidos la extradición de Osiel Cárdenas, pero el proceso tomó un par de años luego de los procesos que Cárdenas Guillén debía enfrentar en México; tras agotar todas las instancias posibles de amparo, finalmente fue extraditado el 19 de enero de 2007.

Con la ausencia de Osiel Cárdenas, las traiciones no se hicieron esperar. Los Zetas dejaron de ser el grupo armado del Cártel del Golfo y pactaron con los hermanos Beltrán Leyva, quienes a su vez habían traicionado al Cártel de Sinaloa, comandado por Ismael "el Mayo" Zambada y Joaquín Guzmán Loera, "el Chapo". La guerra librada entre el Cártel del Golfo y el Cártel de Sinaloa ha llenado de sangre principalmente las calles de Reynosa y Nuevo Laredo, en Tamaulipas, entre otras ciudades de México. Se dice que en Reynosa el Cártel del

Golfo se ha aliado con La Familia para poder combatir así al grupo disidente de Los Zetas, que son apoyados por los Hermanos Beltrán Leyva y comandados por Heriberto Lazcano Lazcano, alias "el Lazca", uno de los hombres más buscados hoy en día. Resulta imposible mantenerse al día de las cabecillas de cada cártel, sus nuevas alianzas, traiciones, además de los nuevos cárteles que surgen a partir de la fractura de otros, como astillas. El mapa cambia cada día, pero la reseña anterior nos ubica temporalmente, al menos, en el Tampico que vivimos hoy.

Tampico, puerto, es clave para el ingreso de cocaína desde Colombia y tránsito para los Estados Unidos. También es uno de los tantos lugares a recorrer para los migrantes centroamericanos antes de llegar a la frontera México-norteamericana e intentar cruzarla. En el mundo de los narcotraficantes, sicarios y delincuentes sádicos y oportunistas, esto es una mina de oro. A mí me tocó ver llegar la violencia así como una ola grande se ve llegar a lo lejos: anunciada, presentida. Después cayó con fuerza sobre la ciudad, haciendo todos los destrozos posibles, y al parecer, ahora, comienza a retirarse poco a poco, paulatinamente. Eso no quiere decir que no vuelva a llegar, pero al menos, la curva de la violencia ha sido una campana. A pesar de que en otros estados la violencia se ha recrudecido (Nuevo León y Guerrero, por ejemplo), donde a veces se suman hasta cuarenta o cincuenta muertos por día, en Tamaulipas se han tomado ciertas medidas que al parecer han tenido resultados. Es aquí donde entra mi historia, la que me ha tocado vivir todos estos días.

Recuerdo que hace dos años, casi tres, poco antes de las vacaciones de Semana Santa, estando en una fiesta infantil escuché a otras madres decir que la violencia del narco había llegado al fin a nuestra ciudad. Una aseguró que en la avenida principal se había colgado una manta en la que los narcos prevenían a la población de que el siguiente viernes (justo el previo a las vacaciones) se efectuaría "una balacera", por lo que pedían a todos resguardarse en sus casas. Yo jamás la vi, argumenté, pero eso no importaba para ellas: un primo, un amigo, un pariente, alguien la había visto; ergo, tenía que ser verdad. A pesar de que yo decía que anunciar con tiempo y por escrito un ataque contra los enemigos era completamente estúpido como táctica de guerra, que el día que sucediera nos íbamos a enterar sin aviso alguno, aquellas madres estaban completamente convencidas. Es muy sospechoso, además, dije, que sea justamente en viernes, un día antes de las vacaciones. Fuera de unas miradas fulminantes, mi comentario no recibió respuesta alguna. Cuando llegó el esperado viernes, la escuela de mis hijos estaba para todos fines prácticos, vacía. Más de ¾ del salón, según me contaba mi hijo, no habían asistido ese día, o bien, sus padres habían ido a recogerlos mucho antes de la hora de salida. En la tarde, la mayoría de los comercios estaban cerrados, incluso las franquicias, las grandes cadenas. Los rumores y la paranoia llegaron a todos los tampiqueños, causando grandes pérdidas a la actividad económica de la ciudad. La tan anunciada "balacera", por supuesto, no llegó. Comenzaron las vacaciones y por un par de semanas, las buenas conciencias y los padres de familia se olvidaron del peligro del narco y las playas tampiqueñas se abarrotaron como siempre.

A riesgo de sonar como profeta de las malas noticias, cuando comenzaron los verdaderos enfrentamientos armados, los narcos no tuvieron la decencia de anunciarlos con tiempo a la ciudadanía de Tampico. Uno de los primeros incidentes fue que unos sicarios fueron a tirar una granada a un cuartel militar: una provocación nada inteligente, por supuesto. Los narcos fueron alcanzados y abatidos por los soldados, tras una persecución. Después vinieron tiroteos en los "table-dance", en bares y centros nocturnos, casas incendiadas, balaceras a lo largo de varias calles que siempre culminaban en muertos y sangre. También se secuestraban criminales o miembros del cártel rival y aparecían torturados, mutilados y asesinados en frente de sus propias casas. Taxistas que trabajaban para el narco vendiendo drogas o de "halcones", espiando y avisándoles de las actividades del ejército y la policía federal, comenzaron además a asaltar a sus clientes, a violar mujeres, y a desechar los cuerpos en cualquier lugar. Se popularizaron los narco mensajes, en mantas o cartulinas, que explicaban ciertas muertes o amenazaban a grupos o personas en particular. Iniciaron los secuestros de gente de todo nivel económico y con ello, el éxodo de la gente rica fuera del país. Después nos dimos cuenta de lo que los grupos de derechos humanos venían diciendo desde hace tiempo: que a los migrantes centroamericanos los secuestraban y los extorsionaban: nos enteramos porque muchos de sus cuerpos fueron encontrados en fosas. Y eso sería la punta del iceberg, porque las fosas siguen apareciendo en varias partes del país, sistemáticamente.

Esta vez, el peligro era verdadero y no anunciado. De los cientos de incidentes, unos cuatro o cinco, quizá por su notoriedad, alcanzaban a llegar a los medios nacionales. El resto era para nuestro propio horror, nuestro propio secreto. Una amiga que trabajaba para un diario local en ese entonces, me explicó que todos los jefes de los periódicos estaban amenazados por el narco: nadie podía reportar nada. Lo único que les permitían era reproducir las declaraciones oficiales que llegaba hacer la policía o el ejército, pero nada más. O bien, muchas veces, los diarios estaban obligados a publicar las notas que los sicarios redactaban ellos mismos, con sus propias y favorecedoras versiones de los hechos. En otras palabras, sólo nosotros sabíamos lo que sucedía: para el resto del país, para los capitalinos, apenas unas cuantas cosas trascendían y llegaban hasta su conocimiento.

Algo que siempre trasciende y además vende muchos diarios, es el magnicidio. El 28 de junio de 2010, a una semana de las elecciones estatales por gobernador, el candidato del PRI, Rodolfo Torre Cantú, virtual ganador aún antes de la votación, en un estado gobernado desde siempre por el PRI y en donde todos los recursos del gobierno se usan para ganar, fue asesinado junto con sus guardaespaldas y varios colaboradores, dos diputados entre otros. Estaba cerrando su campaña e iba camino al aeropuerto de Ciudad Victoria, la capital. Apenas hace dos semanas yo había sido invitada por el ayuntamiento de Tampico a una comida del candidato con los artistas, maestros y otros sectores. Nos saludamos de mano, nos hicimos la foto juntos. Me acuerdo de su cara, de su bigote: fue difícil comprender cómo alguien así, con el poder absoluto de un gobernador electo, para todos fines prácticos, del partido más poderoso del país, con gente que estaba allí para protegerlo, era tan vulnerable como el resto de los ciudadanos. Con ese golpe, los cárteles dejaron claro quién mandaba en Tamaulipas. Si los políticos siempre negociaban con los narcos para obtener beneficios mutuos, algo quedaba claro ahora: alguien muy poderoso estaba sintiéndose incómodo y mandaba un mensaje para el gobernador saliente, el candidato muerto, o el partido en general. En el proceso, la población estaba a merced de todo, desvalida. Ese día lloré por Rodolfo Torre Cantú, no por el priista que era y el hombre poderoso que pudo haber sido, tan igual a otros tantos, sino por lo que su muerte simbolizaba para todos los demás.

Después de eso la violencia se volvió más cotidiana, más cercana y más personal. Las balaceras comenzaron a ser tan frecuentes, que prácticamente a cualquier tampiqueño ya le había tocado una. Todos teníamos historias que relatar. Por el puente por el que tengo que cruzar todos los días para ir a casa, un día amanecieron cuatro personas colgadas. Eran tres hombres y una chica de catorce años. Una noche cuando cenábamos con mi hija pequeña en un puesto de tacos, comenzamos a escuchar el ruido de las balas, algo que sonaba como palomitas en el horno microondas, acercándose cada vez más. Todos los comensales corrimos a refugiarnos: estuvimos allí hasta que ya no escuchamos nada. No perdí la compostura, ahora pienso, porque allí estaba mi hija y su mirada de terror. Por dentro, sólo sentí las vísceras hechas un nudo, el miedo más primitivo que recorre el cuerpo. Semanas después, saliendo de un evento en la escuela de mis hijos, casi a las diez de la mañana, al dar vuelta por una calle me encontré con que no podíamos avanzar: a unos treinta metros de mí había dos vehículos chocados, varios cuerpos, unos asomados por las ventanas, otros desparramados por el suelo, y un gran charco de sangre. Un convoy de soldados apuntaba a los muertos, tal vez esperando un ataque, pero después de un rato, se fueron de allí. Era una persecución entre grupos delictivos que culminó en aquella matanza; los soldados habían sido avisados, pero cuando llegaron al lugar de los hechos, los vivos ya habían huido. Poco después llegaron unos taxis a llevarse los cuerpos: ¿trofeo de guerra o para darles sepultura? Quién sabe. Quedaron los vehículos, la sangre, los vidrios, nuestro terror y el tráfico vehicular. Unas horas después, cuando pasé para recoger a los niños de la escuela, sólo estaba la sangre. Era imposible evitarla: las llantas de mi carro pasaron por arriba de aquel líquido pegajoso.

Yo no sé si el secuestro de varios estudiantes de una conocida universidad privada haya tenido que ver con las medidas que se aplicaron poco después en Tamaulipas, pero coincide en el tiempo. Se tuvo noticia de que varios estudiantes fueron secuestrados y a sus familias se les pidió dinero por ellos. Al parecer, uno de los chicos era hijo de alguien importante, porque vino la policía federal a resolver el asunto. Resultó al final que los jóvenes habían sido secuestrados por elementos de la policía local, quienes usaban las mismas instalaciones de la policía para realizar este tipo de ilícitos. Era lo más común, por supuesto, para un cuerpo de policías que trabajaba directamente para el narco. Sin embargo, poco después de este incidente, llegaron nuevos elementos del Ejército y la Marina a reforzar la seguridad del estado. En Tampico, en específico, se desarmó a la policía local y se comenzó a investigar a los agentes, así como a sus armas, para ver si estaban involucradas en asesinatos perpetrados por el crimen organizado. Al tiempo, se les aplicaron a los agentes exámenes de confianza, antidoping, etc. Mientras duraba el proceso, el Ejército tomó su lugar: vestidos como policías y en los vehículos de los mismos, los soldados comenzaron a realizar funciones policíacas.

Desde el centro el país la gente común, pero sobre todo los "intelectuales" y gente de izquierda, quienes desde siempre cuestionaron la legitimidad del actual presidente, clamaban por la desmilitarización del país. Aseguraban, sin pruebas, que el Ejército se dedicaba a masacrar a la población civil: un escenario más o menos como el de Assad en Siria, hoy por hoy. Si bien ha habido caso de abusos del Ejército, lo cierto es que para quienes vivimos acá, la supuesta militarización fue un gran alivio. Después de todo, quienes liberaban a los secuestrados, eran los soldados y los marinos. Además, con ellos haciendo el papel de policía, la criminalidad en sí bajó en toda la ciudad. Primero, porque los delincuentes comunes temían enfrentarse a los hombres entrenados del Ejército; segundo, porque los mismos policías corruptos cometían gran parte de los ilícitos y ahora estaban cesados. De esta manera, la calma regresó poco a poco a la ciudad. Si bien el problema del narcotráfico persiste, los sicarios han tenido que ser más discretos al hacer su trabajo. Ya no pueden andar por la ciudad en sus camionetas, las armas por fuera, en sus convoyes, con la impunidad con la que antes lo hacían, con la protección y complicidad de las mismas autoridades locales.

Mientras en otros estados y ciudades de México la violencia sigue incrementando, acá la vida ha vuelto casi totalmente a la normalidad. Tanto, que a muchos se nos comienza a olvidar. Si bien la presencia militar no es la solución ideal, quienes la critican no tienen una propuesta mejor. Está claro que será imposible "arreglar" un problema que lleva gestándose y creciendo más de ochenta años y en el que todos hemos sido cómplices de una u otra manera. Porque mientras no se vieron afectados directamente, o mientras pudieron beneficiarse, muchos ciudadanos, en puestos políticos o no, dejaron que los narcotraficantes llegaran a un poder desmesurado, casi comparable al del Estado Mexicano, y peor, pues en muchos casos, eran uno con el gobierno. No se vislumbra una solución sencilla o rápida; no se trata de disposición al diálogo. Cuando uno mira el cinismo, el carisma y la crueldad de algunos de los capos capturados, así como la pleitesía que los medios les rinden y la admiración que generan en parte de la población, uno se pregunta hasta donde ha llegado la metástasis de la corrupción. Al mirar a los jóvenes europeos y norteamericanos disfrutar de sus drogas sin culpa, al mirar a algunos intelectuales mexicanos acusar de asesino al presidente mientras consumen drogas sin sentir que contribuyen de alguna manera al problema, me llega un profundo desaliento.

De momento sólo puedo decir, que me alegra tener menos miedo cada vez que tengo que salir a la calle. Que prefiero pasar junto a un convoy de la Marina, que a uno de los Zetas. Me gusta escuchar a la gente común quejarse solamente del calor y de los altos precios del aguacate, que de los muertos en un tiroteo entre narcos. No diré que estamos mejor, pero puedo decir que hemos llegado a estar mucho peor. Acá, a seis horas de Estados Unidos, en la frontera más ancha del mundo.

THE WIDEST OF BORDERS

Liliana V. Blum
Translated by Nicolás Kanellos

I have lived for years in Tampico, Tamaulipas, a port famous for its crab and also famous as the jumping off location for middle-class shopping excursions to McAllen, Texas, just a six-hour ride up the highway. Tampico, the sister city to Madero and Altamira, is more of an oil-zone than a tourist destination, with Gulf waters that are black and cold. This is my home, although I was born in Durango, birthplace of Doroteo Arango, the revolutionary better known as Pancho Villa. I remember my grandmother telling me how the "Centaur of the North" would visit her father, his half-brother, or so they said. As a relative of Villa (or not), I am a northern Mexican, a *norteña*. Because Mexico is a centralized nation, as it has always been, even before the Spanish appropriated the territory, it should not be surprising that the North, so far from the Center (which is always characterized as cultured and civilized), is thought to be barbarous. It's as if the violence, mythic and historic, real and present, has always been a part of northern Mexico, just like the sand and scorpions in its deserts.

The criminality with which the Mexican-U.S. border is historically associated didn't extend beyond the limits of the immediate border region of the two distant neighbors. Thus, until relatively recently, I could say that I am a *norteña* but not a *fronteriza*, a border-dweller. Nevertheless, more recently, the border has exceeded its limits, expanding by hundreds of kilometers, devouring us. What devours us is not just any kind of violence; it's specifically the violence generated by the drug traffickers. I'm referring to decapitated bodies hanging from bridges, severed hands, disfigured faces, dismembered bodies, mutilated genitals—all messages. But also what I call the para-drug violence, which are the other activities that affect the common person as a derivative of the main violence: the kidnappings, the robberies, the stray bullets that sometimes find their mark. What was once confined to certain cities, infamous for crime, such as Juárez or Tijuana, has now expanded to areas of the nation that many thought were exempt. Now, for example, the dead women of Juárez have disappeared in a sea of unpunished assassinations; each city maintains its own account of cadavers, nothing more.

But despite all of the brutal evidence, let's not err by thinking that this is something recent. Just like the smoker's cough is nothing more than an audible symptom of damaged lungs, what we see now in Mexico is the result of a society that has been rotting for many years. Indifference, corruption, poverty, negligence, ambition, complicity, omission, as much by the authorities as by society in general, have been fermenting for decades in the compost heap of putrid, polluting and inflammable gases that is narco-violence. What's certain is that drug trafficking is not new in this country, nor are the actions to stem it, nor the violence generated around it. Neither is the complicit and passive attitude of the populace and its governments that have permitted narcotics to grow into such monstrous proportions. Given the complicity and impunity, assassinations and crime have returned, if not with greater brutality, then certainly with more boldness. Violence also became the language that the drug cartels employ to communicate with their rivals, with civil society and the government. The difference is that when they were protected under the totalitarianism of the PRI regimes, the cartels communicated in whispers, more discreetly, more hushed. Now, it seems, they scream at each other from one corner of the country to the other, from territory to territory, at the top of their lungs. Suddenly, those who had been distracted by other rumblings of daily life and politics have begun to listen to this terrible dialogue. But those bloody words, the language of violence, have always been with us.

We can trace the war on drugs to 1971, when Richard Nixon declared that drugs were America's number one enemy. The present violent status of Mexico and the high consumption of drugs in the United States, as well as in Mexico (once a country of production and transport but now also an important consumer of drugs) and Europe, indicate the war has been a complete failure. Many would say that it is not our war but that of our neighbors to the north. But we cannot ignore that the common border unites us, for better or for worse: we are Siamese twins, we share vital organs. It is impossible to underestimate, undercut or ignore the problem, especially since Mexico produces but also traffics in drugs from other countries, such as Colombia, to introduce them into U.S. territory, where they are enthusiastically consumed, especially since it is the United States that produces the majority of the weapons used by the cartels to commit all of its crimes. Call it war, call it struggle, effort, problem, situation, whatever; it is of concern to both countries and it concerns us deeply.

It's not as easy as pointing a finger to blame third parties, washing our hands and going on as before. We've already done that for many decades and now it's impossible to hide from reality. It's not enough to allege that our narcos exist only to supply the demand of young North American addicts. If only it were so simple. There's evidence that in the 1930s, in various Mexican cities, such as the capital city, Juárez, Mexicali, Tampico and Tijuana, there were establishments where opium could be smoked. In the following decade, in the peaceful region made up of Sinaloa, Durango and Chihuahua (today called the Golden Triangle of Drugs), marijuana and poppies were grown. The reputation of those states as the land of narcos began then.

My dusty childhood memories recall some of the context, but years later I am astonished that armed men in Durango were as common as the scorpions, fig trees and plums in our gardens, as the ducks in Guadiana Park, as cowboy hats and boots. A simple traffic incident, a fender bender or just some insult uttered by a car horn would be enough to cause a man to get out of his vehicle and threaten someone with a pistol. The city has belonged to them since then, but the hegemony over specific regions by certain cartels imposed a kind of peace. Nevertheless, arms, violence and violent men with arms were already a reality there. My father recalls that before I was born, he had to travel for work to the Technical Institute of Durango, one of the seats of state government. The driver and my father were traveling in a panel truck owned by the Institute when they were stopped by some armed men. In brief, they needed a vehicle to take some wounded men to a clinic. My father and the driver agreed—they didn't have any other choice. After serving them thusly, my father and the driver were paid generously in dollars. Those were the "golden days," so people say, when the drug traffickers had values. I don't think that's necessarily true; rather, their profits were so great that they had the luxury of sharing, a lá Pablo Escobar. So much wealth splashed onto the population that it was seen as benefiting, directly or indirectly, from the drug trafficking. That's why people were so disposed to blissfully ignore, cover up or cooperate. We may not want to admit it, but the narcos were and have been an active and palpable part of our communities. And they were "so good" . . . some people say with nostalgia.

Those people who are so nostalgic are referring to the narcos who would buy vehicles with cash from the dealerships instead of robbing them, as they do now. The narcos who would throw parties for the whole town, or who filled the collection plates at church and kept the priests happy, or went to the agricultural supply and bought without negotiating the price nor applying for credit like farmers do. They purchased everything in quantity and paid up front, or those who bought bicycles for all the town's children. It was the era of narco-glamor: pistols incrusted with precious stones, mansions with stone lions at the entry, trips to Las Vegas, the prettiest women, tigers for pets, luxury vehicles, gold watches and gold chains, private jets. That's why so many children and teens aspired to that life; it looked really good. It was, in a sad and twisted way, the "Mexican dream" of many.

But let me go back to when some big fish began to be caught. In 1983 during the "Moral Renewal" campaign of then-President Miguel de la Madrid, "El Negro Durazo" was captured, Mexico City's Chief of Police and Traffic in López Portillo's government. He was affiliated with the drug traffickers; the police and the traffickers were working together. People are still surprised today when entire local and state police forces are revealed to work for and are hired by the narcos. It's now well-known that this was already a well-grounded tradition in our country. In 1989, Ángel Félix Gallardo, who controlled the cocaine business in Mexico, was arrested and that unleashed a bloody competition to see who would take his place. That same year, General Jesús Gutiérrez Rebollo arrested Amado Carrillo Fuentes, "Lord of the Skies." The general's reward was being named director of the National Institute to Combat Drugs. But, just eight years later under President Ernesto Zedillo, Rebollo was accused and found guilty of reporting to (great surprise) the Lord of the Skies. And let's not forget Joaquín Guzmán Loera, el "Chapo" (Shorty), captured in 1993, and who escaped from a maximum security prison in 2001 during the presidency of Vicente Fox.

The gifts of the narcos and their violence is nothing new. But the direct struggle against them is, starting with the presidency of Felipe Calderón Hinojosa. Everything that had been fermenting all those years was bottled up, and it exploded when it was finally uncorked. The apparent calm that had been maintained through the partnership of the government with the cartels ended. With the arrest of important leaders of various cartels, the cartels began fragmenting and engaged in bloody internal battles for the leadership of each cartel. At the same time, the cartels began fighting with each other over territories for trafficking, as well as for sales of drugs.

I have to admit that during the last presidencies, Mexico became a leading consumer of drugs. It was no longer just a producer of drugs to be sold in other countries, but also an important market. With all the palace intrigues and the competition for assuming the key links in the narco-chain, business flourished.

Because of the Mexican war on the drug cartels, the narcos were attacked on various fronts. This war, nevertheless, caused the destabilization of the country and, according to many observers, the blaming of the various presidents for all of the deaths that occurred. Of course, the drug traffickers did not react well to the launching of a war against them. During many Mexican presidencies, they had operated freely and with impunity. They had conspired with the politicians, paid off the police and the judges. Suddenly, here was an unforeseen war; of course, they weren't happy. On the one hand, the numerous and systematic seizures of drugs and cash ate into their earnings. On the other, as I stated above, they faced a battle among the cartels and, at the same time, against the federal government. It was a war on two fronts at once, which was extraordinarily costly to maintain, and that presupposed extraordinary measures for raising funds. The narcos have had to reduce their expenses; the ostentatious lifestyle of the capos had to be put on pause. Luxury SUVs now had to be stolen instead of purchased. The millions lost to the seizures of drugs and cash had to be replaced, one way or another. The losses were considerable; just read the SEDENA (National Defense Secretariat) web page and you'll see a detailed list of all the seizures since the war began. Faced with these circumstances, the drug traffickers lashed out against the vulnerable and defenseless in society and, until recently, against the condescending or, at least, uninterested.

Next came the assaults, kidnappings and assassinations of the kidnapped. It's an open secret that the authorities collaborate directly with the kidnappers. That's why, when the victims are killed despite their ransoms being paid, there is no way to find out who's responsible, unless someone is close to the case. In Tampico, two ex-mayors, who were business owners at the port, were kidnapped and then freed. Rich people, afraid and terrorized, began immigrating to Texas and administered their businesses and ranches from there. All of this has taken place within the context of community silence, with only whispered rumors. Nevertheless, it was not until the unmarked graves were found in San Fernando, for example, that things were brought into the light of day—almost pornographically—because the graves were not only filled with Central American trans-migrants but also with people previously kidnapped in Tampico for whom no ransom had been paid. Almost every day, the army liberates "safe houses" in which dozens of people are held captive as they wait for families to raise their ransom, without knowing if they too will end up in hidden graves. A couple of blocks from my house, the federal police captured a female member of the Zetas. She was the woman assigned to charge the Central American trans-migrants for their passage through the state of Tamaulipas. In other words, she was the one who decided on the life or death of the migrants, reminiscent of Nazis awaiting the death trains. Assassins, monsters, torturers are our neighbors. Right here in Tampico.

I repeat the name of my city because, although one can make certain generalizations about narco-violence, each city has its idiosyncrasies that make it unique. Much has been written about this phenomenon in the newspapers, especially in those places where the violence is seen as equivalent to that in the Middle East, and thought of as "far away." Television viewers in the capital see the news, march on the Zocalo and demand the demilitarization of the country, comparing the campaign against drugs without experience to the Argentine military dictatorship, which has nothing to do with what the North is experiencing. They speak out of ignorance, from a distance of hundreds of kilometers and from the security that comes from not living here. It is impossible to understand our reality without first-hand experience. It's very easy to judge from a distance and confuse political party rivalries and, sadly, prostitute them by exploiting those who died from this violence as cannon fodder for party politics. There are those who blame the president for the more than forty thousand deaths. The narcos, the criminals, the real assassins couldn't be happier at the news created by the enemies of the regime, especially those who live so far from the bullets and who don't have to throw themselves to the ground every day to avoid them.

Tampico, as well as the entire state of Tamaulipas, is the battleground for the main cartels. Like scenes from a bad soap opera, it's about a mother and daughter who wind up hating each other. In one corner, we have the Gulf Cartel and in the other, the Zetas. In brief and without naming all the individuals who have died by the sword, the history goes more or less like this. The Gulf Cartel started as a gang of criminals that smuggled whiskey through Matamoros during Prohibition in the United States. In the seventies, under the leadership of Juan Nepomuceno Guerra, the organization successfully infiltrated national politics; it developed absolute control over police chiefs and prison wardens, and achieved a mutually beneficial arrangement with the politicos in Tamaulipas. In the nineties, after internal conflicts and assassinations in the cartel, Juan García Ábrego took over in 1996. When he fell, a fight broke out for control of the cartel, a number of pretenders to the throne were assassinated until Osiel Cárdenas Guillén became the Gulf Cartel boss.

It was precisely Osiel Cárdenas, in 1999, who began recruiting military veterans known as the Zetas to form his armed force. These veterans were deserters from the Air Special Forces and the Amphibious Special Forces of the Mexican army, which were founded in 1994 to deal with the Zapatista revolt in Chiapas. They had been trained by experts from the United States, France and Israel in the use of sophisticated weapons and counter-insurgency. In 2003, Osiel Cárdenas Guillén was arrested, but from the maximum security prison of

La Palma, located in Almoloya, he continued directing the activities of his cartel. On March 7, 2005, the Mexican government approved his extradition to the United States, but this did not happen until his trials in Mexico had taken place; after expending all possible resources to free himself, Guillén was extradited on January 19, 2007.

With Osiel Cárdenas gone, soon there were defections. The Zetas left the Gulf Cartel and allied themselves with the Beltrán Leyva brothers, who had betrayed the Sinaloa Cartel, led by Ismael "El Mayo" (Mr. May) Zambada y Joaquín Guzmán Loera, "El Chapo" (Shorty). The war that ensued between the Gulf and Sinaloa cartels flooded the streets with blood in Reynosa and Nuevo Laredo, in Tamaulipas, among other Mexican cities. In Reynosa, it's said that the Gulf Cartel has become an ally of La Familia (The Family) in order to combat the Zeta dissidents, who are supported by the Beltrán Leyva brothers and are led by Heriberto Lazcano Lazcano, alias "El Lazca," one of today's most wanted criminals. It's really impossible to keep abreast of the names of the leaders of each cartel, given new alliances and betrayals, not to mention the appearance of new cartels splintering off from the others. The map changes each day; however, the above summary serves for now, at least in Tampico where I live.The port of Tampico is a key to the importation of Colombian cocaine and its transport to the United States. It is also one of many places crossed by Central American trans-migrants, heading north to cross the U.S.-Mexican border. In the world of the drug traffickers, mobsters and sadistic criminals and opportunists, all of this is a gold mine. I personally felt the rumbling of, and then witnessed, the arrival of violence like an ocean wave from afar. It fell upon the city with force, wrecking everything in its way and, apparently, is beginning to recede little by little, slowly. This doesn't mean that it won't return, but at least the bell curve is on the descent, even as the violence in other states has worsened (in Nuevo León and Guerrero, for example), where, at times, forty or fifty deaths are counted per day. In Tamaulipas, certain measures appear to have had some success. This is where my personal story begins, the story of my life during these days.

I remember that two or three years ago, a little before the Easter holidays, while I was at a children's party, I heard some mothers say that the narco-violence had finally arrived in our city. One woman assured the others that on the city's main thoroughfare the narcos had hung a banner warning the citizens that the following Friday (the day our vacation was to begin), bullets would be flying and everyone should stay in the safety of their homes. I hadn't seen it, I argued, but they didn't pay any attention to me. A cousin, a friend, someone had seen it; therefore, it had to be true. Despite my reasoning that announcing in writing such an attack against enemies ahead of time would be a stupid tactic and that it was more likely to happen without any warning, those mothers were totally convinced. It was very suspicious, I also said, that it would happen on Friday, on the eve of vacation. Aside from some hateful glares, my comments did not merit any response. On that Friday, for all intents and purposes, my children's school was deserted. More than three-quarters of my son's classroom, he reported, was empty that day, and many parents had gone to pick up their children ahead of time. By that afternoon, most of the stores in town had closed, even the large chain stores. Rumors and paranoia had taken over the citizens of Tamauplipas, resulting in large losses for the city's businesses. The alleged "rain of bullets," of course, did not happen. The two weeks of vacation started, and the good consciences and memories of the families forgot about the threat of the narcos; the beaches of Tamaulipas overflowed, as usual.

When the real armed confrontations took place, the narcos did not have the decency to announce it ahead of time to the citizens of Tampico. In one of the incidents, a gangster hurled a grenade into a military garrison. Not a very intelligent provocation, of course. This was followed by shootings in strip bars, taverns and nightclubs; houses were burned down and along a number of streets there were gun battles that ended in blood and deaths. Criminals and rival cartel members were also kidnapped, mutilated and assassinated in front of their homes. Taxi drivers who served as "falcons" or spies on the activities of the military and the federal police began assaulting clients, raping women and discarding their bodies anywhere. Narco messages became common, on banners and posters, explaining certain killings or threatening specific groups and individuals. They started kidnapping people of every social class, and this initiated the out-migration of the wealthy. Later, we learned what the human rights groups had been saying for some time— that Central American trans-migrants were being kidnapped and extorted. We found this out when their cadavers were discovered in unmarked graves. And that was the tip of the iceberg, because the graves continue to be systematically discovered in various regions of the country.

This time the danger was real and unannounced. Of the hundreds of incidents, only some four or five were covered in the national media, possibly because of their notoriety. The rest were for our own secret horror. A friend who was working at that time for a local newspaper explained to me that all newspaper directors were being threatened by the narcos—no one could report anything. Newspapers were limited to printing official announcements of the police or the army, nothing else. And often the daily papers were forced to publish communiqués written by the criminals themselves, with their own, favorable accounts of events. In other words, only we knew what was going on, only a few news items ever reached the rest of the country and the citizens in the capital.

One item that always reaches audiences and, what's more, sells newspapers, is wholesale slaughter. On June 28, 2010, a week before the elections for state governors, the PRI candidate, Rodolfo Torre Cantú, the expected winner of the election in a state always governed by the PRI and in which all government resources are invested in winning, was assassinated along with his bodyguards and his team, two legislators among them. He was ending his campaign and en route to the Ciudad Victoria airport. It was just two weeks earlier that I had been invited by him and the Tampico city government to a dinner with artists, teachers and others. We shook hands and posed for photos. I remember his face, his moustache; it was hard to comprehend how someone like him, possessing the practically absolute power of an elected governor, a member of the most powerful political party, with bodyguards present, was as vulnerable as the rest of the citizens. With that coup, the cartels made it clear who was in charge in Tamaulipas. Although the politicians had always benefitted from negotiating with the narcos, it was now clear that someone very powerful was feeling uncomfortable and was sending a message to the governor elect, the dead candidate, or the party in general. In the process, the population in general was at their mercy. That day, I cried for Rodolfo Torre Cantú, not because he belonged to the PRI and was as powerful as could be, like so many other governors, but for what his death symbolized for all of the rest of the politicians.

After that, violence became an everyday occurrence, close and more personal. Gun battles became so frequent that almost every Tampico resident had been touched by them. We all had stories to tell. On the bridge that I have to cross to get home every day, there were four persons lynched one day: three men and a fourteen-year-old girl. One night as we were eating with my youngest daughter at a taco stand, we heard shots, something that sounded like popcorn in the microwave, getting closer to us. All of the customers ran for cover; we stayed hidden until we could no longer hear anything. I didn't lose my composure, I remember, because my daughter was there, terrified. I only felt my insides tied in knots in the most primordial reaction to fear. At ten in the morning, weeks later, as we left an event at my daughter's school, we turned a corner and could not proceed; some thirty meters ahead there were two crashed vehicles, with some dead bodies hanging out the windows and others strewn on the street amid a large pool of blood. A detachment of soldiers was aiming guns at the bodies, possibly expecting an attack, but after a while they left. It had been a battle between two groups of criminals that ended in a slaughter. The soldiers had been tipped off, but by the time they arrived, the survivors had already fled. Soon thereafter, some taxis arrived to take away the bodies. Were they war trophies or were they to be buried? Who knows? What remained were the vehicles, the blood, the broken glass, our terror and the usual traffic. There was no way for me to get around the blood; my car wheels rode over that sticky liquid.

I don't know if the kidnapping of some students at a well-known private university had anything to do with policy created after the Tamaulipas event, but they occurred about the same time. It was known that the students were kidnapped, and a ransom was extorted from their families. Seemingly, one of the youngsters was the scion of an important family, because the federal police came in to resolve the issue. It turned out that the young people had been kidnapped by members of the local police force who were using the local police station to carry out these crimes. This was very common, of course, among police that worked directly for the narcos. However, shortly after this incident, Army and Marine reinforcements were deployed to reinforce the state police. In Tampico, specifically, the local police were disarmed and subjected to an investigation to see if they were involved in assassinations perpetrated by the criminal syndicates. Then, they were subjected to loyalty tests, drug tests, etc. While this was going on, the Army replaced them, dressed as local police and drove their same vehicles, taking over the police responsibilities.

In the center of the country, common citizens and especially "intellectuals" and leftists, who all along had questioned the legitimacy of the president, were calling for the demilitarization of the country. They were claiming, without any proof, that the Army was massacring the civilian population—something like what Assad is doing in Syria today. While there may have been cases of abuse by the Army, the truth is that for those of us who live here, the supposed militarization was a great relief. After all, it was the soldiers and the Marines who were liberating the kidnapped. Also, with them assuming the role of policemen, crime plummeted in the city. First, because common criminals were afraid to confront men trained in the Army; second, because the corrupt police were the ones who had committed a major part of the crimes and now they were fired. Calm was restored to the city, little by little. While it is true that narco-trafficking still exists, the gangsters have had to become more discrete in their work. They can no longer cruise the city in their pick-ups and convoys, displaying their weapons with the impunity they had been accustomed to, with the protection and complicity of the local authorities.

While in other Mexican cities and states violence continues to rise, our lives here have almost returned completely to normal, so much so that many of us are forgetting the past.

Although the military presence may not be an ideal solution, its critics have not proposed a better one. It is clear that it will be impossible to solve a problem that has been eighty years in the making and continues to grow, one in which we have all been complicit in creating, one way or another. Because many citizens were not directly affected, and because many benefitted from it (through political employment or in other ways), they allowed the narcos to achieve unlimited power, power almost as great as that of the Mexican government, and even greater, given that, in many cases, they were the government. No easy or quick solution can be foreseen; it's not a matter of opening up a dialogue. When one considers the cynicism, charisma and cruelty of some of the captured capos, as well as the homage rendered to them by the media and the admiration from certain sectors of our population, we have to ask ourselves, how far has corruption metastasized? When one considers how European and American youth guiltlessly enjoy their drugs, and also considers how some Mexican intellectuals accuse their president of assassination while they consume drugs without realizing they are contributing to the problem, I become very discouraged.

For now, I can only state that I am content to feel a little safer every time I go out into the street. I prefer to go by a Marine convoy instead of a Zeta convoy. I'm happy to hear common folk complain only about the heat and the high price of avocados instead of people killed in a narco shoot-out. I won't say that things are now better, but I can say that they have been worse. Down here, just a six-hour drive to the United States, in the broadest border in the world.

LA GUERRA, NOSOTROS,
LA PAZ

Lolita Bosch

1

Hace casi dos años, aunque este haya sido un tiempo que ha pasado lento y ha avanzado casi como remolque, abrí Nuestra aparente rendición (NAR), cinco días después de que fueran hallados en un rancho de Tamaulipas los cuerpos maniatados y asesinados con un tiro en la frente de 72 migrantes. Y lo hice porque quise, tuve la oportunidad y necesité reaccionar de algún modo. No soportaba más que mi perplejidad ante la violencia me mantuviera paralizada y absorta, y pensé que era momento de aprovechar el hecho de estar fuera del país para tratar de pensarlo todo con cierta distancia, de aprovechar el hecho de pertenecer a un colectivo de gente con acceso a la voz pública y de sentir la responsabilidad y la capacidad social, moral y emocional de usarla.

El filósofo Theodor W. Adorno había escrito en 1969: "La exigencia de que Auschwitz [léase: el horror] no se repita es la primera de todas en la educación. Hasta tal punto precede a cualquier otra que no creo deber ni poder fundamentarla". Y yo creo firmemente en esta afirmación contundente: La exigencia de que el horror no se repita es la primera de todas en la educación, la transmisión, la vida. Esa debería ser nuestra lucha.

Y no lo ha sido.

México no es un país con derechos iguales para todos y lo que hoy vivimos no es del todo inesperado, sino la reacción histórica a años de racismo, desigualdad, xenofobia, pobreza, machismo, corrupción y un clasismo tan apabullante que casi nos parece natural. Hemos arrinconado a la mitad de nuestros conciudadanos durante años, siglos. Y la pobreza ha sumido a millones de familias mexicanas a un presente sin opciones. Y frente a eso, en muchos casos: sólo existe la posibilidad de cruzar al otro lado (pa' los States) o trabajar para el narco. Ganar dinero, mantener a una familia, salir adelante. Y si bien la pobreza, aunque resulte a veces incomprensible, no exime de la ley y no todo lo que vemos en estos tiempos es su consecuencia directa, el nuestro es un país con cientos de miles de gentes desesperadas, adictas y a veces, y también, rendidas. Personas sin derechos, con graves enfermedades mentales, carencias emocionales, una ignorancia aplastante y sin solución posible a menos que la sociedad civil se implique, con seriedad, en lo que (nos) está sucediendo.

Miles de presos en México no tienen derecho a un juicio justo, no existen programas serios de rehabilitación física ni social en las cárceles ni fuera de ellas y la reinserción, hoy, es una fantasía.

Y aunque nos cueste verlo de este modo y sigamos responsabilizando de todo lo que ocurre a los criminales (y también, lamentablemente, a las víctimas), miles de personas se han visto obligados a rendirse: muchos de ellos amenazados a trabajar para el narco, con una necesidad económica urgentísima, adictos, acorralados y olvidados por nosotros: sus paisanos. Lo hemos visto en NAR, donde hemos tenido la oportunidad de leerlos, de saber cómo han llegado hasta el día de hoy. Y hemos querido mantener y defender que todos ellos, víctimas y también victimarios, tienen derecho a un juicio justo, a una condena justa y a ser escuchados. Porque en muchos casos los criminales son también, aunque nos cueste asumirlo, víctimas. La avaricia de la clase política y financiera mexicana ha opacado su derecho a ser ciudadanos con plenos derechos y durante años ha utilizado las carencias del pueblo para manipularlo.

Pero lo que hoy nos ocurre, es inmenso.

Y no podemos seguir esperando que el Gobierno Federal reaccione (si acaso todavía sabe hacerlo, si acaso todavía tenga capacidad) y lo detenga. Ni tampoco que el Gobierno Estadounidense asuma su responsabilidad en este gravísimo conflicto y colabore en su finalización. Sino que debemos tomar conciencia de que formamos parte de una sociedad que incluye a gentes distintas a nosotros y con otras oportunidades, que debemos aprender a escuchar (y perdonarnos) y que debemos de ser consecuentes con lo que creemos, con lo que amamos.

Es por todo esto que cuando leí sobre el macabro descubrimiento de los setenta y dos cuerpos de Tamaulipas, que para muchos de nosotros fue un banderolazo de salida, pensé qué era lo que yo quería hacer: Crear un espacio en el que, como si fuera un milagro en medio de esta vorágine, este miedo y esta incredulidad, pudiéramos hablar, donde nos diéramos el tiempo para escucharnos. Aprender a pensar qué nos estaba ocurriendo, cómo habíamos llegado hasta aquí, qué podíamos hacer. Dónde estábamos. Quiénes éramos.

Qué ocurre.

Porque México nos estaba doliendo a todos de un modo tan íntimo y tan esencial, que nos ha costado y nos sigue costando contarlo, asumirlo, hablarlo e incluso creerlo. No estábamos preparados para una debacle como ésta en la que vivimos sumidos desde que la contienda electoral de 2006 partió un país, que ya arrastraba una herencia política terrible, bruscamente en dos y muchos quisieron posicionarse con modelos absolutos y totalitarios. No estábamos preparados para el terrible incremento de la violencia en 2008. No estábamos preparados para ser la reacción de nuestra historia de impunidad y corrupción políticas. No sabíamos lo que era una guerra. Y no supimos prever las consecuencias —en muchos aspectos irreversibles— de tanto resquemor y tantísima avaricia. La nueva y débil democracia mexicana ni nos ayudó ni nos animó a asumir nuestra responsabilidad civil, y tampoco nos hizo sentir ciudadanos y ciudadanas con pleno derecho para construir un país nuevo. En el año 2000, después del PRI, no se modificaron los métodos represivos y corruptos de las autoridades, y no se convirtió en prioridad nacional el combate a la pobreza, la desigualdad y la injusticia. Ni tampoco el acceso a la educación, la nutrición y la salud. Porque muchos de nosotros, casi de modo inconsciente, sabíamos habitar un país así. Habíamos crecido encima de este patrón desigual y seguíamos asumiéndolo, prácticamente, como un rasgo de nuestro carácter nacional. O continental, dirían algunos. En definitiva: sin remedio.

Pero esto no es así.

Porque no es cierto que hayamos perdido. Sino que estamos apenas comenzando a luchar.

Hemos contado más de 60 mil muertos y más de 20 mil desaparecidos en cuatro años —desde 2008. Hay pueblos abandonados, miles de huérfanos, cientos de miles de víctimas y millones de personas (léanlo bien: millones de personas) que pasan miedo a diario. Que se sienten tristes. Que a menudo no le ven un fin a este infierno. Pero aún así: no hemos perdido. No nos han arrinconado a ser, únicamente, el tristísimo torso de la mujer que cuelga de un puente de Tamaulipas, las víctimas inverosímiles de la pederastia, los cuerpos de los migrantes amontonados en las fosas comunes, las personas atrapadas por el fuego en el Casino Royale de Monterrey, los treinta y cinco cuerpos arrojados en una calle de Veracruz, los hombres y mujeres caídos en las balaceras ni nuestros amigos y familiares asesinados. Ni siquiera nuestros amigos y familiares asesinados. Sino que somos más, mucho más y tenemos una capacidad infinita para reinventarnos. Es por eso que debemos asumir ese poder, utilizarlo y reconstruir nuestro país íntimamente herido.

Y si todavía somos capaces de plantearnos un cambio como éste es, únicamente, porque no estamos solos.

En la primera de las marchas convocadas tras el asesinato del hijo del poeta Javier Sicilia, la del 6 de abril de 2011, una joven de Morelos sujetaba una pancarta entre las manos donde podía leerse: "Ustedes los llaman daños colaterales, nosotros los llamábamos amigos". Y éste, a mi parecer, es el cambio de perspectiva esencial y necesario que debemos hacer hoy como ciudadanos y ciudadanas. Un cambio que, de hecho, ya estamos haciendo. Y para el que cientos, miles de personas ya estaban trabajando desde hacía muchos años. Aunque nunca, como hoy, hubiéramos sido conscientes del inestable país que hemos venido construyendo.

De cuánta falta nos hemos hecho los unos a los otros.

Así que harta de la violencia pero también harta de la apatía y de la respuesta inmediata de "es increíble que nadie haga nada" (que niego, por convicción, de forma rotunda), yo, como muchísimos otros ciudadanos y ciudadanas, quise hacer algo. Porque estoy convencida que México necesita hoy del voluntariado y que sólo la sociedad civil tiene el poder para lograr una reacción, política, económica e internacional, que nos ayude a mitigar lo que estamos viviendo.

Fue entonces cuando abrí el portal y mandé una carta a varios amigos que se puede sintetizar con el primero de sus párrafos:

> *a raíz de los últimos acontecimientos, pero también como respuesta a meses, años de desgaste, los artistas, pensadores, lectores, escritores, profesores, estudiantes, críticos y demás ciudadanos interesados, mexicanos de nacimiento o de corazón, debemos comenzar a criticar, protestar, imaginar y proponer, de una manera activa y sistemática. Creemos que nos urge inventar recursos para ser quienes somos y no quienes nos están acorralando a ser. Tratando de superar, nosotros también, nuestra aparente rendición ante lo que nos sucede.*

Y dos semanas después, el 12 de septiembre de 2010, tras pensar cómo abordar algo qué consideraba urgente, abrí un segundo proyecto que resultó el paralelo imprescindible de NAR: Menos días aquí, un nombramiento de los de muertos por violencia que a día de hoy ha contado a más de 25 mil muertos, a los que tratamos de ponerles nombres o marcarlos con alguna seña que los identifique para que sus familiares y amigos puedan encontrarlos.

Y que a menudo pedimos, públicamente, que descansen en paz.

En los días anteriores a la creación del blog, algunos amigos mexicanos y también extranjeros quisieron desanimarme diciendo que México no era un país de voluntarios, que estar fuera me desautorizaba para entenderlo o que yo no podía comprender que el *nuestro* (y algunos cuando decían nuestro, me excluían a mí: que soy mexicana por decisión) era un continente así. Pero no es cierto que seamos "así" y basta. Nuestro mundo no es un duelo de cowboys. Tenemos el mismo derecho a vivir en paz que cualquier otro lugar del mundo. Y debemos aprender a confiar en todas las personas que merecen nuestra confianza. Sentirnos capaces de hacer algo. Porque estamos, literalmente, hartos. Hasta la madre.

2

Pero trabajar contra la violencia es agotador porque nunca sientes que estás haciendo suficiente. Y porque visto de cerca, diariamente, México se ha convertido en un paisaje tristísimo. Y es algo con lo que es muy difícil, íntimamente, lidiar.

Así que cuando me embarqué (sin saber donde me embarcaba) en el portal, que desde que comenzó no ha dejado de crecer y sumar propuestas, pedí consejo a personas que habían generado otras propuestas y posturas críticas, personas que habían atravesado estas mismas dudas, este mismo miedo. Y fue Rossana Reguillo —probablemente sin saberlo— quien me dio el empujón que me faltaba, cuando me dijo que entendía la tristeza y la impotencia pero que no tenía derecho a dejarlo. Que ya no era una opción. A pesar de que México, casa, se hubiera convertido de pronto en un pantano de cosas pendientes que no sabía cómo empezar a ordenar.

Y entonces mataron a un amigo de una forma brutal y yo traté de imaginar su final y no supe. Ésta es nuestra incredulidad, pensé. Y lo más terrible de todo es que no sabemos reaccionar: tenemos miedo, no queremos creerlo, pensamos que a nosotros no nos va a tocar. No a los nuestros. De modo que tras la muerte brutal de mi amigo, mi relación con la violencia cambió radicalmente. Había vivido yo misma y había visto infringir estados de miedo y acorralamiento a amigos y familiares, pero cuando traté de imaginar a mi amigo muriendo: no pude. Y eso, misteriosamente, lo cambió todo.

Y empezaron a llegar manos, ayuda, propuestas, voces.

No doy abasto para contarles todas las personas que generosamente se han ofrecido a colaborar con nuestro proyecto y que confían en él. Tenemos voluntarios que mantienen blogs permanentes, responsables de proyectos de paz o de un mapa de asociaciones de voluntariado, por nombrar dos de las cosas que hacemos. Pero además, tenemos colaboradores que reportean, reflexionan, advierten y nos acompañan. Poetas, fotógrafos, moneros, ilustradores, académicos, periodistas, amas de casa, herreros, estudiantes, jóvenes, niños . . . Y tenemos, además, voluntarios que cada noche, por una semana, hacen el nombramiento de muertos por violencia que podemos localizar en todo el país. Y que se sientan, durante siete noches terribles, a escribir entradas como éstas:

> *Santiago Jamiltepec, Oaxaca, 29 de octubre. Dos niños, Jesús Jorcaef y Oldemar Amadeo, ambos de apellidos Carmona Vázquez de 5 y 8 años, murieron ejecutados cuando su familia regresaba a casa. Jesús y Oldemar iban acompañados de sus padres y su hermano de 1 año a bordo un vehículo Volkswagen Crossfox de color negro y sin placas de circulación, cuando una camioneta Voyager les dio alcance y 5 sicarios tiraron a matar. En medio de la lluvia de balas, su padre salió de la unidad y corrió entre la maleza, de la misma manera su madre tomó entre sus brazos a su hijo más pequeño, logrando escapar y resultando únicamente con heridas leves; sin embargo, esa suerte no la corrieron los otros dos pequeños que fueron alcanzados por las balas.*

Los nombres o las señas de nuestros amigos, nuestros familiares, nuestros compatriotas. Indignamente expuestos en su momento final, brutalmente torturados e impunemente olvidados por nuestras autoridades y también por muchos de sus conciudadanos. Olvidados ellos, olvidado su contexto y olvidados también sus familiares, sus amigos, nosotros: Espectadores atónitos frente a torturas increíbles que varían en sus métodos, que se aplican de modo distinto en cada estado y que se precipitan hacia una crueldad cada vez más inimaginable.

3

Una de las intenciones iniciales del proyecto era convocar a gente que quisiera curar proyectos especiales sobre hechos concretos (las consecuencias de la violencia en la infancia, las enfermedades mentales, la soledad, el trabajo en las prisiones, la atención a las víctimas . . .), y esta invitación sigue permanentemente abierta. Pero hemos querido prestar especial atención a lo que les ocurre a los migrantes que cruzan México para llegar hasta los Estados Unidos. Porque donde antes encontraban en México un país hermano, hoy, como dice el cronista salvadoreño Óscar Martínez: encuentran el infierno. Nuestro banderolazo de salida había sido el asesinato de los setenta y dos migrantes en Tamaulipas y quisimos mantenernos fieles a ese tributo. Y sin embargo, desde que inicié NAR, se han encontrado tantas fosas comunes en México y hemos visto tantísimos migrantes maltratados que todavía sorprende la entereza y la alegría con la que personas absolutamente necesarias (y permanentemente amenazadas) hoy en nuestro país, como las patronas de Veracruz o el Padre Alejandro Solalinde desde Ixtepec, Oaxaca, siguen pensando que la de los migrantes es una situación que puede cambiar. Que debe cambiar.

Y ha sido gracias a la convivencia y el ejemplo de estos seres extraordinarios —y también a la de otras convocatorias como la protesta de los estudiantes contra la militarización en Juárez o las acciones de Por un México sin violencia, basta ya— que trabajan en pos de bien común y que están convencidos que lo que nos sucede lo podemos cambiar, que siempre he pensado que debemos hacer más. Que sabemos cómo. Y que hay tanto trabajo pendiente, que no es momento de limar asperezas, sino de recurrir a todas las formas de voluntariado posibles. De invitarlos, a todos ustedes, a trabajar con nosotros.

Porque nos hacen falta.

Hoy hemos alcanzado entre todos los proyectos alrededor de 1 millón de visitas. Y para mi sorpresa, NAR es ya una casa en donde habitamos muchos de nosotros para tratar de comprender este México inesperado. Hemos presentado el proyecto en lugares como el centro cultural del Palacio de la Moneda o la Casa de Pablo Neruda en Chile, el Centre de Cultura Contemporània de Barcelona, el Auditorio de las Madres de la Plaza de Mayo en Argentina, el Centro Cultural de España en Montevideo o Columbia University y el Hemispheric Institute de Nueva York. Hemos recibido invitaciones para hablar con Amnistía Internacional o con la UNESCO. Dentro de México hemos sido convocados en muchos lugares de la república para hablar con víctimas, estudiantes y responsables de otros proyectos. Y en los dos años que llevamos trabajando debemos agradecer que en tantos y tantos lugares nos hayan recibido con los brazos abiertos.

Porque necesitamos cómplices. Todo el rato.

Aunque quiero contarles que sí rechazamos una invitación: la que nos extendió el Departamento de Estado estadounidense, inmediatamente después del inicio de la revolución pacífica de Egipto, para hablar desde la Embajada de los Estados Unidos en Ciudad de México, vía videoconferencia, con Hillary Clinton. Invitación, precipitada y a puerta cerrada, que rechacé con esta carta:

Señora Hillary Clinton, Señor John Feely,

Les agradecemos la lectura de esta carta y les hablamos con absoluta sinceridad, tal y como creemos que tenemos derecho a ser escuchados y tal y como esperamos que puedan respondernos:

Nuestra Aparente Rendición es un portal que ha recibido cien mil visitas en cuatro meses y sigue creciendo a una velocidad vertiginosa y esperanzadora. Un portal que se erige como un cementerio virtual en el que dejamos el recuerdo de nuestros compatriotas asesinados y creamos un espacio de diálogo y construcción de paz. Nos estamos convirtiendo en una plataforma única, sólida y estable que permite entrelazar proyectos de toda la República, devolver el derecho a la expresión a todos los mexicanos, coordinar proyectos por la paz, crear foros de debate y construir nuestra esperanza de futuro. Confiamos en la capacidad de todos nosotros para pensar y actuar en consecuencia, en la inteligencia, la curiosidad y la responsabilidad de miles de lectores. Y estamos dispuestos a trabajar en la construcción de un proceso de paz y recuperación del país justo, ecuánime y sustentable.

No estamos vinculados a ninguna institución ni partido político. Sino que estamos, como muchos de nuestros lectores y los millones de mexicanos que no pueden permitirse el acceso a la cultura y la información, acompañando a las víctimas de la violencia, de la pobreza, del femicidio, de la pederastia, de la impunidad y de la corrupción. Somos posibles muertos.

Creemos, muchos de nosotros, que esta debacle social en la que vivimos sumidos, ante la indiferencia internacional y la impunidad nacional, sólo la podrá arreglar la sociedad civil mexicana. Pero necesitamos que el gobierno mexicano, el estadounidense y la comunidad internacional tomen medidas estrictas y urgentes que frenen las ventas de armas, el consumo de droga, el lavado de dinero y la corrupción. Tienen, como tenemos nosotros, la obligación de apoyar las propuestas civiles que luchan por la paz, protegen a las víctimas y combaten la censura. Tienen la obligación de enfrentarse a la pobreza y el abandono que padecen millones de niños y familias mexicanas ante la brutal economía de mercado que las está acorralando y olvidando. Y, por decencia y humanidad, su gobierno y el gobierno mexicano pueden y deben posicionarse del lado de los ciudadanos y no de las corporaciones y los grupos delictivos. Pueden y deben romper las complicidades y la hipocresía y hablar con la ciudadanía con respeto e igualdad. Pueden y deben reconocer que el problema de la violencia y el narcotráfico están íntimamente relacionados con el tráfico de migrantes, la pobreza, la prostitución, el secuestro o la trata de personas, problemas gravísimos y crueles que afectan con una crueldad y una impunidad inimaginables a la sociedad mexicana y que ustedes tienen la capacidad y la obligación de combatir. Por decencia y humanidad, estas son obligaciones que tenemos todos. Ustedes, el gobierno mexicano y la comunidad internacional. Pero también nosotros.

Y eso es exactamente lo que estamos haciendo. Porque estamos tristes, estamos asustados y estamos hartos. Es por eso que vamos a seguir trabajando hasta recuperar nuestro inalienable derecho a vivir en paz. Somos una sociedad civil capaz y organizada que está comenzando a reaccionar ante el impacto que ha supuesto esta ola de violencia para el pueblo mexicano, y a recuperar la fuerza que nos da nuestra seguridad de que somos capaces de convertirnos en un país mejor. Juntos.

Hoy seguimos increíblemente en el mismo sitio. Pero por alguna razón casi perversa nos sentimos menos solos cuando estamos juntos y terriblemente solos cuando pensamos esto de manera individual. Hemos logrado crear una comunidad a la que recurrir y que a mí ya no me pertenece. NAR es hoy un proyecto que llevamos a cabo más de veinte personas que trabajamos de manera permanente —por nosotros y por nuestros conciudadanos. Los que tienen acceso a la palabra y los que no.

Y a pesar de la tristeza y la impotencia, debemos mantenernos de pie y tener confianza en que todo saldrá como ha ido saliendo: lenta, pero sólidamente. Porque aunque pueda parecer incomprensible, confiamos en México y en sus ciudadanos. Y sobretodo confiamos en nuestra capacidad de construir un país mejor. Hemos visto a la sociedad civil mexicana reaccionar con solidaridad y empatía en otros momentos, y esperamos (de verdad lo esperamos) que también ocurra ahora, aunque el miedo nos impida una respuesta masiva e inmediata. Necesitamos tiempo, y los necesitamos a todos ustedes. Queremos que cuenten lo que está ocurriendo, que se impliquen en un proceso de paz que está íntimamente vinculado con los Estados Unidos, que se solidaricen con las víctimas de esta tragedia sin precedentes en América Latina y que se sumen a nuestro portal.

Porque tras estos dos años lentos que han avanzado a velocidad de remolque, lo único que sé es que la guerra es también apatía, también egoísmo, también negación. Pero que en México hay muchísimas personas dispuestas a trabajar por la paz, y también hay muchísimas que no saben cómo hacerle, hacia dónde voltear, como actuar. Y, sin embargo, todos los proyectos que están trabajando por la paz necesitan ayuda y hay mucha gente a las que nosotros necesitamos para construir un destino común que nos incluya a todos. Porque sobre todo sé, constato a diario, que en México hoy residen millones de ciudadanos tristes, perplejos, asustados e indignados (escuchen de nuevo: millones.) Y no podemos, no debemos y no tenemos derecho, a dejarlos solos (a dejarnos solos.) Lo digo con un profundo respeto y con la honestísima intención de entender todas las formas de reacción ante lo que hoy nos ocurre. Porque créanme que trato de entender la apatía, el miedo, la incredulidad e incluso la burla que reciben los defensores de los derechos humanos en muchos lugares. Pero, a título personal, en verdad pienso que tenemos una obligación moral y social con todas las personas sin privilegios. Porque a nosotros, con todo: hoy nos queda la palabra. Podemos difundirla.

Lo único que queremos es volver a casa: aquel México que echamos tanto de menos y que hace sólo cinco años no hubiéramos imaginado que nos reuniría hoy en este libro para hablar de cosas tan tristes.

THE WAR, US, THE PEACE

Lolita Bosch
Translated by Sergio Troncoso

1

Two years ago, even though this has been a time that has passed slowly and has advanced like a semi-trailer, I opened the platform *Nuestra Aparente Rendición* (NAR), five days after seventy-two bodies of migrant workers, bound and assassinated with a shot to the forehead, were found on a ranch in Tamaulipas. I did it because I wanted to, had the opportunity and needed to react in some way. I could no longer tolerate that my perplexity amid the violence left me paralyzed and stunned, and I thought it was the moment to take advantage of being outside the country to attempt to think about everything from a certain distance, to take advantage of belonging to a collective of people with access to the public voice and with a sense of responsibility, and the social, moral and emotional ability to use it.

The philosopher Theodor W. Adorno wrote in 1969: "The demand that Auschwitz [read: the horror] not be repeated is the first of all priorities in education. This priority precedes all others that I believe I need not and should not justify it." And I believe firmly in this blunt statement: The priority that the horror not be repeated is the first priority before all others in education, values, life. This should be our struggle.

And it has not been.

Mexico is not a country with equal rights for all, and what we experience today is not wholly unexpected, but the historic reaction to years of racism, inequality, xenophobia, poverty, machismo, corruption and a class discrimination so overwhelming that it almost seems natural to us. We have oppressed half of our fellow citizens for years, for centuries; poverty has drowned millions of Mexican families in a present without options. And before this reality, in many cases, the only option is to cross to "*el otro lado*" (to the United States) or to work for the narcos, in order to earn money, to feed and clothe a family, to build a future. And while poverty, even though it is often incomprehensible, does not exempt one from the law, nor is everything we see in these times the direct consequence of poverty, ours is a country with hundreds of thousands of desperate, addicted and often, too, defeated people. People without rights, with serious mental illnesses, emotional needs and a crushing ignorance, and without a possible solution unless civil society becomes involved, with seriousness of purpose, in what is happening (to us).

Thousands of prisoners in Mexico do not have the right to a fair trial. No serious programs for physical or social rehabilitation exist in prisons, nor outside of prisons, and reintegration into society is today a fantasy.

Although it may cost us to look at it this way and we keep blaming everything that happens on the criminals (and unfortunately, also on the victims), thousands of persons have been obligated to surrender: many of them threatened into working for the narcos, with a very urgent economic need, addicted, oppressed and forgotten by us, their fellow citizens. We have seen it in NAR, where we have had the opportunity to read their stories, to know how they have arrived to this day. We have wanted to argue and defend that all of them, victims and also perpetrators, have the right to a just trial, to just sentencing and to be heard. Because, in many of these cases, the criminals are also, although it is difficult to accept this, victims. The greed of the Mexican political and financial class has obscured their duty to be citizens with all rights and duties, and for years this class has used the needs of the people to manipulate the masses.

But what is happening today is profound.

We cannot keep hoping that the federal government will react (if in case it still knows how to, if it still has the ability to) and so stop this conflict. We cannot also hope that the U.S. government will assume its responsibility in this very grave conflict and collaborate on its end. Instead, we should become conscious that we form part of a society that includes people different from us and with varying opportunities, we should learn to listen (and to forgive), and we owe it to ourselves to follow what we believe, what we love.

For all these reasons, when I read about the macabre discovery of the seventy-two bodies in Tamaulipas, which for many of us was like a flag at a starting gate, I thought about what I wanted to do: create a space—as if it were a miracle amid this vortex, this fear and this incredulity—in which we could talk, a space where we could give each other the time to listen. A space to learn to think about what was happening to us, how we had arrived here, what we could do, where we were, who we were.

A space to understand what is happening.

Because Mexico was hurting for all of us in a way so intimate and so essential that it has cost us, and continues to cost us, to recount the drug violence, accept it, talk about it, and even believe it. We were not prepared for a debacle like the one in which we live, overwhelmed since the electoral contest of 2006 ripped apart a country abruptly in two, a country already hobbled with a terrible political inheritance. Many wanted to position themselves to take advantage with absolute and totalitarian political models. We were not prepared for the terrible increase in violence in 2008. We were not prepared to be the reaction to the culmination of our history of political impunity and corruption. We did not know what was a war, and we did not know how to foresee the consequences—in many irreversible aspects—of so much resentment and so much avarice. The new and fragile Mexican democracy did not help us and did not encourage us to assume our civil responsibility, and it did not help us to feel like citizens with the right to construct a new country. In the year 2000, after the PRI, the repressive and corrupt methods of the authorities were not changed, and the fight against poverty, inequality and injustice did not become a priority, nor did access to education, nutrition and heath care. Many of us knew, almost unconsciously, how to live in a country this way. We had grown up with this unequal standard, and we continued accepting it, practically, like a trait of our national character, or a continental one, some would say. Definitely without a cure.

But this is not the case.

It is not true that we have lost. Instead, we are only just beginning to fight.

We have counted more than sixty thousand dead and more than twenty thousand disappeared in four years, since 2008. There are towns that have been abandoned, thousands who have been orphaned, hundreds of thousands of victims and millions of persons (read it well: millions of persons) who endure daily fear. Who are overwhelmed with sadness. Who, at the very least, do not see an end to this hell. And even so: we have not lost. They have not reduced us to be only the very tragic torso of the woman who hangs from a bridge in Tamaulipas, the improbable victims of pedophilia, the bodies of migrants stuffed into common graves, the people trapped by the fire in the Casino Royale of Monterrey, the thirty-five bodies flung into a street in Veracruz, the men and women fallen in the shootouts, nor our friends and family members who have been assassinated. Not even our friends and family members who have been assassinated. Instead, we are more, much more, and we possess the infinite capacity to reinvent ourselves. That is why we should accept this power, and utilize it, and reconstruct our intimately wounded country.

And if we are still capable of proposing for ourselves a change as this is, it is only because we are not alone.

In the first of the protests organized after the assassination of the son of the poet Javier Sicilia, on April 6th, 2011, a young woman from Morelos held a sign in her hands which read: "You call us collateral damage, we called them our friends." And this, to me, seems the essential and necessary change of perspective that we should, as citizens, make today. A change that, in fact, we are already making. A change for which hundreds of thousands of people have already been working to achieve for many years. Yet never like today have we been conscious of the unstable country we have been creating.

So much blame we have bestowed upon each other.

So fed up with the violence but also fed up with the apathy and the immediate response that "it is incredible that nobody does anything" (a response I deny, with conviction, wholeheartedly). I, like many other citizens, wanted to do something. I am convinced that Mexico today needs civic volunteers, and because only civil society has the power to achieve a political, economic and international response that will help us mitigate the situation we have been living.

That was when I opened the NAR platform and I sent a letter to various friends, which can be summarized by the first of its paragraphs:

> . . . because of the past events, but also as a response to months, years, of waste, artists, thinkers, readers, writers, professors, students, critics and even interested citizens— Mexicans by birth or by heart—we should begin to criticize, protest, imagine, and propose in an active and systematic manner. We believe it is urgent for us to invent resources to be who we are and not who they are forcing us to be. We are trying too to overcome our apparent surrender in the face of what is happening to us.

Two weeks later, on September 12th, 2010, after thinking about how to tackle something I considered urgent, I opened a second project that became an essential parallel to NAR: Menos Días Aquí, a naming of those dead by the violence that up to this day has counted more than twenty-five thousand dead, for whom we have attempted to find names, or to mark them with a sign that will identify them so that their families or friends can find them.

We, at the very least, publicly ask that they may rest in peace.

In the days after the creation of the platform, some Mexican friends and also foreign friends wanted to discourage me from this project, saying that Mexico was not a country of volunteers, that to be outside the country automatically prevented me from understanding it, or that I could not understand that *ours* (and some when they said *ours* excluded me, because I was a Mexican by choice) was a continent like that. But it is not true that we are "like that," end of story. Our world is not a duel of cowboys. We have the same right to live in peace that any other place has in the world. And we should learn to have confidence in all those persons who deserve our confidence. We should learn to feel capable of doing something, because we are literally fed up. Fed up as hell.

2

But working against the violence is exhausting, because you never feel that you are doing enough. And because seen from up close daily, Mexico has become a very sad landscape.

And it is something that is very difficult to fight against intimately.

So that when I embarked on the platform (without knowing where I was going), which from the beginning has not ceased to grow and to add proposals, I asked for counsel from persons who had generated other proposals and critical positions, persons who had endured similar doubts and this same fear. And it was Rossana Reguillo, who, without even knowing it, gave me the push I needed when she told me she understood the sadness and importance of NAR and that I did not have the right to abandon it. That it was not an option anymore. In spite of the fact that Mexico, home, would soon become a swamp of things outstanding which it did not know how to begin to order.

And then they killed a friend in a brutal manner, and I attempted to imagine his end, and I did not know how. This is our incredulity, I thought. And the most terrible thing of all is that we don't know how to react: we are afraid, we do not want to believe it, we don't think the violence will touch us.

Not our loved ones. In that manner, because of the brutal death of my friend, my relationship with the violence changed radically. I myself had lived it, and I had seen the states of fear and surrender infringe on my friends and family, but when I tried to imagine my friend dying, I couldn't. And that, mysteriously, changed everything.

People began to arrive to lend a hand, to help: proposals, voices.

It is impossible to mention all the people who have generously offered to collaborate with our project and who have faith in it. We have volunteers who maintain permanent blogs on our site, who are responsible for peace projects or for a myriad of volunteer associations, to name two of the things we do. More than that, we have collaborators who report, reflect, and witness, and who accompany us. Poets, photographers, cartoonists, illustrators, academics, newspaper people, housewives, blacksmiths, students, young adults, kids. . . . Moreover, we also have volunteers that each night, one week at a time, create the list of the dead by violence whom we have located throughout the entire country. These volunteers also sit down, for six terrible nights, to write entries like this one:

> *Santiago Jamiltepec, Oaxaca, 29th of October. Two children, Jesús Joracaef and Oldemar Amadeo, both with a last name of Carmona Vásquez, five- and eight-years-old, died execution style when their family returned home. Jesús and Oldemar were accompanied by their parents and one-year-old brother, in a black Volkswagen Crossfox car without license plates, when a Voyager SUV reached them and five hit men shot at them. Amid the rain of bullets, their father escaped and ran into nearby weeds, in the same way their mother grabbed her youngest child in her arms, managing to escape with only superficial injuries; however, the*

other two children did not have such luck, and the bullets found their mark.

The names, or the last signs left by our friends, our family members, our compatriots. Indignantly exposed in their final moments, brutally tortured and forgotten with impunity by our authorities and by many of our fellow citizens. They are forgotten, their context forgotten, and also forgotten are their families, their friends, and even ourselves: astonished spectators face-to-face with incredible tortures which vary in their methodology, which are applied in every state in a unique way, and which rush toward a cruelty each time more unimaginable.

3

One of the initial intentions of the project was to gather together people who might want to administer special projects on concrete data (the consequences of violence in infancy, the mental health problems, the problems of solitude, the work in the prisons, the care for victims . . .), and this invitation remains permanently open to anyone. But we have wanted to lend special attention to what happens to migrants who cross Mexico to reach the United States, because before migrants found Mexico to be a brotherly country, today, as the Salvadorean chronicler Oscar Martínez writes: they find an inferno. Our starting flag had been the assassination of seventy-two migrants in Tamaulipas, and we wanted to remain loyal to that beginning. Nevertheless, since the start of NAR, so many common graves in Mexico had been found, and we have seen too many migrants mistreated that it is surprising the strength and happiness with which people absolutely necessary (and permanently threatened) today in our country—like the humble housewives of Veracruz or Father Alejandro Solalinde from Ixtepec, Oaxaca—keep having about the migrants, that their situation can change. That it should change.

It has been thanks to the community and the example of these extraordinary individuals—and also thanks to other organized events like the student protests against the militarization of Juárez and the actions of Por un México sin violencia, basta ya—that they work in pursuit of the community good and that they are convinced that what is happening to us can be changed. Because of that, I have always thought that we should do more. Because of that, I believe we know how. There is so much pending work that it is not a moment to smooth things over, but to appeal for all forms of possible volunteerism. We want to invite all of you to work with us.

We need your help.

Today, we have reached, with all of our projects, around one million website visits to NAR. To my surprise, NAR is now a home in which many of us live to try to understand this unforeseen Mexico. We have presented our project in places like the cultural center of El Palacio de la Moneda, La Casa de Pablo Neuruda in Chile, El Centre de Cultura Contemporánia in Barcelona, the Auditorio de las Madres de la Plaza de Mayo in Argentina, the Centro Cultural de España in Montevideo, Columbia University and the Hemispheric Institute of New York. We have received invitations to talk with Amnesty International and with UNESCO. Within Mexico, we have convened to talk with victims, students and organizers of other projects in many places. In the two years we have worked, we owe our gratitude to many who have received us with open arms in so many places.

We need accomplices. All the time.

I do want to tell you that we did reject one invitation: the one extended to us by the State Department of the United States, immediately after the initial peaceful revolution in

Egypt, to talk from the embassy of the United States in Mexico City by teleconference with Hilary Clinton. A rushed and closed-door invitation that I rejected with this letter:

Ms. Hilary Clinton, Mr. John Feely,

We thank you for reading this letter and we address you with absolute sincerity, such as we believe that we have the right to be heard and such as you might respond to us:

Nuestra Aparente Rendición is a platform that has received hundreds of thousands of visits in four months, and that continues to grow at a dizzying and hopeful velocity. It is a portal that is built like a virtual cemetery in which we keep alive the memories of our assassinated compatriots, and in which we create a space for constructive dialogue for peace. We are becoming a unique platform, solid and stable, which permits the interrelation of projects from all the republic, returns the right of expression to all Mexicans, coordinates projects for peace, creates forums for debate, and constructs our hope for the future. We are confident in the ability of all of us to think and act effectively, with the intelligence, curiosity, and responsibility of thousands of readers. And we are ready to work for the construction of a process for peace and renewal of country that is just, impartial, and sustainable.

We are not linked with any institution or political party. Rather we are accompanying—like many of our readers and the millions of Mexicans who are not able to access culture or information—the victims of violence, poverty, femicide, pedophilia, impunity, and corruption. We are the possible dead. Many of us believe that this social debacle that oppresses us, in the face of international indifference and national impunity, could only possibly be fixed by Mexican civil society. But we need that the Mexican government, the U.S. government, and the international community take strict and urgent measures to stop the sale of arms, the consumption of drugs, the laundering of money, and corruption. You have, much like we do, the obligation to support these civic efforts that fight for peace, protect victims, and combat censorship. You have the obligation to confront poverty and the abandonment that millions of Mexican children and families suffer in the face of the brutal free market that is silencing them and forgetting them. Furthermore, for the sake of decency and humanity, your government and the Mexican government can and should position themselves on the side of the citizenry, and not of the corporations and criminal groups. You can and should destroy the complicities and hypocrisy, and talk to the citizenry with respect and on equal terms. You can and should realize that the problems of violence and narcotrafficking are intimately related with the traffic of migrants, poverty, prostitution, kidnapping, and the slave trade, problems very grave and cruel which affect Mexican society with an unimaginable cruelty and impunity, problems for which you have the capacity and obligation to combat. In the name of decency and humanity, these are obligations we all have. You, the Mexican government, and the international community. But also us. And that is exactly what we are doing, because we are sad, fearful, and fed up. That is why we will continue to work to recover our inalienable right to live in peace. We are a civil society capable and organized that is beginning to react to the impact endured by the Mexican people from this wave of violence. We will continue to recover the strength given to us by our certainty that we are capable of creating a better country. Together.

Today we continue in the same site. But for some perverse reason we feel less alone when we are together with others, and terribly alone when we think about this in an individual manner. We have managed to create a community to appeal to, and which does not anymore belong to me. NAR today is a project that more than twenty people carry out who work in a permanent manner, for ourselves and for our fellow citizens. Those who have access to the word, and those who do not.

Despite the sadness and impotency, we should remain on our feet and have confidence that everything will unfold the way it has always unfolded: slowly, but solidly. Although it may seem incomprehensible, we believe in Mexico and its citizens. Above all, we believe in our capacity to construct a better country. We have seen Mexican civil society react with solidarity and empathy at many moments, and we hope (truly we hope) that this will happen again today, even though fear impedes a massive and immediate response. We need time, and we need all of you. We want you to tell the stories of what is happening, to involve yourselves in a peace process that is intimately linked with the United States, to have solidarity with the victims in this unprecedented tragedy in Latin America, and to ask you to join our portal.

During these two slow years that have reached the speed of a semi-trailer, the only thing I know is that the war is also apathy, also selfishness, also denial. In Mexico, there are very many people willing to work for peace, and also very many who know how to do it, where to turn to, how to act. Nevertheless, all the projects that are working for peace need help, and we need many persons to create a common destiny that includes all of us. Above all, I know, confirmed daily, that today in Mexico live millions of citizens mournful, perplexed, and fearful, and indignant (listen anew: millions). We cannot, we should not, and we don't have the right to leave them alone (to leave ourselves alone). I say this with profound respect and with the very honest intention to understand all the different forms of reaction to what is happening to us today. Believe me, I have tried to understand the apathy, the fear, the incredulity, and even the laughter that the defenders of human rights receive in many places. But, personally, I truly believe that we have a moral and social obligation to all the people without privileges. Because for us, with everything that has happened, today we still have the word. We can spread it.

The only thing we want to do is to return home: to a Mexico which we miss so much, and where only five years ago we would not have imagined it would reunite us in this book to talk about such sad things today.

LA BATALLA DE CIUDAD MIER

Diego Osorno

Ésta es la historia de un pueblo de la frontera con Estados Unidos arrasado en silencio por la guerra de Tamaulipas.

1. La Esquina de los Degollados

La mañana del 22 de febrero de 2010, cuando Ciudad Mier se preparaba para las fiestas anuales, quince camionetas con las siglas del Cártel del Golfo entraron por el acceso de la carretera de Reynosa como caballos desbocados. Los pistoleros enfilaron a la comandancia de la policía municipal, bajaron de sus vehículos y comenzó a sonar el tableteo de sus ametralladoras contra el viejo edificio. La gente que estaba alrededor echó el cuerpo a tierra y como pudo fue a refugiarse.

El tiroteo amainó. Seis policías municipales asustados, golpeados, jadeando con la boca abierta, rojos de sangre y con el miedo en la mirada, fueron sacados de la comandancia por los pistoleros, quienes gritaban consignas contra los Zetas. Ésa fue la última vez que se vio a los seis policías y fue también la última vez que hubo policías municipales en Ciudad Mier.

El comando instaló pistoleros en los tres principales accesos al corazón de Ciudad Mier; montaron un cerco para que cuatro camionetas exploraran las calles en busca de casas y negocios a los que hombres de rostro parco entraban por personas específicas. En ese lapso, la plaza principal, ubicada frente a la comandancia, fue usada como paredón. Vaciándose de sangre, dos hombres detenidos por los pistoleros fueron llevados a la plaza. Ahí los acribillaron y después los decapitaron. Sus cabezas terminaron colocadas en un rincón de la plazoleta. Con el paso del tiempo, por el uso frecuente que se le dio, aquel rincón sería conocido como "La Esquina de los Degollados".

Un par de horas después de que los pistoleros abandonaron el pueblo, el Ejército hizo un rondín fugaz y desapareció antes de que oscureciera. Toda la semana siguiente el pueblo vivió con somnolencia. El silencio de las noches era cortado por voces lejanas y disparos aislados. Las calles estaban sucias y ruinosas, sencillamente no hubo cómo realizar los festejos anuales del 6 de marzo, los cuales fueron cancelados en ese 2010, algo que no sucedía desde la época de la Revolución.

2. Pueblo Mágico

Aunque no veo a nadie, sé que hay alguien viéndome. Lo siento mientras camino entre el metal escupido por las bocas de los fusiles, regado entre vidrios rotos que, pese a mi cautela, es inevitable hacer que crujan con la pisada de las botas. Debo apurarme a terminar de mirar las gruesas manchas de sangre seca y los miles de impactos de bala que aún quedan en las paredes de las casas. No puedo dejar que caiga la noche mientras busco recuperar más testimonios de lo que sucedió estos meses aquí. La oscuridad de una zona de guerra no es lo mismo que la oscuridad a secas, además, no existe ningún hotel o sitio al cual meterte a pasar la madrugada. Por ahora, éste no es el *Pueblo*

Mágico que se anuncia a la entrada: a juzgar por la destrucción existente, es la primera línea de la guerra de Tamaulipas.

Se supone que los bandos en pugna emprendieron la retirada hace unas semanas a los campamentos que han montado en ranchos cercanos, y, aunque no vengas empotrado a una unidad del Ejército, portando casco y un chaleco antibalas pesado y caluroso, puedo caminar por estas calles donde se ven construcciones cubiertas de ceniza, con basura chamuscada en el suelo y sin señal aparente de vida en su interior. Pero sé que estoy en un pueblo fantasma y es posible que los fantasmas me estén observando.

3. El alzamiento

Lo de Ciudad Mier no fue un estallido de violencia irracional. La incursión del 22 de febrero de 2010 formaba parte de un plan más ambicioso para tomar el control de la franja divisoria entre Tamaulipas y Texas, conocida del lado mexicano como la Frontera Chica. Zona clave para cualquier tipo de tráfico ilegal a Estados Unidos, aquí se localiza también la Cuenca de Burgos, la principal veta de gas natural con que cuenta México.

Las cabeceras de pueblos como Miguel Alemán, Camargo, Valle Hermoso y Nueva Ciudad Guerrero fueron asaltadas de la misma forma en que ocurrió con Ciudad Mier. El inicio de esta ofensiva que el país tardó en identificar, tiene varios nombres: quienes la emprendieron —los integrantes del C.D.G.— reivindicaron su ataque sorpresa como "La Vuelta"; mientras que el blanco de su ofensiva, los Zetas, marcaron esa fecha del calendario con el título de "La Traición". En cambio, la gente, simplemente lo llamó "El Alzamiento".

Los ataques coincidieron con la divulgación en México de unas palabras de arrepentimiento de Osiel Cárdenas Guillén, quien lideraba ambos grupos antes de ser extraditado a Estados

Unidos, donde a cambio de una pena reducida de 25 años de prisión en una cárcel de mediana seguridad, proporcionó información clave contra los Zetas, agrupación que él mismo fundó una década atrás.

Cuando estalló la guerra en Tamaulipas —un estado cuyo tamaño es cuatro veces mayor que el de El Salvador, y cuyas costas abarcan buena parte del Golfo de México— no hubo referencia ni posicionamiento particular de las corporaciones policiacas estatales y federales para dar cuenta de lo que estaba sucediendo. Ante las preguntas de algunos periodistas sobre los reportes de balaceras y enfrentamientos en la región, el entonces gobernador Eugenio Hernández, dijo que se trataba de pura psicosis. En la bitácora pública de actividades, la Comandancia de la Octava Zona Militar del Ejército, apenas reconoció tres enfrentamientos, en los cuales cayeron un soldado y otros once fueron heridos. Finalmente, basados en un reporte de la DEA, funcionarios del gobierno federal filtraron a columnistas de la ciudad de México que lo que sucedía se debía a una alianza de el cártel del Golfo con el cártel de Sinaloa y la Familia Michoacana, bajo un lema que —según decían— convenía a todos: "México unido contra los Zetas".

4. Pepino

Estoy frente al Hotel El General, bautizado así en honor a Francisco Villa: un edificio blanco de tres pisos, ubicado en el cruce de las calles Allende y Colón, a menos de 20 kilómetros de distancia del puente internacional de Roma, Texas, uno de los accesos que tiene Ciudad Mier a Estados Unidos. Puedo reconocerlo por el mural que representa a Pancho Villa. Durante los días de combate, en una de las ventanas contiguas al mural se instaló un francotirador en busca de cabezas. Las construcciones de mayor solidez en el pueblo fueron usadas como lugar de resguardo durante las batallas callejeras, y las que no fueron incendiadas, acabaron con más hoyos que un queso *gruyère* y aún se encuentran severamente dañadas.

Ciudad Mier fue sitiada por lo menos en tres ocasiones a sangre y fuego en 2010, pero los francotiradores no fueron los que sembraron el mayor terror. En una de las incursiones, uno de los grupos armados capturó a un peón apodado *Pepino* y lo sometió a juicio sumario. A plena luz del día lo llevaron hasta la plaza principal, donde lo estuvieron golpeando bajo la acusación de ser un *halcón* (vigía) del bando rival. Él alegaba que esto no era cierto mientras le cortaban un brazo. Todos los habitantes del casco principal podían oír su gritadera mientras lo descuartizaban. Nadie se asomó. Tanto era el miedo, que pasaron casi 12 horas antes de que alguien se atreviera a descolgarlo de la rama del árbol donde lo ahorcaron.

5. Guatemala

Un hombre de aire campesino llamado José Concepción Martínez participó en "El Alzamiento" del 22 de febrero. Antes de ser reclutado para la guerra de Tamaulipas estuvo ocho años en la Marina Armada. Patrullaba Ciudad Mier en una camioneta con logos del C.D.G. cuando se topó con un convoy de los Zetas que lo capturó y lo hizo su prisionero. En un video enviado en agosto de 2010 por sus captores por medio de mensajes electrónicos masivos, y subido y bajado de You-Tube de forma intermitente, se ve a Concepción y a otros tres pistoleros vestidos con uniformes de camuflaje, hincados, con las manos amarradas a la espalda y los ojos vendados, mientras eran interrogados por un comandante de los Zetas. Concepción relata que estaba en Reynosa en espera de indicaciones junto con otros diez pistoleros antes de integrarse a una estaca, nombre que dan los grupos criminales de la región a sus equipos de vigilancia más pequeños. Su sueldo quincenal era de ochocientos dólares. Había sido capturado mientras trataba de escapar de un enfrentamiento durante su bautismo de fuego en la guerra. Aunque contraatacó con una ametralladora, tropezó en la retirada y el arma se le encasquilló. No tardó mucho en ser sometido.

El segundo de los prisioneros que aparece es José Abel Rubí. Abel nació en Baja Verapaz, un pueblo del norte de Guatemala. En la ciudad de Zacapa lo contactó un hombre de apodo el *Paisa*, quien andaba buscando gente que quisiera irse a una guerra que iba a empezar en el noreste de México, para la cual se necesitaban personas que supieran matar sin que eso les afectara el sueño a la hora de dormir. Les decía que a cambio el sueldo era de 1,500 dólares al mes. Abel aceptó y se embarcó con otros hombres en el puerto De Ocos hasta llegar a las costas de Oaxaca después de ocho horas de navegación. En Oaxaca los esperaba un autobús, al cual se subieron junto con salvadoreños, nicaraguenses y hondureños, incluyendo algunas mujeres. El vehículo llegó sin mayores problemas hasta Reynosa, donde los recibieron y les avisaron que trabajarían para el cártel del Golfo. A Abel lo asignaron a la plaza de Ciudad Mier. Una tarde en la que vigilaba la carretera apareció un convoy rival. Cuando quiso subirse a la camioneta en la que patrullaba, su compañero arrancó y lo dejó ahí, junto a otros compañeros de aventura bélica, muertos y atravesados por las balas.

El tercero de los prisioneros de guerra que aparecen es un hombre que dice ser de Ciudad Victoria, Tamaulipas, y haber sido contactado ahí por Jesús Martínez Hernández, un joven reclutador a quien apodaban el *Binomio*, quien, semanas después de iniciados los combates, se dio un tiro en la cabeza, debido a un ataque de paranoia. El prisionero de Ciudad Victoria relata que la mayoría de los hombres reclutados en México son de Michoacán; son ellos quienes integran los comandos que recorren la región acompañados por algún nativo de Tamaulipas, elemento que a su vez suele tener la función de guía.

El cuarto de los prisioneros se llama Miguel López Rodríguez y es del puerto de Veracruz. Cuenta que después de un enfrentamiento fue capturado en Ciudad Mier. Tenía once días de estar de guardia ahí y se movía por las carreteras de los alrededores, junto con otras tres decenas de hombres, a bordo de siete camionetas. Cuando sus captores se lo llevaban, de reojo vio que atrás quedaba un reguero de muertos, tiesos como el cuero. Saldo mudo de la batalla.

Tras dieciocho minutos de proyección el video acaba abruptamente sin que hasta la fecha se sepa el destino de los prisioneros. Por el momento hay que agregarlos al número de las desapariciones forzadas en la región, y preguntarse si sus restos aparecerán algún día, cuando sean desenterradas las fosas comunes cavadas por ambos grupos para maquillar el horror de su lucha encarnizada.

6. La carretera

Aunque aquí suelen matar a alguien a diario, casi no hay muertos. Tamaulipas, una de las regiones más violentas del país, tiene reservada la palabra muerte para otras cuestiones espirituales (algo curioso tomando en cuenta que el mundo que se ve hoy por estos rumbos no incita precisamente a ser espiritual). En lugar de muertos, se habla de acribillados, encajuelados, encobijados, rafagueados, entambados y sobre todo de ejecutados. El verbo matar casi nunca se conjuga: más bien se dicen —y se practican— sus sinónimos. Pienso en eso mientras viajo por la carretera que va de Monterrey a Ciudad Mier, considerada una ruta algo más que peligrosa, donde a veces recorro tramos tan largos y solitarios que se podría jugar en ellos un partido de futbol en pleno lunes al mediodía.

Recuerdo un viaje lejano, allá en la adolescencia, cuando de repente al coche lo asaltaban por las ventanillas el sonido de una polka norteña o el olor denso de arracheras asándose sobre el carbón y chiles serranos tostándose entre las brasas. Ahora no hay nada de aquello. Oigo las roncas combustiones emitidas por el motor del coche y el aire me parece asfixiante.

Marín, Doctor González, Cerralvo, General Treviño, son los nombres de pueblos sin vida que quiero dejar atrás cuanto antes, mientras me dirijo a Ciudad Mier enumerando cada uno de los 158 kilómetros de esta carretera que la guerra convirtió en un camino de sombras.

7. El negocio

A diferencia de Sinaloa y Chihuahua, en Tamaulipas no se cuenta con una larga tradición en el tráfico de drogas. No al nivel de Sinaloa, que desde los treinta ha surtido de importantes cantidades de heroína, marihuana y cocaína a estados como California, el lugar del mundo con más consumidores de drogas por metro cuadrado, y por ende el mercado más codiciado entre esa empresa armada que es el narco. En el noreste de México, sobre la ruta a ciudades como Nueva York, si bien existía el contrabando, el narcotráfico tuvo un crecimiento importante hasta hace apenas dos décadas, en un principio bajo el control omnipotente de la policía federal y de un grupo de traficantes al que se le denominó "El Cártel del Golfo", por la ubicación de Tamaulipas en el mapa.

Un profesor llamado Óscar López Olivares, quien fuera socio del capo Juan García Ábrego —y que más tarde se convirtió en testigo protegido del gobierno estadounidense— tiene una historia que contar. En sus memorias, aún inéditas, relata la forma en la que García Ábrego le dio un giro empresarial a la organización que había fundado el tío de éste último, Juan Nepomuceno Guerra.

De cara a lo que vendría después, las ambiciones del contrabandista Juan N. Guerra, eran sin duda modestas. Cuenta López Olivares:

En el año de 1980 quedó establecido el puente aéreo Mata-moros-Oaxaca, con un promedio de 4 vuelos por semana de 400 kilogramos de cañamo indígena (mota, marihuana, grifa, hierba verde) en ese tiempo contaba con 40 años y jamás en mi vida había visto la hierba, pues apenas acaba-ba de conocer la cocaína, que los mismos agentes federales me habían enseñado a utilizar, contra el cansancio del vuelo. En Matamoros, la Policía Judicial Federal, estaba compuesta únicamente por tres elementos y todos eran ami-gos de Juan García Ábrego desde la infancia. Les con-seguíamos oficinas, muebles, armas y les pagábamos la luz así como una gratificación por cada viaje. Durante los años siguientes se hizo una constante que a cada comandante nuevo que llegaba, había que comprarle nuevamente todo, pues el que se iba no dejaba nada.

Este tipo de operaciones fueron las que predominaron y se afianzaron durante el gobierno de Carlos Salinas de Gortari, cuando se incluyó al cártel de Cali como el gran proveedor de la cocaína colombiana vendida a los consumidores estadouni-denses. En enero de 1996, García Ábrego fue detenido y extra-ditado a Estados Unidos, y el cártel del Golfo vivió su primera transición. Por esa época, a finales de los noventa, Osiel Cár-denas Guillén tomó el control y empezó a oírse hablar de los Zetas, pero lo que se decía sobre ellos parecía más leyenda que realidad.

En un inicio, los Zetas eran un grupo de escoltas encarga-dos de cuidar la vida del capo. Sin embargo, a partir de 2003, cuando Osiel Cárdenas Guillén fue detenido y encarcelado en una prisión de máxima seguridad, el grupo conformado por ex militares de élite entrenados en Estados Unidos, creó una organización de corte marcial dirigida por Heriberto Lazcano, cabo de infatería desertor con entrenamiento especial en combate, inteligencia y contrainsurgencia. La extradición de Cárdenas Guillén a Estados Unidos acabó por darles la autonomía total como un nuevo grupo en el mapa del narcotráfico nacional, convirtiéndose, incluso, en una especie de marca registrada de la violencia extrema. Su fama hoy es tal que un zeta no es solamente quien forma parte de dicha organización, sino también lo es aquel sicario o narco que pone la violencia por delante del "negocio".

Hasta febrero de 2010, el cártel del Golfo prácticamente había desaparecido. Fue entonces cuando ocurrió "El Alzamiento" y cuando el grupo que lo encabezó revivió las siglas C.D.G., para nombrar la alianza de algunos traficantes tamaulipecos con el cártel de Sinaloa y la Familia Michoacana en contra de los Zetas.

8. San Fernando

Como Ciudad Mier, hay otros pueblos a la redonda colapsados por la guerra. Uno es San Fernando; como cualquiera podría imaginar después de que ahí se encontraran, el 23 de agosto de 2010, los cadáveres de setenta y dos migrantes. Lo sé también porque gente de ahí me ha contado cómo la plaga de la guerra y los enfrentamientos llegaron a trastocarlo todo desde febrero; arrojaron decenas de muertos y con ello impactaron la vida de los habitantes del casco de San Fernando. Sin embargo, sé también que lo peor ocurrió en las carreteras y brechas donde se cree que los asesinatos se cuentan por cientos. De esto se sabe muy poco con certeza, debido a que la prensa regional no puede informar de ello, y los enviados de la prensa nacional y extranjera, estarían en grave riesgo si intentaran pisar la zona para investigar.

Las brechas son espacios ideales para moverse y esconderse en una guerra como la de Tamaulipas; y más que un pueblo, San Fernando es, en cierto sentido, un casco urbano con un laberinto interminable de brechas. La gente que debe transitar por algunas de éstas, relata cómo el olor a muerto tiene impregnado los caminos, y cómo los zopilotes ya pasan más tiempo pisando la tierra que volando. ¿Cómo hacer que la curiosidad venza al miedo, para ir a verificar si lo que se dice sobre las brechas es verdad y no una exageración?

Me cuentan también que en los primeros días de la guerra era común ver la ciudad patrullada por convoyes de pistoleros de uno u otro bando, apuntando sus armas hacia la calle y las casas. Esas manadas de vehículos que irrumpían en el pueblo llegaron a estar formadas hasta por cuarenta camionetas *pick-up* doble cabina, en las cuales se movían cuatro pistoleros en cada una: ciento sesenta hombres con armamento seguramente adquirido en Estados Unidos. A veces los convoyes paraban su marcha e instalaban retenes en las carreteras para vigilar el ingreso a la zona. Otras veces desataban el trueno de sus fusiles contra cualquier cosa que les pareciera amenazante.

Hasta antes de la matanza de los setenta y dos migrantes, ocurrida en un rancho del ejido El Huizachal, la presencia del Ejército era reducida en San Fernando. Después de la tragedia la zona se militarizó, pero sólo unos días. Cuando los soldados se fueron los ánimos de los habitantes que todavía no huían, se volvieron a desmoronar. Me dicen que quizá no voy a encontrar un solo sanfernandense que no haya perdido amigos, familia o conocidos de toda la vida, a causa del conflicto. Me aseguran que no todos los muertos son narcos, que hay muchos inocentes, que no debo olvidar que en las guerras la muerte es pareja, y que siempre hay dramas terribles como los que han sucedido en ésta; dramas como el de esas familias que han hecho funerales y enterrado solamente las cabezas de sus parientes muertos, porque el resto de los cuerpos jamás los pudieron encontrar.

9. La soledad

Basta echar una ojeada a un mapa de México para darse cuenta de que Ciudad Mier es la línea divisoria entre dos grupos en guerra. Reynosa, área de influencia de C.D.G., queda al oriente, y Nuevo Laredo, bajo control de los Zetas, al este. Ciudad Mier está justo a la mitad, por eso es explicable que ahí se librara la batalla más importante de la guerra de Tamaulipas. Lo que no es explicable es que Ciudad Mier fuera abandonado a su suerte, que las autoridades lo dejaran morir lentamente, durante casi nueve meses.

Al menos eso creen algunos de sus pobladores, quienes sospechan que uno de los grupos está haciendo la guerra que debería hacer el gobierno, y que se preguntan que si esto no es así, por qué no entraron antes los militares de forma permanente, como lo hicieron hasta finales de año, el 2 de noviembre, tras un enfrentamiento que provocó el éxodo de prácticamente todos los habitantes.

En la Octava Zona Militar responden a esta pregunta diciendo que era imposible hacerlo debido a que la mayoría de la tropa estaba concentrada en otras operaciones ordenadas desde la ciudad de México, y que Ciudad Mier no era el único lugar en guerra. Algunos de los pobladores no creen en esto, y argumentan que hubo negligencia gubernamental. A su juicio, la lógica fue dejar que los narcos se destruyeran entre ellos, y al hacerlo, de paso, se permitió que destruyeran Ciudad Mier.

En ese lapso, los muertos de la guerra de Tamaulipas se quedaron sin acta de defunción. De febrero a noviembre de 2010 hubo masacres, asesinatos selectivos y balaceras pero no hubo parte informativo de las batallas ni comunicado o vocero que diera cuenta de lo sucedido o de sus causas. En medio de los bandos en pugna, los habitantes eran juguetes de un azar indescifrable, y fuera de Tamaulipas pocos se enteraban de lo que sucedía. La información de la zona salía a cuentagotas vía internet. Una mujer se atrevió a grabar la forma en que quedó la La Ribereña —la carretera que comunica a Ciudad Mier con el poblado de Camargo— luego de un enfrentamiento que duró toda la madrugada. Días después de subir las imágenes a las redes sociales, el video se convirtió en noticia de portada en los diarios nacionales y tema de conversación por unos días. Luego se reanudó, otra vez en silencio, la guerra de Tamaulipas: cadáveres tirados, harapos ensangrentados, esqueletos de camionetas calcinadas, miles de cartuchos percutidos y militares peinando la zona aparecen en la grabación de un enfrentamiento cuyo registro oficial no existe, pero que ocurrió y se supo gracias al teléfono celular de una mujer desconocida.

Algún día alguien contará la historia de tantos anónimos valientes que también ha producido la guerra de Tamaulipas, como esta mujer.

Durante ese tiempo, Ciudad Mier no sólo fue un pueblo sin policías: fue un pueblo sin escuela, sin bancos, sin carnicerías, sin médicos y sin farmacias, porque los principales establecimientos estuvieron cerrados buena parte de los nueve meses. Camionetas cargadas de gente con maletas y bultos abandonaban al pueblo. La Arquidiócesis estuvo a punto de dejar a Ciudad Mier también sin cura, pero —pese a la orden de sus superiores— el sacerdote del pueblo fue el único de la Frontera Chica que se rehusó a abandonar su templo durante los enfrentamientos. El tamaño de la soledad de Ciudad Mier era tal que el alcalde sólo visitaba la presidencia municipal dos veces por semana, y el resto de los días los pasaba en Roma, Texas, o en cualquier otro lugar lejano y seguro.

En 2010 no sólo no se celebró el aniversario del pueblo, tampoco hubo fiestas de Semana Santa, Día de las Madres, y ni siquiera Grito de Independencia. La vida civil en Ciudad Mier se fue extinguiendo de forma callada y cruel, hasta que en noviembre apenas quedaban mil de los 6,117 habitantes de los que habla el censo oficial. Fue entonces cuando el país le prestó un poco de atención a la tragedia del pueblo, ignorando lo que le había ocurrido a lo largo de los meses anteriores.

10. El periodista

Cuando empezó la guerra, uno de los pocos periodistas que viajaron de la ciudad de México a Tamaulipas a ver lo que pasaba fue un buen amigo mío. Serio como persona y más como reportero. No es de esos que hacen periodismo porque andan buscando la misma adrenalina que puedes conseguir si te subes a la Montaña Rusa, o de los que creen que las guerras son como en las películas de Hollywood, o que se trata de un asunto poético. Antes estuvo en Líbano, y sabe que los campos de batalla están llenos de sangre, de cuerpos mutilados, de dolor y de pánico; que la palabra guerra no tiene el mismo significado para un político que la usa como un elemento más de su retórica, que para quien la padece en carne y hueso.

Mi amigo Raymundo Pérez Arellano estuvo trabajando al principio sin demasiados aspavientos en esos días de marzo de 2010 en Reynosa, junto con un camarógrafo de Milenio Televisón. Hicieron un reportaje sobre el hip-hop que le canta al narco y otro sobre la cuenta de Twitter del gobierno de la ciudad. Cuando trataban de corroborar unos datos —precisamente sobre periodistas locales desaparecidos a causa de la guerra— se toparon con un convoy de hombres armados que circulaba a plena luz del día por un lugar céntrico. Los pistoleros pasaron al lado de ellos. A los pocos minutos, los volvieron a topar por segunda ocasión, unas calles adelante. Los pistoleros detuvieron a mi amigo y al colega camarógrafo, les pusieron pistolas en la sien y cortaron cartucho, los golpearon, los llevaron a una casa de seguridad y los interrogaron. Antes de dejarlos en libertad les ordenaron: "Váyanse y avisen que la prensa no venga a calentarnos la plaza". Pocos minutos después Raymundo me llamó y soltó a bocajarro: "A la mierda el periodismo: no sirve para nada lo que hacemos".

11. El Dorado

Un par de años después de la firma del Tratado de Libre Comercio entre México, Estados Unidos y Canadá, se intensificaron los trabajos de explotación de gas de la Cuenca de Burgos, al permitirse de forma parcial la participación de empresas privadas. No es poca cosa la infraestructura gasera que ha sido levantada en la zona desde entonces, aunque la guerra la ha puesto en un segundo plano: hay 127 estaciones de recolección, veintiocho de trasiego y diez de entrega, así como 108 ductos de gas húmedo y 114 tuberías de gas seco con una longitud total de 2,789 kilómetros. En su conjunto, colocadas en línea recta, la totalidad de las instalaciones equivaldría a la distancia en carretera del Distrito Federal a Arizona. Aún así, la red de explotación todavía es muy limitada para la riqueza que hay en la región. En el vecino estado de Texas, por ejemplo, hay noventa mil pozos explorados y diez mil produciendo, mientras que en Tamaulipas existen once mil explorados y solamente 1,900 produciendo, de los cuales, la mitad pararon sus actividades a causa de la guerra.

Ciudad Mier y los demás poblados de la zona de guerra se localizan en una de las principales regiones energéticas del país. Hace unos años, luego de que se anunció una fuerte inversión de Pemex en el área, y de que se prometió un esquema de privatización parcial, la Frontera Chica empezó a ser conocida como un nuevo *El Dorado*. La expectativa de una explotación masiva del gas generó un *boom* económico: empresas y trabajadores emigraron a los pueblos de la región, provocando que aumentaran todos los precios, desde los tacos de carne asada hasta el de la hectárea de tierra.

Sin embargo, en 2010 el panorama cambió radicalmente: la guerra ahuyentó a pueblos enteros, hizo que bajara el precio de los predios, y en lugar de bonanza llegó la miseria y con ella la región comenzó a ser identificada como una tierra inhóspita.

En medio de la guerra, una cuadrilla de trabajadores estaba dando mantenimiento a la estación de compresión de gas de Pemex llamada Gigante 1, construida en un tramo de Nueva Ciudad Guerrero, municipio vecino de Ciudad Mier. De repente apareció un grupo de hombres armados y les advirtió que se fueran de ahí. Los técnicos obedecieron y reportaron a sus superiores lo que les había pasado ese 16 de mayo de 2010. No trabajaban directamente para la empresa paraestatal Pemex, sino para Delta, una de las compañías subcontratadas.

Junto con la estadounidense Halliburton, compañías como Delta llegaron hace tiempo a la zona, atraídas por la promesa de bonanza que dejaría la explotación de la Cuenca de Burgos, en la que Pemex calculaba en 2003 que se invertirían veinte mil millones de dólares durante los años siguientes.

Los jefes de la cuadrilla descreyeron el relato de los trabajadores y les ordenaron regresar la semana siguiente a la estación de compresión, si no serían despedidos. Así lo hicieron, y cuando apenas tenían unas horas de haber vuelto a la estación Gigante I, apareció uno de los grupos en guerra y, sin más, se llevó a seis de los trabajadores que estaban ahí. No hubo resistencia alguna. Los demás empleados alcanzaron a correr y esconderse. A la fecha nada se sabe del paradero o destino del mecánico Anselmo Sánchez Saldívar, de los ayudantes de mecánico, Martín Franco y Martín Zuñiga, del instrumentista de máquinas de compresión, Saúl García Ayala, y del operador de plantas de compresión, Christopher Cadena García. Rancheros que vivían en los alrededores de las instalaciones de la Cuenca de Burgos, como Gerardo García, César García y Adán de la Cruz Santiago, también fueron secuestrados y, al igual que los trabajadores de Pemex, siguen desaparecidos al día de hoy. El número de personas desaparecidas cerca de estaciones de Pemex es mayor, casi tan grande como el miedo a denunciarlas.

Tal y como lo comentan algunos conocedores de la región, suena a teoría de la conspiración suponer que en medio de la lucha de intereses que se disputan el estado de Tamaulipas, se encuentren también ciertas compañías petroleras de Texas. Sin embargo, cabe recordar que además del negocio de la guerra, Afganistán e Irak, representaron muy buenas inversiones en cuanto a energía se refiere para las mismas empresas estadounidenses que hoy —y desde hace tiempo— tienen los ojos puestos en la Cuenca de Burgos.

También suena a teoría de la conspiración ese afán de justificar todos los males de la zona como el resultado de un enfrentamiento entre un cártel y otro, ignorando los intereses políticos y económicos que existen en la Frontera Chica, intereses que, de algún modo, quedaron en medio de la disputa por el control del tráfico de drogas a Estados Unidos.

Conspiración o no, nada se sabe con certeza sobre lo que pasará con el tesoro nacional que hay bajo el teatro de la guerra en Tamaulipas.

12. El silencio

En una situación de guerra, negarse a prestar testimonio es una de las maneras que los testigos tienen de salvar sus vidas. Fingir ignorancia es una forma de sobrevivir. Y en esta guerra, los bandos en pugna exigen un silencio a su favor.

Por lo general las revueltas buscan hacer visible algo. Lo de Tamaulipas es otra cosa: lo contrario.

Me cuentan que hace poco estuvo por aquí la televisora Al Jazeera, y que lo que decían los periodistas enviados era que nunca habían estado en un terreno tan fangoso, donde el riesgo y el desconcierto lo dominaran todo. Los de Al Jazeera, que en los años recientes han estado en las líneas de fuego de los principales conflictos bélicos del planeta, no pudieron recorrer la carretera de La Ribereña. Ni los funcionarios locales ni los militares les dieron mínimas garantías de que saldrían vivos si lo intentaban. Optaron por hacer un reportaje sobre la forma en que los *sheriffs* fronterizos texanos viven el drama tamaulipeco.

¿Qué más? Nadie sabe cómo cubrir lo que sucede aquí. Por mucho, la tarea más difícil del periodismo la tienen mis colegas locales. En los periódicos de Tamaulipas lo que debe callarse supera a lo que se puede contar. Enciendo la radio del coche. Hay canciones de Rigo Tovar o de Cuco Sánchez, o comentarios sobre los resultados del torneo de futbol nacional, pero no se informa de las cinco personas asesinadas hace unas horas en el centro de Reynosa, ni tampoco de los ataques con lanzagranadas en un ejido de Camargo. Me pregunto: ¿cómo va a documentarse cincuenta años después, lo que hoy sucede en Tamaulipas si no existe registro alguno al día siguiente?

Sé que el silencio que hoy existe en Tamaulipas no se generó de forma espontánea. Para funcionar, el silencio requiere de un sofisticado aparato de represión. Necesita de fosas clandestinas, de gobernantes ilegítimos, del monopolio de los cuernos de chivo, de la degradación económica, de policías corruptos y de una sociedad civil aletargada. "Quien se impone mediante el ruido debe hacer un mayor esfuerzo para mantener su hegemonía que quien lo hace a través del silencio". Kapuscinski decía eso y decía también que por tal motivo, la palabra "silencio" casi siempre aparece asociada con palabras como "sepulcro" (silencio sepulcral) o "mazmorras" (el silencio de las mazmorras).

No se trata de asociaciones gratuitas.

Sé que a *Pepino* lo mataron sin que nadie hiciera nada y en silencio. Uno de los hombres que oyó todo —y que lo vio al día siguiente colgado antes de entrar a misa— me contó que desde ese día no ha podido dormir bien. Ese hombre ha entrado ya al laberinto negro de los insomnios que producen todas las guerras.

La batalla de Ciudad Mier, de todo Tamaulipas, es sobre todo una batalla contra el silencio.

13. Un millón de balas

El 2 de noviembre de 2010, cuando los Zetas lanzaron una contraofensiva para recuperar el control de Ciudad Mier, Matilde González Puente estaba en la sala de su casa viendo la telenovela de las cuatro de la tarde. Al escuchar los primeros balazos se levantó de la silla para ir a cerrar primero la puerta principal y luego la del patio. Los balazos se siguieron oyendo e imploró: "¡Virgen, líbreme!", mientras lamentaba en sus adentros que hubiera gente con una piedra en lugar de corazón. Después dos balas pasaron cerca de ella y se estrellaron al lado de un viejo ropero, dejando un par de hoyos en el concreto. Matilde González se apresuró a entrar a una pequeña bodega dentro de la casa, donde había un colchón, el cual se colocó encima para tratar de sentir menos miedo y calmar el temblor de su artritis. A sus ochenta y dos años, Matilde no había podido abandonar el pueblo como la enorme mayoría lo habían hecho ya. Uno de sus hijos vive en Monterrey, y sus dos hijas en Estados Unidos, una en California y la otra en Texas. "Vivo de milagro, por pura cosa de diosito", me dijo el día que la conocí. Matilde nació el 18 de diciembre de 1928, cuando no tenían mucho de haber menguado las batallas revolucionarias en México y estaba en pleno auge la lucha cristera. Fue una de las pocas personas que nunca abandonó Ciudad Mier, y me dijo que ya estaba resignada a morir como nació: en medio de la guerra. Creía que lo que le sucedido al pueblo tenía una explicación divina y que los responsables recibirán algún día lo que merecen: "Dios sólo espera el momento indicado".

Pasaron varias horas hasta que amainó la tormenta de pólvora ocurrida ese Día de Muertos que Matilde González pasó encerrada. Toda la noche hubo humo saliendo de la esquina norte del pueblo, y en las calles del acceso a Reynosa quedaron los esqueletos de tres camionetas calcinadas y un camión recolector de basura volteado tras ser improvisado como barricada. En algunas paredes aparecieron pintas de *graffiti* con mensajes como: "Su plaza Ja ja ja", "Sálganle Golfas, ya llegamos" y "Pónganse vergas porque ya llegamos los zetas a quedarnos".

Otro hombre, de ojos color avellana, Gregorio Olivo Salinas, nacido por los mismos años que Matilde González, también estuvo cuando sucedió la batalla del Día de Muertos. Mientras platicábamos, a varias semanas de los sucesos, unos albañiles trabajaban en Hidalgo, una de las calles principales donde había fachadas de casas que tenían las paredes negras por el fuego, y otras que guardaban todavía tantos impactos de bala en el concreto, que parecían estar enfermas de sarampión.

"¿Cuántos balazos se habrán disparado ese día?" pregunté.

"¿Aquí? Millones de cartuchos que se recogían ahí. Hasta para venderlos por kilo, pero no se mataba tanto porque todos estaban bien escondidos, arriba de las casas."

"¿Le había tocado a usted una cosa así?"

"Fui jefe de la policía vario tiempo, tres etapas. Pero no, había otras cosas duras, nada cómo esto."

"¿Cómo qué?"

"La (policía) federal era la que andaba aquí encargada de ese asunto. Yo estuve del 86 para atrás y ya después arreglé mi pasaporte y me fui a trabajar para allá." (Señala en dirección a unos mezquites detrás de los cuales está el Río Bravo).

Gregorio Olivo empezó a fastidiarse de la conversación. Se movía de un lado a otro y se tocaba el ala izquierda del sombrero vaquero que llevaba puesto.

"Ojalá que se mejore la situación de Ciudad Mier," le dije.

"Ojalá, qué más quisiéramos porque pues apenas se está arrimando la gente al pueblo. Aquí estaba antes solo, solo. En esta calle nada más yo me quedé. Ahora bueno, pues ya comienza a haber familias."

"¿Y usted por qué no se fue?"

"¿A dónde me voy? Al cabo lo que no te pasa de joven, de viejo no te escapas. [Risas]. Yo no tenía a donde correr."

14. Ciudad Mier

En este instante, la única compañía que siento en la solitaria carretera por la que voy es la de unas cruces monumentales ubicadas en el kilómetro 35. Son del tamaño de una casa de tres pisos y están a la entrada de un cementerio.

Unos kilómetros más adelante aparece, en el carril de sentido contrario, el único vehículo con el que te has topado en media hora de recorrido. Es una vieja *pick-up* conducida por un hombre de bigote y camisa celeste, quien enciende y apaga las luces un par de veces justo cuando su coche está frente a mi. Quiere decirme algo. En cualquier otra carretera pensaría que me avisa que tengo una llanta ponchada, o que más adelante te vas a topar con un accidente o con un tramo en mal estado, pero en esta carretera lo que se viene a la mente es que adelante hay un enfrentamiento o un retén de alguno de los grupos de la guerra. Sigo la marcha y lo que encuentro es una obra en construcción que parece abandonada, por lo que debo salir de la carretera unos metros y andar entre la tierra antes de retomar el camino de asfalto. Solares yermos, arbustos verdigrises, corrales vacíos, tristes nopales, bodegas de alimento para vacas derrumbándose: el paisaje de un campo agonizante va quedando atrás.

Poco antes de entrar a Ciudad Mier, en el municipio contiguo de General Treviño, veo a mi costado izquierdo un rancho donde hay algo de vida y una imagen que parece un espejismo: avestruces y ponys compartiendo cautiverio entre los mezquites retorcidos de troncos gruesos y follaje abundante que les regalan sombra. Más adelante, asomándose por el valle, advierto unas columnas de humo negro, denso y brumoso. Otra vez se activa discretamente un alarma dentro de mi.

Así se recorre esta carretera, bajo tensión.

El coche continúa su marcha. Paso a un lado de la humareda y me doy cuenta de que fue causada por basura quemada. La siguiente imagen con la que me topo es la de pequeños montículos con costales llenos de tierra y tambos atiborrados de rocas en ambos lados de la carretera, trincheras que por el momento no dan refugio a nadie.

He llegado al sitio que andaba buscando: Bienvenido a Ciudad Mier.

15. CDG y Zetas

El C.D.G. inició la ofensiva contra los Zetas divulgando un canto de batalla con ritmo de hip hop. Un rapero fronterizo cuyo nombre artístico es Sr. Cortés grabó la canción de propaganda. Se llama "El Reto" y busca explicar el por qué del inicio de la guerra en febrero de 2010.

Dice así:

> *Recuerda ciudadano: no todo es violencia, por eso el CDG, también en eso piensa. Respeto a tu familia, no te metas conmigo, insisto y te recuerdo: yo no soy el enemigo.*
>
> *Esto va de parte de CDG, esto es un llamado, así es que escuchen bien: el pleito no es contigo, ni con el gobier-*

no, pero si nos buscas, arderás en el infierno. El que mata a mujeres y niños es un cobarde. Hay que ir de frente, porque así es el jale. Confunden la valentía con la felonía, cuando en verdad, es pura cobardía. Los que se creen valientes, allá ellos con su fama, mienten y quitan la vida a gente inocente. Los invito: topón de frente. Ya saben: escojan el puente, la hora, el día para desaparecerlos como los dinosaurios, extinguirlos en masa con la metraca, tacataca-taca.

Pa que el pueblo sepa que el CDG respeta, en todo el planeta, pa que se den cuenta que aquí va la vuelta, pa los que secuestran.

Y con el gobierno evitamos la fricción, pero si así lo quieren nos damos un tocón. Es por eso que con ellos evitamos balaceras, para que así gente inocente no se muera. Pueblo no confundan al cártel con cobardes; si el CDG no mata más que a los cobardes.

Ya lo saben, acabemos con la escoria. Y protejamos bien nuestras colonias. Así es que los retamos a que se la fleten al estilo bravo, líderes enfrente, no manden achichincles para que los mate, amárrense las bolas, bola de cobardes.

Matamoros, Reynosa y Laredo, todo Tamaulipas, también el mundo entero, en el entrenamiento el cártel no escatima, por eso en Tamaulipas, el CDG domina. Flétense cabrones, nos damos un tocón, y donde ustedes quieran, les damos un juntón. Maten pero el hambre, y déjense de pedos, y por si necesitan, yo les presto mi dedo. Esto es un reto.

A su vez, los Zetas, poco después de iniciados los ataques, enviaron a los buzones de los correos electrónicos de funcionarios locales, periodistas y empresarios, el siguiente escrito, explicando su posición ante la guerra:

Este es un comunicado oficial de parte de La Compañía.

Sabemos que en todas las ciudades están molestos con todo lo que está pasando, y están hartos de ver cómo esto no se termina, pero aquí esta la realidad de lo que querían saber:

A nosotros nos tachan de secuestradores, extorsionadores, asesinos y demás, pero les recuerdo que nosotros, antes de que iniciara todo esto, estábamos a las órdenes del Cártel del Golfo (CDG), y por lo cual recibíamos órdenes. Ahora que ellos nos declararon la guerra, aún así nos culpan de quemar casas, de matar gente inocente y demás, como si ellos no hicieran eso.

Se tachan de finos, estudiados y buena gente, que hasta roban tiendas de ropa para vestir bien. Queman casas porque creen que así nos iremos para siempre, matan a gente inocente para echarnos la culpa de eso y que toda la ciudad se ponga en contra de nosotros, y ellos queden bien. Ponen comunicados en diferentes medios para tapar el sol con un dedo.

Nosotros no necesitamos andar diciendo a la gente que nos apoye, ni mucho menos reclutamos alumnos de secundarias como ellos lo hacen. Nosotros somos gente preparada para combate y no necesitamos de gente que no sabe ni manejar una arma.

Ellos nos declararon la guerra y ahora no la ven llegar porque están situados en territorios donde no se pueden mover para ningún lado y por eso necesitan de sus alianzas con otros cárteles para defenderse, pero no saben que sus aliados los terminarán exterminando primero a ellos.

Así que espero que les quede claro la realidad de quién recluta gente no preparada, de quién asesina gente inocente para culparnos a nosotros, de quién arma sicosis en la ciudad para que la ciudadanía crea que con ellos las extorsiones, secuestros y asesinatos terminarán, de quiénes publican miles de "comunicados" y pagan mucho dinero para que sus videos sean publicados.

Somos lo que somos pero estamos conscientes de nuestras acciones y antes de realizarlas, le añadimos inteligencia.

Sólo nos resta decirles que no salgan de sus casas si no tienen nada a que salir, y ante cualquier evento en la calle, traten de resguardarse, pero tengan por seguro que nosotros sí tenemos entrenamiento, no como ellos, que no saben actuar ante una situación así. Con esto no les estamos pidiendo que nos apoyen ni que anden poniendo gente, solo que no se metan con nosotros y que nos dejen trabajar. Al final de esto, saldrá victorioso quien tenga más poder y más estrategia para poder realizar su trabajo.

Estamos conscientes de que perderemos gente, pero ellos perderán todo. Nosotros podemos realizar nuestro trabajo sin necesitar el apoyo de la población inocente.

Atentamente: La compañía Z.

16. Guerra

La primera vez que vine a Ciudad Mier después de que pasó la parte más intensa de la guerra que desplazó a casi todos los habitantes del pueblo fue con Santos, un experimentado camarógrafo de Multimedios Monterrey que, junto con el periodista Daniel Aguirre, entró antes que nadie a la zona para corroborar la diáspora provocada por los enfrentamientos del 2 de noviembre. Las noticias sobre lo sucedido ese día aparecieron con tibieza en los diarios nacionales, donde no hay nunca el espacio suficiente para recoger todo el caudal de la violencia nacional.

Si estás allá, en ese raro oasis de paz en el que se convirtió hoy el Distrito Federal, puedes abrir el periódico casi cualquier mañana del año y leer que ayer en (aquí puedes poner Ciudad Mier o Guasave, o Fresnillo . . .) han sido ejecutados (aquí puedes poner cinco o diez o cincuenta) sicarios en (una cárcel, un rancho o tal plaza principal) y que . . . Tras empezar a leer la noticia te darás cuenta de que es la misma que leíste hace unos días, y la semana pasada también, y el año anterior, y mejor darás la vuelta a la página para enterarte de otra cosa más novedosa. Masacres de jóvenes, crímenes contra niños, asesinatos de alcaldes y las desapariciones de periodistas ocurren tan lejos de la capital del país, y son ya tantos que se olvidan al día siguiente.

Santos me contaba que cuando llegó a Ciudad Mier, tras los enfrentamientos del 2 de noviembre, él y su compañero iban con chaleco antibalas y casco, acompañados por soldados. Estaban conscientes de que si les pasaba algo, habría lamentaciones públicas y condenas por parte de los políticos unos días, pero que después sus muertes acabarían perdidas en la montaña de estadísticas.

Cuando él y yo viajábamos hacia Ciudad Mier, Santos contaba que la otra ocasión estuvo poco tiempo en el pueblo, pero que alcanzó a grabar muchos esqueletos de camionetas calcinadas y casas llenas de hoyos. Los soldados que lo escoltaban le daban tres minutos para grabar en cada parada. Le advirtieron que podía haber francotiradores, emboscadas o asaltos imprevistos, pero por suerte no hubo nada de aquello. Santos te hablaba de lo que para él significa reportear en esta zona, y de repente hizo una lista en su mente con los nombres de periodistas desaparecidos o asesinados que él conoció.

El día del viaje con Santos la mayor parte de la carretera estaba recubierta por neblina. Gotas de lluvia ligera perlaban el cristal del coche, pero de cualquier forma se podían ver los llanos dorados de la orilla del camino. Santos y yo suspendimos abruptamente la conversación en la gasolinera de Cerralvo, donde un grupo de veinte soldados, en dos camionetas, montaba guardia, con los dedos muy cerca del gatillo, listos para el combate.

La situación nos devolvió a la realidad del camino: hasta para ir a cargar combustible había que hacerlo preparado para la guerra.

17. El alcalde

Alberto González nunca había tenido ningún cargo de elección popular hasta que fue electo alcalde de Ciudad de Mier a media guerra. La disputa no obsequió saldo blanco a la clase política local: una semana antes de los comicios celebrados el 4 de julio, fue asesinado el candidato del PRI a la gubernatura, Rodolfo Torre Cantú, quien prácticamente tenía ganadas las votaciones. Alberto González, un hombre de pelo cano y lentes de profesor de biología, era el supervisor escolar de la zona comprendida por Ciudad Mier; en 2010 aceptó ser el aspirante priista a la alcaldía de un pueblo que nunca ha sido gobernado por otro partido que no sea el PRI. Para las elecciones del 4 de julio de 2010, Ciudad Mier ya estaba semivacío debido a los enfrentamientos. Ochenta por ciento del padrón registrado no votó; de los 6,009 electores registrados, apenas acudieron a las urnas 1,486 y de esos, 1,210 eligieron al candidato priista. Sólo cincuenta y cuatro habitantes votaron por el aspirante del PAN.

A principios de 2011, Alberto asumió el cargo de presidente municipal. Una de las primeras cosas que hizo su administración fue organizar cuadrillas de albañiles que remozaran los impactos de bala —miles de ellos— que había, principalmente, en las casas del casco y en los monumentos de las tres principales entradas al pueblo. Por esos días acompañé al alcalde en un recorrido a bordo de su camioneta. Fuera de las calles principales, el panorama lo componían casas abandonadas, calles tristes, sin personas ni perros, y comercios cerrados con los neones apagados.

Justo cuando el nuevo presidente municipal me explicaba que ya habían remozado la mayor parte del pueblo, pasamos a un lado del Hotel El General, la construcción favorita de los francotiradores, la cual se veía todavía muy dañada.

"Bueno," dijo el alcalde antes de que yo comentara algo, "en esta parte, pues el edificio fue destruido y fue quemado y ahora presenta como quiera otra cara, pero bueno, se siguen llevando a cabo obras de reconstrucción."

El edificio más afectado por la batalla de Ciudad Mier fue la comandancia municipal, cuya construcción era atacada constantemente, pese a que desde el inicio de la guerra ya no había policías dentro de ella. Durante el último enfrentamiento que se registró, el cual incluyó un ataque con lanzagranadas, ocurrió algo curioso: el edificio se incendió y de la fachada principal cayó material de estuco que se había sobrepuesto a la pared. La fachada original, con arcos, columnas y un águila republicana en el centro, quedó así a la vista, dándole un aire histórico y más solemne al edificio en ruinas, cuya antiguedad era de casi ciento treinta años.

Le conté después el hallazgo de este "tesoro" en medio de la guerra al escritor tamaulipeco Martín Solares, quien me dijo que para él la caída de la fachada de la comandancia de Ciudad Mier era la metáfora perfecta de lo que pasaba en el país: las balas estaban haciendo que cayera el barniz de la realidad que durante muchos años había sido ocultada superficialmente, y que ahora se estaba desmoronando, porque no aguantaba un balazo más.

Entré con el alcalde al viejo edificio y me topé con trozos de cables y las paredes ennegrecidas. En un escritorio había una televisión, un teléfono, una taza y una lámpara de mano achicharrados; estaban ahí también los papeles y plásticos que alimentaron el fuego.

"¿Vio la película *El Infierno*?" pregunté de repente al alcalde.

"No la he visto, pero ya me han dicho que lo de Mier es algo parecido," contestó con cierto fastidio.

"¿Por qué quiso ser alcalde de Ciudad Mier en un momento así?"

"Estamos muy motivados porque la gente también está muy motivada, está muy entusiasmada precisamente por recuperar esto, y eso te hace más fácil la situación. Además, el ambiente que vive Mier, yo creo que no es exclusivo de Mier, es nacional . . . Pero bueno, vuelvo a repetir, me siento contento porque me siento respaldado por la gente, y también tenemos el respaldo de otras dependencias: Pemex por ejemplo, que ha estado muy atento para ayudarnos en la reconstrucción de nuestro querido Ciudad Mier."

18. Tarantino

Ésta es la tercera vez que viajo a Ciudad Mier en lo que va del año. Ahora lo hago con dos colegas de Monterrey y con Daniel Aguilar, un fotógrafo al que me han tocado algunas balaceras en Oaxaca y en otros sitios de la atribulada geografía nacional. Pero no hablamos de eso durante el viaje. Platicamos de estos paisajes fronterizos, usados varias veces por Tarantino y Robert Rodríguez para filmar sus películas, de lo bonita que es la colonia Condesa allá en la Ciudad de México, del grupo musical Intocable, de lo caro que es el equipo fotográfico, y de cosas así.

19. Pollos asados

El domingo 6 de marzo de 2011 Ciudad Mier cumplió 258 años de haber sido fundada. Si la celebración del aniversario anterior se había cancelado debido a la guerra, ahora un grupo de pobladores, junto con el flamante alcalde, Alberto González, habían decidido organizar los habituales festejos para devolverle la vida al pueblo. Ese domingo al mediodía, bajo el resguardo de sesenta soldados, por la plaza principal caminaron duquesas, princesas y reinas, con grabaciones de música del piano de Raúl Di Blassio de fondo.

Aunque todavía se percibía el cataclismo de la guerra en algunos edificios, decenas de los pobladores exiliados en Texas y en Monterrey regresaron momentáneamente a Ciudad Mier. Una jovencita preparatoria con vestido color merengue y peinado de salón, fue nombrada reina Emily I, recibió una corona y un cetro y su primera actividad como Reina del pueblo fue decretar que Ciudad Mier debía seguir manteniéndose unida pese a la difícil situación.

Tras la coronación, frente a la comandancia municipal —ya algo restaurada— fue colocado un arriate con carbón encendido para asar en unas cruces de acero, 258 pollos, uno por cada aniversario del poblado.

"¿Por qué festejar con pollos asados?" pregunté a Diego Treviño, el secretario particular del alcalde.

"Porque era para lo que había, ¡pero para el otro año vamos a asar cabritos!" contestó emocionado al ver que más de quinientas personas se encontraban en la plazoleta que meses atrás había atestiguado horrores que no venía al caso recordar en ese momento.

La fiesta por el 258 aniversario de Ciudad Mier sólo incluyó el primer cuadro de la ciudad. Fuera de ahí el panorama sigue siendo desolador. Un fraccionamiento de casas Geo construido en 2003 está completamente abandonado, sin vida alguna. El resto de las calles y la devastación del paisaje advierten que quizá por ahora, lo que hay sólo es un periodo de entreguerra.

Por la tarde, el cura ofició una misa en la que imploró por la paz del pueblo. Los fieles oraron junto con él: "Señor, ayúdanos a combatir el miedo y la inseguridad, consuela el dolor de quienes sufren, da acierto a las decisiones de quienes nos gobiernan, toca el corazón de quienes olvidan que somos hermanos y provocan sufrimiento y muerte".

El alcalde Alberto González era quizá la persona más eufórica esa tarde, mas no por la fiesta. Unos días antes recibió una llamada telefónica de Julián de la Garza, uno de los directivos de Pemex encargados del proyecto de la Cuenca de Burgos. La cita entre ambos ya había ocurrido y el funcionario petrolero le había informado que le entregarían a su administración una buena cantidad de recursos económicos para sacar adelante a Ciudad Mier; le confirmó también que en la primavera se reactivaría la explotación de varios pozos de la Cuenca de Burgos, y que la compañía texana Halliburton, estaba muy interesada en afianzar su presencia en este 2011.

La esperanza del alcalde era tan grande, que calculaba que dentro de unos meses Ciudad Mier podría volver a tener policías.

20. Respirar

Antes de irnos de Ciudad Mier fuimos al entronque con la carretera La Ribereña, donde un enorme monumento con forma de campana recibió miles de impactos de bala y cerca del cual absolutamente nadie se atreve a vivir. Daniel Aguilar quería hacer unas fotografías del sitio, que en realidad es un cántaro monumental que alude a la leyenda de la creación del poblado. Mientras Daniel hacía sus fotos, uno de los colegas que nos acompañaban gritó: "¡Ya valió madre!" y señaló al horizonte de la carretera. Voltee y vi una camioneta blanca *pick-up* de reciente modelo, luego otra igual atrás, y después otra, y otra . . . "¿Son ellos?", preguntó Daniel. Yo callé. Ninguno sabía que hacer. Nos quedamos de piedra. El convoy se fue acercando, hasta que pasó a un lado de nosotros y alcancé a ver que las camionetas tenían en el costado un pequeño logotipo de Pemex. Eran once y pasaron de largo. Volví a respirar.

THE BATTLE FOR CIUDAD MIER

Diego Osorno
Translated by Nicolás Kanellos

This is the story of a town on the U. S.-Mexico border that
was squelched into silence by the war in Tamaulipas.

1. Street Corner of the Beheaded

On the morning of February 22, 2010, when Ciudad Mier
was preparing for its annual celebration, fifteen pickup trucks
bearing the Gulf Cartel logo entered the city like wild horses
from the Reynoso highway. The gunmen drove up to the
municipal police headquarters, got out of their vehicles and
the sound of machine guns firing at the ancient headquarters
building began. Everyone nearby dropped to the ground and
ran for cover.

When the firing ceased, six municipal policemen, beaten,
their mouths open, bloodied and with fear written on their
faces, were pulled out of the headquarters by the gunmen,
shouting slogans against the Zetas. That was the last seen of
the six policemen, and that was the last time that there were
municipal police in Ciudad Mier.

The cartel command placed gunmen at the three main entrances to downtown Ciudad Mier; they set up a perimeter inside of which four pickups explored and where sullen-faced men entered houses and businesses looking for specific people. Meanwhile, the main plaza in front of police headquarters was used by firing squads; two bleeding men were taken by the gunmen to the plaza. There, their bodies were riddled with bullets and their bodies decapitated. Their heads were mounted at a corner of the little plaza. Over time and after frequent use, that corner, henceforth, became known as "The Corner of the Beheaded."

A couple of hours after the gunmen had left the town, the Army made a quick round and disappeared before dark. All of the following week, the town could hardly sleep. Far-off shouts and shots cut the silence of the night. The streets were dirty and crumbling. There was no way to carry on with the planned March 6, 2010 celebration, which had to be cancelled, something that had not happened since the Revolution of 1910.

2. Magic Town

Although I don't see anyone, I know that someone is watching me. I feel him as I walk among the metal bullets strewn from the barrels of firearms and mixed with the broken glass that, despite my wariness, I cannot help but crunch under my boots. I have to hurry to finish looking at the broad blood stains and the thousands of bullet marks that remain on the walls of houses. Nightfall catches me as I try to collect more testimonies about what happened here these months. The darkness in a war zone is not the same as the dark; besides, there is no hotel, no place to hide to spend the night. For the time being, this is not the "Magic Town" on the sign to the town's entrance. Judging from the present destruction, this is the front line in the Tamaulipas war.

Supposedly, the two fighting gangs retreated to camps on nearby ranches some weeks ago. Even if I'm not embedded in an Army unit, wearing helmets and heavy, hot bulletproof vests, I can travel these streets where everything is covered in ash, the ground covered in burned garbage. There is no sign of the living in the houses. I know I'm in a ghost town and that the ghosts are watching me.

3. The Uprising

What happened in Ciudad Mier was not an irrational outbreak of violence. The attack on February 22, 2010 was part of a more ambitious plan to take control of the stretch of border between Tamaulipas and Texas, which is known on the Mexican side as the "Little Border." As a key zone for any type of illegal trafficking to the United States, this is also the location of the Burgos Field, the main source of Mexican natural gas.

The headquarters of such towns as Miguel Alemán, Camargo, Valle Hermoso and Nueva Ciudad Guerrero were assaulted in the same way as Ciudad Mier. The beginning of this offensive, that the government was late in identifying, has various names. For the Gulf Cartel, which initiated this war, the surprise attack is known as "The Return," but for the targeted Zetas that calendar date is known as "The Betrayal." On the other hand, most common people just call it "The Uprising."

The attacks coincided with the dissemination in Mexico of words of repentance by Osiel Cárdenas Guillén, who was the leader of both groups before he was extradited to the United States, where in exchange for a reduced sentence of twenty-five years in a medium security prison he rendered key information against the group he had founded a decade earlier: the Zetas.

With the outbreak of the war for Tamaulipas—a state four times as large as El Salvador and whose coast makes up a large part of the Gulf of Mexico—the state and federal police forces took no position on what was happening. When asked by journalists about the shootouts and armed conflict in the region, then governor Eugenio Hernández said it was "imagined." In public discourse, the Command of the Eighth Army hardly acknowledged the three battles in which one soldier was killed and eleven others were wounded. Finally, various government members leaked parts of an American DEA report to journalists: what was happening was an Alliance of the Gulf and Sinaloa Cartels with the Michoacan Family under the banner of "Mexico United against the Zetas."

4. "Pepino"—the Cucumber

I'm standing in front of the Hotel El General, named in honor of Francisco Villa. It is a white three-story building located at the junction of Allende and Colón Streets, less than 20 kilometers from the international bridge at Roma, Texas, one of the ports of entry for Ciudad Mier to the United States. I recognize the hotel because of the Pancho Villa mural on its exterior. During the days of the battle, a sniper installed himself in one of the windows beside the mural to aim at people's heads. The most solidly constructed buildings in town served as bunkers during street battles, and those that were not burned down ended up with more holes than Swiss cheese and are today still severely damaged.

Ciudad Mier was under bloody and fiery siege at least three times in 2010; however, the snipers were not the source of greatest terror. During one of the invasions, one of the armed groups captured a peon by the name of Pepino and submitted him to summary judgment. In broad daylight, they took him to the main plaza, where the beat him and accused him of being a spy for the rival gang. He denied the accusation while they cut off his arm. All the inhabitants downtown could hear his screams as they dismembered him. No one dared come outside. Their fear was so great that twelve hours went by before someone dared to cut the peon down from the tree where he had been hung.

5. Guatemala

A man with a campesino background, José Concepción Martínez, participated in "The Uprising" on February 22, 2010. Before he was recruited for the Tamaulipas war, he had served eight years in the Mexican Marines. He was patrolling Ciudad Mier in a pickup when he ran into a Zetas convoy that captured him and took him prisoner. In a video disk sent in August of 2010 by his captors to major media, and replayed periodically on YouTube, Concepción and others dressed in camouflage uniforms, were seen hanging with their hands bound behind them and their eyes blindfolded, while they were being interrogated by a Zeta commander. Concepción recounts that he and ten other gunmen were waiting for orders in Reynosa to join a small squad. He was earning $1,600 a month. He had been captured while trying to escape an onslaught during his baptism of fire in the war. Although he counter-attacked with a machine gun, he tripped in his retreat and his weapon got jammed. It did not take long for him to be overcome.

The second prisoner on the video was José Abel Rubí, who was born in Baja Verapaz, a town in northern Guatemala. He was contacted by a man nicknamed Paisa, in the city of Zacapa, who was recruiting men to go to a war that was about to start in northern Mexico, for which they needed men who knew how to kill without losing sleep over it. He was told that the salary was $1,500 a month. Abel accepted and he shipped out with other men from the Port of Ocos. After eight hours, they arrived on the coast of Oaxaca. There, a bus was waiting for them, which they boarded along with Salvadorans, Nicaraguans and Hondurans, including some women. The vehicle arrived without incident in Reynosa, where they were greeted and told that they would work for the Gulf Cartel. Abel was assigned to the plaza in Ciudad Mier. One afternoon when he was guarding the highway, a rival convoy appeared. As he was getting into the pickup he used for patrol, his partner took off and left him standing there, along with other soldiers of fortune who were shot dead.

The third prisoner of war in the video was a man who said he was from Ciudad Victoria, Tamaulipas, and had been contacted there by Jesús Martínez Hernández, a young recruiter nicknamed Binomio who, within weeks after the start of hostilities, shot himself in the head in an attack of paranoia. The prisoner from Ciudad Victoria recounts that the majority of the men recruited in Mexico were from Michoacán. They are the commandos who patrol the region accompanied by Tamaulipas natives, who usually serve as guides.

The fourth prisoner was Miguel López Rodríguez from the port of Veracruz. He said that after a shootout, he was captured in Ciudad Mier. He had worked as a guard there for eleven days, patrolling the highways with dozens of men in pickups. As his captors were taking him, out of the corner of his eye he saw that there were bodies littered all over the place, stiff as boards, the now silent remains of the battle.

After eighteen minutes, the video ends abruptly and to date no one knows the fate of the prisoners. For now, they should be added to the number of the forcefully disappeared in the region. Their remains will appear someday, when they are disinterred from the mass graves that both groups dug as adornment for their bloody struggle.

6. The Highway

Although someone is killed every day here, there are no dead. Tamaulipas, one of the most violent regions in the country, has reserved the word "death" for other spiritual issues (something strange given that life in this place does not seem very spiritual). Instead of speaking of dead men, you hear about the bullet riddled, the shrouded, the boxed up, the blown away and, more than anything, the executed. The verb to kill is almost never conjugated; rather, its synonyms are spoken—and practiced. I'm thinking about that as I travel the highway from Monterrey to Ciudad Mier, a route that is seen as more than dangerous with such long and lonely stretches that you could have a game of soccer on them at noon on a Monday.

I remember a trip long ago, when as a teenager I'd hear *norteño* polkas as I drove by and smell the beef loin barbecuing and hot peppers being grilled. Now there is nothing like that. I hear the hoarse roar of the car motor, and the air entering the window is asphyxiating.

Marín, Doctor González, Cerralvo, General Treviño are the names of lifeless towns that I speed away to leave behind me on my way to Ciudad Mier, counting every one of the 158 kilometers of this highway that the war has converted into a road of shadows.

7. The Business

In contrast to Sinaloa and Chihuahua, Tamaulipas has never had a tradition of drug trafficking. Never at the level of Sinaloa, which, since the 1930s, has been a supplier of large quantities of heroin, marijuana and cocaine to California, the place with the highest concentration of consumers and, therefore, the most attractive market for armed narcos. In addition, drug trafficking did exist in the northeast of Mexico, especially along the route to such cities as New York. There, trafficking grew rapidly up until two decades ago, first under the complete control of the federal police and a group of traffickers known as the "Gulf Cartel," because of the geographic location of Tamaulipas.

A professor by the name of Óscar López Olivares, who was an associate of the capo Juan García Ábrego, and who later became a witness protected by the U. S. government, recounts in his unpublished memoir how García Ábrego took the organization founded by his uncle, Juan Nepomuceno Guerra, and ran the cartel as a business enterprise.

Initially, in comparison to what the organization became, the intentions of smuggler Juan N. Guerra were modest:

In 1980, the route by air from Matamoros to Oaxaca was established, with an average of four flights a week, transporting 400 kilos of a native plant called marijuana. Back then, I was forty years old and had never seen that herb in my life. I had only then become familiar with cocaine, because federal agents had taught me to use it to combat the fatigue of flying. In Matamoros, the Federal Judicial Police was made up of only three officers, all of whom were friends of Juan García Ábrego since childhood. He paid for their offices, furniture, weapons, and even their electric bills as a gratuity for each shipment of drugs he sent north. This became such a custom that, over the years, for each new commander, García Ábrego had to buy him a new set-up —the outgoing commander usually took everything with him.

These were the types of operations that predominated and were customary during the presidency of Carlos Salinas de

Gortari, when the Cali Cartel became the largest provider of cocaine to U. S. consumers. In January 1996, García Ábrego was arrested and extradited to the United States, and the Gulf Cartel experienced its first transition. At that time, the late 1990s, Osiel Cárdenas Guillén took control and we began to hear about the Zetas, but what we heard seemed more like legend than reality.

At first, the Zetas worked as a group escorting and guarding the capo's life. Nevertheless, from 2003 on (after Osiel Cárdenas Guillén had been arrested and sent to a maximum security prison), this group made up of ex-military elite trained in the United States created a militaristic organization directed by Heriberto Lazcano, an infantry corporal who had deserted and who had special training in combat, intelligence, and counter-insurgency. The extradition of Cárdenas Guillén to the United States resulted in this group gaining its complete independence as a new narco organization on the Mexican map, quickly gaining for itself a reputation for extreme violence. Its infamy today is such that a Zeta is not only someone who belongs to that organization, but also any gangster or narco who places violence before "business."

Until February 2010, the Gulf Cartel had practically disappeared off the map. That is when the "Uprising" took place and when the group who revived the organization started using the logo of C. D. G. (Cartel del Golfo) to indicate the alliance of drug traffickers from Tamaulipas with the Sinaloa Cartel and the Michoacán Family against the Zetas.

8. San Fernando

Like Ciudad Mier, there are other towns in the area that have been destroyed. One is San Fernando, where on August 23, 2010, the bodies of seventy-two migrants were discovered. I know of this town's demise because people from there have told me how the plague of shootouts and conflicts had turned everything upside down since the previous February with dozens of dumped cadavers, impacting the lives of the inhabitants and creating great disorder in downtown San Fernando. Besides this, I also know that the worst occurred on the highways and open spaces where hundreds of assassinations are thought to have taken place. Very little is known about this because the regional press was prohibited from reporting on it. Correspondents from the national and international media were also at grave risk if they tried to enter the area to investigate.

Open spaces are ideal for moving about and hiding in a war like that of Tamaulipas; and San Fernando is somewhat of an unlimited series of open spaces more than a town. People who have to cross these spaces tell how the stench of death pervades the roads and that vultures spend more time on the ground than in the air. How can we overcome our fear to go and verify if what they say is true or just an exaggeration?

They also tell me that during the first days of the war it was common to see convoys of gunmen of one group or the other patrolling the town, aiming their weapons at streets and houses. Those lines of vehicles crossing through town were composed of up to forty four-door pick-ups carrying four gunmen each: one hundred-sixty men armed with weapons assuredly obtained in the United States. At times, the convoys would stop and drop off men to guard the entrance to the area. At other times, their weapons would explode at anything they thought to be threatening.

Up until the time of the slaughter of seventy-two migrants on El Huizachal ranch, the presence of the military did not extend beyond San Fernando. After that tragedy, the whole area became militarized for a few days. When the soldiers withdrew, the morale of the inhabitants that had remained disintegrated. I'm told that I may not be able to find a single San Fernando resident who has not lost an acquaintance, friend or family member in the conflict. They assure me that not all of the dead were narcos, that there were many inno-cents, that in war death is ubiquitous, and that there are always tragedies like this one, tragedies in which families only have the head of a loved one to bury, because the rest of the cadaver has never been found.

9. Solitude

It only takes a brief glance at the map of Mexico to reali-ze that Ciudad Mier is the dividing line between both warring groups. Reynosa, within the sphere of influence of the Gulf Cartel, lies to the west, and Nuevo Laredo under control of the Zetas lies to the east. Ciudad Mier is right in the middle; that's why it's understandable that the most important battle for Tamaulipas broke out there. What is hard to explain is why Ciudad Mier was left to its own devices, why the authorities let it die a slow, painful death over nearly nine months.

Some of Ciudad Mier residents believe that one of the narco groups was waging the war that the government should have. They ask, if this is not so, then why didn't the Army deploy permanently, as it did by the year's end on November 2, after a showdown that resulted in the exodus of almost all the residents.

In the Eighth Command Zone, the Army answers that it was impossible to deploy because most of the troupes were concentrated in other operations ordered by Mexico City, and Ciudad Mier was not the only war zone. Some inhabitants find this hard to believe and argue that the government was negli-gent. They think that the decision was to let the narcos des-troy each other and, in doing so, they also permitted the des-truction of Ciudad Mier.

During that time, the dead in the Tamaulipas were not interred. From February to November 2010, there were massacres, targeted assassinations and shootouts, but there was no news nor communiqués informing the nation about what was happening and why. Caught between the two warring bands, the inhabitants were the playthings of unknown fate, and outside Tamaulipas, few knew what was happening. Yet, information began slowly seeping out over the Internet. One woman dared record the condition of the La Ribereña highway between Ciudad Mier and Camargo after a shootout that had lasted all morning. A few days after uploading her images onto social networks, her video became the source for front page reports of the national dailies and commentary for some days. Soon, silence was restored as the Tamaulipas war continued: abandoned corpses, bloodied rags strewn, skeletal remains of burned pickups, thousands of cartridges littered everywhere, and soldiers combing through the area—all of this appearing in a video documenting a battle that officially never happened. But it did happen, and we know about it thanks to an unknown woman on a cell phone.

Someday, someone will tell the story of so many anonymous heroes, like this woman, that were also produced by the Tamaulipas war.

During that time, Ciudad Mier was not only a town without a police force, but it also was a town without a school, banks, butcher shops, doctors and drug stores, because all of the main establishments were closed for most of nine months. Vehicles full of people and their luggage continually abandoned the town. Even the archdiocese was about to leave Ciudad Mier without a single priest, but despite the orders of his superiors, the local priest was the only one in the whole region who refused to abandon his church during the battles. The solitude of Ciudad Mier was so profound that even the mayor only went to city hall twice a week, and he'd spend the rest of the time in Roma, Texas, or some other place, far away and safe.

In 2010, not only was the town's founding not celebrated, but there were also no celebrations for Holy Week, Mother's Day and not even for Independence Day. Civic life in Ciudad Mier was dying out cruelly and silently, until by November, there were only one thousand inhabitants left of the 6,117 recorded by the census. That's when the nation finally paid some attention to the town's tragedy, in total ignorance of all that had happened in the previous months.

10. The Journalist

When the war started, a good friend of mine was one of the few journalists who traveled from Mexico City to Tamaulipas to see what was happening. He was a serious person and even more a serious reporter. He's not one of those who pursue journalism for the same adrenaline rush available from riding a roller coaster, or one of those who think that war is like what you see in Hollywood movies, or that war is poetic. He had worked in Lebanon and knew that battlefields are covered in blood, mutilated bodies, pain and panic. He knew that the word "war" doesn't have the same meaning for a politician, who makes rhetorical hay out of it, as for someone who experiences it in the first person.

This friend, Raymundo Pérez Arellano, had been working with a videographer from Millenium TV in Reynosa, at first without much fanfare during those days in March 2012. They did a report on a hip-hop number dedicated to a narco and another story on the Twitter account of the municipal government. When they tried to verify some facts—precisely on some local journalists who had disappeared because of the war—they ran into a convoy of armed men making the rounds in broad daylight through the center of town. The gunmen drove right by them. Within a few minutes, they ran into them again a little ways up the road. The gunmen detained my friend and his cameraman, they put their guns to their heads, cocked their guns, beat them and took them to a safe house and interrogated them. Before freeing them, the gunmen ordered: "Go and warn the press not to trespass here." A few minutes later, Raymundo called me and blurted out: "Screw journalism. What we do isn't worth shit."

11. El Dorado

A few years after the signing of the North American Free Trade Agreement for Mexico, the United States and Canada, the exploitation of the Burgos natural gas field went into first gear, now that partial participation by private entities was permitted. The natural gas infrastructure that has been created since then is considerable, even if the war has pushed it to the background: there are 127 collection stations, twenty-eight for moving the gas and ten for unloading it, as well as 108 pipelines for liquefied gas and 114 pipelines for dry gas with a total length of 2,789 kilometers. Even so, the network of gas development is very limited compared to the wealth of gas resources in the region. In the neighboring state of Texas, for example, there are 90,000 exploratory wells, with 10,000 of them productive, while in Tamaulipas, there are only 11,000 wells with only 1,900 productive, half of which are inactive because of the war.

Ciudad Mier and the other towns in the area of hostilities make up one of the most productive energy regions in the country. A few years ago, after Pemex had announced a heavy investment in the region, and a concurrent announcement indicated a partial privatization scheme, the Frontera Chica became known as the "new" El Dorado. The anticipation of massive exploitation of natural gas created an economic boom. Businesses and workers migrated to the towns in the region, raising prices for everything from tacos to roast beef and even a hectare of land.

Nevertheless, in 2010 the panorama changed drastically. The war scared entire towns away, the prices of buildings plummeted, and instead of a boom, misery arrived and with it, the region began to be known as uninhabitable.

In the middle of this war, a squad of workers was tending to the Pemex compressed gas station, named Giant 1, constructed in a section of Nueva Ciudad Guerrero, a municipality close to Ciudad Mier. Suddenly, a group of armed men appeared and warned them to get away from there. The technicians obeyed and told their superiors what had happened on May 16, 2010. They did not work directly for Pemex but for Delta, a subcontractor. Along with the U. S. company, Halliburton, companies like Delta had arrived some time ago in the area, attracted by the bonanza the Burgos field would bring. Pemex had calculated in 2003 that some twenty million dollars would be invested there during the next few years.

The technicians' bosses did not believe their story and ordered them to return to the station the next week or they would be fired, so that's what they did. When they had only been a few hours at Giant 1, one of the groups at war kidnapped six of the workers. There was no resistance. The other workers escaped and hid. To date, nothing is known of the whereabouts of the mechanic Anselmo Sánchez Saldívar, his assistants Martín Franco and Martín Zuñiga, the compressor operator Saúl García Ayala and compression plant operator Christopher Cadena García. Ranchers living in the vicinity of the Burgos field installations, such as Gerardo García, César García and Adán de la Cruz Santiago, were also kidnapped and, like the Delta workers, are still missing today. The number of disappeared persons near the Pemex stations is as high as the anxiety about reporting them missing.

Many commentators who know the region theorize that among the conflict of vested interests in the state of Tamaulipas are those of certain Texan oil companies. However, it is worth remembering that the business of war in Afghanistan and Iraq represented great investments for these oil companies, and these same American companies today—and for some time now—have had their eyes on the Burgos field.

They also blame this conspiracy for many of the ills that afflict the region as a result of the conflict between the two cartels, while ignoring the political and economic interests that exist in the Frontera Chica, interests that somehow were mixed in with the battle for control of the drug trafficking routes to the United States.

Conspiracy or not, nothing is known for certain about what will happen to the national treasure that lies below the theater of war in Tamaulipas.

12. The Silence

In war, refusing to bear witness is one way to save your life. To protest your ignorance is a way to survive, and in this war, the warring bands demand silence on their behalf. In general, revolts aspire to make something visible. The Tamaulipas war is something else: the opposite.

They tell me that recently Al Jazeera television was in the area, and that their journalists said that they'd never been in such a dark place, where risk and disappointment dominate everything. The Al Jazeera journalists, who in recent years have been in the line of fire in the largest wars on the planet, could not even travel down the La Ribereña highway. The local government representatives and the military could not minimally guarantee them that they'd come out alive, if they tried. They decided instead to do a story on how sheriffs on the Texas side of the border were surviving the drama in Tamaulipas.

What else? No one knows how to report on what's happening here. By a long shot, the hardest journalistic work is done by my local colleagues. In the Tamaulipas newspapers, there is more to cover up than recount. I turn on the car radio. There are songs by Rigo Tovar or Cuco Sánchez, or the outcome of the national soccer race, but there is nothing about the five persons assassinated a few hours ago in downtown Reynosa, nor about the attacks by grenade launchers on a ranch in Camargo. I ask myself: Fifty years from now, how will they be able to document what's happening today in Tamaulipas, if there's no coverage in the press?

I know that the silence that exists today in Tamaulipas did not generate spontaneously. For silence to work, you need a sophisticated repression apparatus. It needs hidden burials, illegitimate governors, the monopoly on automatic weapons, economic decay, police corruption and a lethargic civil society. "He who imposes himself loudly has to exert more effort to maintain his hegemony than someone who does so through in silence," was said by Kapuscinski, and that's why the word "silence" in Spanish is almost always associated with such words as "tomb" (the silence of a tomb) or dungeon (the silence of a dungeon).

These are not gratuitous associations.

I know that they killed Pepino without anyone doing anything to save him—in silence. One of the men who heard Pepino's torture and death—and who saw the remains the next day before going to hear Mass—told me that since then, he has not been able to sleep well. That man has now entered the black labyrinth of insomnia that all wars produce.

The battle for Ciudad Mier, for all of Tamaulipas, is above all a battle against silence.

13. A Million Bullets

On November 2, 2010, when the Zetas launched a counter-offensive to re-take Ciudad Mier, Matilde González Puente was in her living room watching television at four o'clock. On hearing the first shots, she stood up, first shutting the front door and then the patio door. The bullets kept echoing and she implored, "Virgin Mary, free me!" as she lamented that there were people with a heart of stone. Two bullets landed nearby, crashing close to an old wardrobe and pitting the concrete floor. Matilde González rushed to a small storeroom in the house and covered herself with a mattress so that she would not be so afraid and could calm her arthritic shaking. At eighty-two years of age, Matilde was incapable of abandoning town, like the vast majority of inhabitants had. One of her sons lives in Monterrey and two daughters live in the United States, one in California and the other in Texas. "It's a miracle of God that I'm alive," she told me the day I met her. Matilde was born on December 18, 1928, not long after the battles of the Mexican Revolution had ceased and the Cristero War was in full force. She was one of the very few who had never abandoned Ciudad Mier, and she told me that she was resigned to dying as she had been born: in the middle of a war. She believed that there was a divine explanation for what had happened to her town and that those responsible would one day be punished: "God is just waiting for the right moment."

A few hours passed before the hail of bullets lessened that Day of the Dead that Matilde González spent in hiding. All night long, smoke was billowing from the north side of town, and on the roads to Reynosa there were the remains of three burned out pick-ups and a turned-over garbage truck that had been used as a barricade. Some walls were adorned with graffiti with messages like, "Your central plaza, ha, ha, ha," "Out with the Gulf boys, we're here now," and "Stand up like men, because we Zetas are here to stay."

Gregorio Olivo Salinas, a hazel-eyed man born around the same time Matilde González, was also a witness to the Day of the Dead battle. We spoke a few weeks after the events, when some bricklayers were working in the center of Hidalgo, where the facades of some houses had been blackened by smoke and others were pockmarked from being hit by so many bullets.

"How many bullets do you think were fired that day?" I asked.

"Here? Millions of cartridges were being picked up, so many that they were being sold by the kilo. But not many people were killed, because everyone was covered pretty well on the buildings' roofs."

"Had you ever experienced anything like that?"

"I served as police chief various times, three turns. There were hard times, but no, nothing like this."

"Like what?"

"The federal police were in charge of that deal. I was responsible up until 1986, when I got my passport and went up north to work." (He points to some mesquites bordering the Río Grande.)

Gregorio Olivo was getting tired of our conversation. He was balancing on one leg and then the other and playing with the brim on the left side of the Texan hat he was wearing.

"I hope the situation in Ciudad Mier improves," I told him.

"I wish for even more, so few people are returning to town. I was so alone here, alone. I was the only one who stayed behind in this house. Now, now we're beginning to have a few families."

"And why didn't you leave?"

"Where would I go? After all, what happens to you when you're young, won't happen when you're old. [He laughs.] I didn't have any place to run to."

14. Ciudad Mier

At this instant, my only companions, as I travel down the lonely highway, are the monumental crosses located at kilometer thirty-five. Located at the entrance to a cemetery, they're as tall as a three-story house.

A few kilometers ahead, approaching in the opposite lane, is the only vehicle I've seen in the half hour I've been on the road. It's an old pick-up driven by a man with a mustache and a sky-blue shirt. He turns his headlights on and off as he approaches my car. It must mean something. On any other highway, it would mean that I have a flat tire, or that up ahead there is an accident. But on this highway, what comes to mind is a shootout or a road block set up by one of the warring groups. I keep driving and what I find is construction that has been abandoned, and I have to get off the highway for a bit and drive on a dirt road before getting back on the asphalt. Barren fields, grey-green bushes, empty corrals, sad cacti, silos falling down. The agonizing landscape falls away as I drive.

Shortly before entering Ciudad Mier, in the adjacent city of General Treviño, I see to the left a ranch with some sign of life and an incredible vision: ostriches and ponies side-by-side, corralled between twisted mesquite trunks and abundant foliage that offers them some shade. Up ahead, there are columns of dense, black smoke appearing in the valley. Once again, an alarm goes off in my head.

That's how you travel this highway, tense.

The car rolls on. I drive by the smoke and realize that it's from burning trash. The next sight I encounter is a series of small mounds made of burlap bags filled with dirt and walls of stacked rocks on both sides of the highway, trenches that for now don't protect anyone.

I have arrived at the place I was looking for—the sign reads "Welcome to Ciudad Mier."

15. The Gulf Cartel and the Zetas

The Gulf Cartel initiated the war against the Zetas, to the strains of a battle hymn sung to hip-hop rhythm. A rapper on the border by the name of Sr. Cortés recorded the song as an advertisement for the cartel. Its title is "El Reto" (The Challenge) and attempts to explain the reason for the war starting in February 2010.

It goes like this:

> Keep this in mind, citizen: not everything is violence, that's what the Gulf Cartel thinks.
>
> I respect your family, don't mess with mine, I insist and remind you: I'm not the enemy.
>
> This is on behalf of the Gulf Cartel, this is a call, so listen carefully: we have nothing against you, nor against the government, but if you come after us, you'll burn in hell. He who kills women and children is a coward. You have to move on. That's the job. You confuse valor with crime, when in reality it's just cowardice. Those who think they're tough, let them enjoy their rep, they lie and kill innocent people. I invite them: a face-to-face showdown. Yeah: choose the place, the time, the day when I'll make them disappear like dinosaurs, I'll extinguish them with my machine gun, rat-tat-ta.
>
> So that people learn to respect the Gulf Cartel, all over the world, so that they realize that this is in exchange for people kidnapped.

We avoid conflict with the government, but if that's what they want, we'll get it on. That's why we avoid shootouts with them, so that innocent people don't die. People, don't confuse the cartel with cowards; the Gulf only kills cowards.

Now you know, we get rid of the riff-raff. And protect communities well. That's why we challenge them to let bullets fly like men, with their leaders up front, don't send us kids for us to kill, put your testicles into it, you bunch of cowards.

Matamoros, Reynosa and Laredo, all of Tamaulipas, even the whole world, in training the cartel does not spare anything, that's why in Tamaulipas, the Gulf dominates. Let the bullets fly, cabrones, we'll come at each other, wherever you want, we'll get together. Kill, but kill hunger, and quit the bullshit, and if you need it, I'll lend you a finger.

I challenge you.

The Zetas, a little after the war had started, sent the following message explaining their position to the e-mail accounts of government officials, journalists and businessmen:

This is an official communiqué from The Company.

We know that all the cities are put out by what is happening, and are fed up by how this is turning out, but here is the reality of what you wanted to know:

We are accused of being kidnappers, extortionists, assassins and more, but I remind you that before starting all this, we followed the orders of the Gulf Cartel. Now that they have declared war on us, they even blame us for burning down homes, killing innocent people and more, as if they didn't do these things.

They call themselves refined, educated and good people, who even rob clothing stores to dress well. They burn down houses because they think we'll leave forever, they kill innocent people so that they can blame it on us and so that the whole city will be against us, and they come out fine. They place communiqués in various media, trying to hide the obvious.

We don't have to go around asking people to support us, nor do we recruit high school kids like they do. We're people prepared for combat and we don't need people who don't even know how to use a weapon.

They declared war on us, and now they can't pursue it because they're in territories where they can't move around and that's why they ally themselves with other cartels to defend themselves, but they don't realize that the other cartels will exterminate them first.

So, I hope this clarifies for you the reality of those who recruit unprepared people, of those who kill innocent people to blame it on us, those who create psychosis in the city so that the citizens think they'll end the extortion, the kidnapping and assassination, those who publish thousands of media releases and pay so much money so that their videos are issued.

We are who we are but we are aware of our actions and before implementing them, we add intelligence.

The only thing that's left to say is don't leave your houses if you don't have reason to, and protect yourselves from events you encounter on the street, but be assured that we have been trained, not like those who don't know how to act under similar circumstances. We are not here asking for your support nor to recruit anyone, just don't mess with us and just let us work. In the end, the ones with more power and better strategy for doing their work will be victorious.

*We know that we'll lose some of our own, but they'll
lose it all. We can do our job without the support of the
innocent populace.*

*Sincerely,
Z Company*

16. War

The first time I came to Ciudad Mier, after the most inten-
se part of the war had displaced most of the populace, I was
accompanied by Santos, an experienced cameraman from
Multimedios Monterrey, along with the journalist Daniel
Aguirre. He entered the area to document the diaspora that
had been provoked by the battle of November 2, 2010. The
news about the events of that day slowly appeared in the
national dailies, where there is never enough space to cover
the overwhelming violence in the nation.

If you're up there in the capital city, in that rarified oasis
of peace that has become the Capital, you can unfold the
newspaper almost any morning and read that yesterday in
(here you can insert Ciudad Mier, Guasave or Fresnillo . . .)
there were executed (insert five or ten or fifteen) criminals in
(insert jail, ranch or some main plaza) and that . . . On beginning to read this news, you'll realize that it's the same news
you read a few days ago, and last week also, and last year, and
it's better to turn the page to read about something more
novel. Massacres of young people, crimes against children,
assassinations of mayors and the disappearance of journalists
take place so far from the nation's Capital, and it's old news by
the next day.

Santos told me that when he arrived in Ciudad Mier after
the shootout of November 2, he and his companion were wea-

ring bulletproof vests and helmets and were escorted by soldiers. They were aware that if something happened to them, the politicians would decry it in public for a few days, but afterward their deaths would be lost in a mountain of statistics.

When Santos and I were traveling to Ciudad Mier, he recounted that on another occasion when they had been in the town a short while, he was able to video the skeletal remains of numerous burned-out pick-ups and houses riddled with bullet holes. The soldiers who were escorting them gave them three minutes to do their videoing at each stop. They warned that there could be snipers, ambushes or assaults, but fortunately there was nothing of the sort. Santos was speaking of what it meant to report from that area, and suddenly he made a mental accounting of the disappeared or assassinated journalists that he knew.

The day I traveled with Santos, most of the highway was covered in fog. Light rain drops sparkled on the windshield, but we could still see the golden plains on the sides of the road. Santos and I stopped talking abruptly at the Cerralvo gas station, where a group of some twenty soldiers was on guard duty with their fingers on their triggers ready for combat.

The situation brought us back to the reality of the road— even to get gasoline for your car you had to be ready for war.

17. The Mayor

Alberto González had never been elected to office until he was elected mayor of Ciudad de Mier in the middle of war. The war did not exempt the local political class. In fact, one week before the elections of July 4, 2010, Roberto Torre Cantú, the PRI candidate for governor, was assassinated; he had practically won the election already. Alberto González, a gray-haired man sporting the eye glasses of a biology teacher, was the superintendent of the Ciudad Mier schools. In 2010 he accepted the PRI nomination for town mayor, a town that had always been governed by the PRI. For the July 4 elections, Ciudad Mier was already half-empty because of the gun battles. Eighty percent of registered voters did not vote. Of the 6,009 registered voters, only 1,486 voted, with 1,210 electing the PRI candidate. Only fifty-four had voted for the *Partido Acción Nacional* party.

At the beginning of 2011, Alberto accepted the position of mayor. One of the first things his administration did was to organize squads of bricklayers to fill in the bullet holes—thousands of them—mainly on downtown houses and on the monuments at the three main entrances to the town. During those days, I accompanied the mayor in his pick-up as he made his rounds. Beyond the main streets, there were mainly abandoned houses, sad streets without people, not even dogs left behind, and shuttered stores with their neon signs off.

Just as the mayor was telling me that most of the bullet holes in town had been filled in, we passed by the Hotel El General, the building favored by snipers and which was still pretty damaged.

"Well," said the mayor before I could comment, "over here, well, the building was destroyed and burned and now looks different, but well, the reconstruction is ongoing."

The building most affected by the battle for Ciudad Mier was city hall, which had been attacked continuously, even though from the beginning there were no policemen inside. During the last shootout to take place, which included an attack with grenade launchers, something strange happened: the building caught fire and stucco fell from the façade of the building. The original façade was revealed, with arches, columns and the eagle of the republic in the middle, giving an historical and solemn air to the building in ruins, whose age was nearly 130 years old.

I told this story of finding this treasure in the middle of war to the writer from Tamaulipas Martín Solares, who told me he considered the city hall facade falling as the perfect metaphor for what was happening in our country: the bullets were removing the varnish from the surface to reveal the reality that for many years had been hidden, and now it was crumbling, because it could not take one more bullet.

I entered the old building with the mayor and I encountered pieces of cable and blackened walls. There was a television on a desk, as well as a telephone, a coffee cup and a flashlight, all charred; there was also paper and plastic that had fed the fire.

"Did you see the movie *The Inferno?*" I suddenly asked the mayor.

"No, I didn't see it, but they tell me that Mier is somewhat similar," he answered with certain discomfort.

"Why did you want to become mayor of Mier at a time like this?"

"I was encouraged because our people were encouraged, they're enthusiastic about recovering this, and that makes things easier. Also, what's going on in Mier I don't think is exclusive to Mier, it's national . . . But well, let me repeat, I'm content because I feel supported by our people, and also we have other support: Pemex, for example, which has been keen to help us with the reconstruction of our beloved Ciudad Mier."

18. Tarantino

This is the third time I travel to Ciudad Mier so far this year. Now I'm traveling with two colleagues from Monterrey and with Daniel Aguilar, a photographer with whom I've witnessed some shootouts in Oaxaca and other places of our troubled national geography. But we don't talk about that during our trip. We talk about the landscapes along the border, used various times by Tarantino and Robert Rodríguez in their films, how beautiful the Condesa neighborhood of Mexico City is, about the Intocable musical group, about how expensive photographic equipment is, and things like that.

19. Roast Chicken

On Sunday, March 6, 2010, Ciudad Mier was 258 years old. If the previous year's celebration of its founding had been canceled due to the war, now a group of its citizens, along with its splendid mayor Alberto González, had decided to organize the usual festival in order to resuscitate the town. At midday that Sunday, the main plaza under the protection of soldiers witnessed a parade of dukes, princesses and queens marching to the piano music of Raúl Di Blassio.

Although the cataclysm of war was still evident on some of the buildings, dozens of citizens exiled in Texas and Monterrey had returned momentarily to Ciudad Mier. A young high school student in a merengue-colored dress and with a salon hairdo was crowned as Queen Emily I and awarded a scepter; her first act was to decree that Ciudad Mier should maintain its unity despite the difficult situation.

After the coronation in front of a somewhat restored city hall, a bed of coals was arranged with steel spits for roasting 258 chickens, one for each of the years of the town's anniversary.

"Why celebrate with roast chicken?" I asked Diego Treviño, the mayor's private secretary.

"Because that's what was available, but next year we'll roast baby goats!" he answered full of emotion on seeing that more than five hundred people were crowded onto the plaza that a few months earlier had been the site of the horrors that were not appropriate to recall at that moment.

Ciudad Mier's 258th anniversary was held downtown, but a few blocks away the rest of the town was desolate. The housing development known as Geo, built in 2003, had been completely abandoned, with no signs of life. The rest of the streets and the devastated countryside reveal that what exists presently is perhaps a period between wars.

In the afternoon, their own priest offered Mass, imploring peace upon the town. The faithful joined him in prayer: "Lord, help us to combat fear and insecurity, console the pain of those who suffer, give confidence to those who govern, touch the hearts of those who create suffering and death, and do not forget that we are brothers and sisters."

Mayor Alberto González was perhaps the most euphoric person that afternoon, but not because of the celebration. A few days earlier he had received a phone call from Julián de la Garza, one of the directors of the Pemex Project in the Burgos field. They had already met and the oil executive had informed him that the company would turn over to his administration a large quantity of economic resources to move Ciudad Mier forward. He also confirmed that by spring, various wells in the Burgos field would be reactivated and that the Texas company, Halliburton, was interested in joining the effort in 2011.

The mayor's hopes were so high that he calculated that within a few months, Ciudad Mier would once again have a police force.

20. Breathe

Before leaving Ciudad Mier we reached the crossroads with the highway to La Ribereña, where a large monument in the shape of a bell had been shot by thousands of bullets. No one dares live close to this site. Daniel Aguilar wanted to take some photos of what in reality is a large water pitcher that represents a legend about the founding of the town. While Daniel was taking his photos, one of the colleagues who had accompanied us shouted, "It wasn't worth shit!" as he pointed a distance up the highway. I turned and saw a brand-new pick-up, and then another just like it, and then another, and another . . . "Is it them?" asked Daniel. I kept my mouth shut. No one knew what to do. We were petrified. The convoy continued approaching and passed to one side of us; I was able to see that the pick-ups had the logo of Pemex on their sides. There were eleven of them and they drove off into the distance. I could breathe again.

ESPEJOS, FANTASMAS Y VIOLENCIA EN CIUDAD JUÁREZ

María Socorro Tabuenca Córdoba

Mi familia y yo regresamos a la gran Paso del Norte (Ciudad Juárez) ocho meses después del asesinato del Presidente Kennedy. Manejamos por una angosta carretera de dos carriles llamada "Panamericana" (mucho antes de que fuera una gran avenida y que cambiara de nombre tres veces hasta llegar a alcanzar de nuevo su nombre original "Carretera Panamericana"). Dicen que esta vía comienza en Juárez, apenas pasando "la curva" de San Lorenzo y termina en Tierra del Fuego, en la punta del Cono Sur. El aeropuerto era apenas un cuarto de adobe y entre éste y la ciudad no había casi nada: unos pocos centros nocturnos, algunas casas, el lienzo charro Baca Gallardo y el por inaugurarse Tecnológico de Juárez. En aquel entonces, como niñas/os podíamos jugar en la calle hasta el anochecer y caminar largos trechos sin temer que algo malo nos pudiera ocurrir. Claro que sabíamos que existían los "robachicos" que nos podían llevar si no nos portábamos bien; sin embargo, nos sentíamos seguros en nuestros barrios, en nuestra ciudad. Como niños no sabíamos el verdadero significado de las palabras violencia y crimen.

Durante los setenta organizábamos fiestas en las casas o íbamos a los bailes de la secundaria y la prepa en los distintos salones o casinos de la ciudad. La vida nocturna de Juárez siempre fue famosa por su diversidad. Había centros nocturnos exclusivos en una calle y burdeles a la vuelta de la esquina, pero la gente sabía por dónde andar. Después del estreno de la película "Fiebre de sábado en la noche" las calles de Juárez recobraron el esplendor de la vida nocturna de los cuarenta. Se abrieron discotecas no sólo en la zona de cabarets sino también en otros lugares hacia donde la ciudad se había extendido. Los soldados del Fuerte *Bliss* y adolescentes que aún no tenían la mayoría de edad de El Paso iban a Juárez a divertirse. Entonces podíamos salir a bailar del ocaso al alba sin temer que algo trágico pudiera pasarnos. Como adolescentes no sabíamos el verdadero significado de los vocablos violencia y crimen. Para ese momento la ciudad había cambiado su paisaje étnico y urbano. Muchas mujeres habían llegado de zonas rurales y urbanas con altos índices de pobreza de los estados norteños de Chihuahua, Durango y Coahuila. Llegaron a trabajar en la industria maquiladora muchos años antes del Tratado de Libre Comercio. La clase media juarense también había cambiado la manera de percibir a sus habitantes. Antes de la llegada de la maquila nos mezclábamos fácilmente; sabíamos quiénes eran los ricos, pero era muy difícil distinguir entre la clase media, la media alta y la media baja. Desafortunadamente, los pobres y los que viven en pobreza extrema, como sucede en la mayoría de las sociedades, eran ignorados por el resto hasta la llegada de la maquiladora. La gente pobre padecía la falta de recursos básicos y de servicios, pero no de la violencia social que soportan hoy en día.

A las mujeres obreras se les clasificaba casi automáticamente como "mujeres livianas" pues estaban ganando dinero propio y la mayor parte del tiempo eran *ellas* quienes mantenían a sus familias. Lo peor era que se "atrevían" a ejercer su derecho a divertirse y a salir a bailar. Había varios centros nocturnos en donde la clientela era principalmente de mujeres obreras y eso hizo que las estigmatizaran aún más. Los prejuicios de nuestra sociedad eran a la vez evidentes y extraños. Por una parte, como integrantes de la clase media, nuestra sociedad y la ciudad nos permitía toda clase de libertades: podíamos caminar y manejar por la ciudad, salir a bailar y a tomar, a divertirnos de cualesquiera de las formas posibles y nadie la pensaba dos veces. De hecho, era lo que se esperaba de la juventud clasemediera. Sin embargo, cuando las obreras, las "maquiladoras" o "maquilas", decidieron ejercer ese derecho, se les desprestigió porque eran mujeres pobres. Pero aunque esas actitudes existían, aún podían caminar por la ciudad, ir a trabajar y salir a bailar sin temer que nada terrible les sucediera. Estoy segura de que ellas no sabían tampoco el *verdadero* significado de la violencia y el crimen.

El *boom* de la maquiladora de la década de los años ochenta trajo caras diferentes al paisaje urbano de Juárez. Hombres y mujeres de otros estados de más al sur y de la costa este, particularmente de Veracruz, empezaron a establecerse en la ciudad. Las zonas periféricas del poniente y el surponiente experimentaron un crecimiento rápido y caótico debido a asentamientos irregulares. La infraestructura de la ciudad no estaba preparada para un crecimiento tan rápido y estable en la población y a los nuevos fraccionamientos y colonias les faltaba agua corriente, pavimento, drenaje y transporte público. Quizá fue entonces que la pobreza se empezó a hacer más visible que antes; pero, en aquel tiempo los pobres todavía podían navegar por la ciudad de alguna manera u otra sin temer que algo terrible les pudiera pasar.

La vida en Juárez era todavía "normal" aunque poco más agitada con más gente y más tráfico. El crecimiento no sólo afectó el movimiento dentro de la ciudad sino también el cruce hacia El Paso, Texas. Para quienes acostumbrábamos transitar en ambos lados de la frontera, se volvió más difícil ir al otro lado. El secuestro y asesinato del agente de la DEA Enrique Camarena Salazar en 1985 hizo insoportables las filas de los puentes. De un día para el otro sufrimos la "venganza" del gobierno de los Estados Unidos por medio de los agentes de Inmigración. Ésta es una práctica común en la frontera: cada vez que Washington, D.C. y México, D.F. no están de acuerdo en algún asunto, nosotras/os, las y los habitantes de las fronteras somos el blanco perfecto para las represalias. Las colas de los puentes empezaron a ser más y más lentas; los agentes detenían cada carro y hacían revisiones exhaustivas y una fila de autos que normalmente tomaba veinte minutos en cruzar, tardaba una o dos horas. Entonces las inspecciones en la aduana de los Estados Unidos fueron similares a las que experimentamos en 1969 durante la "Operación Intercepción" de Nixon, aquélla que dio inicio a la guerra contra las drogas de la cual, después de cuarenta y tres años, seguimos sufriendo sus crueles consecuencias. Pero en aquel momento no teníamos miedo, sentíamos rabia por la forma en que nos trataban los agentes. No éramos narcotraficantes así que no teníamos a qué temer. Sabíamos demasiado poco sobre la violencia y el crimen.

Los noventa llegaron con las noticias nacionales sobre la Revolución Zapatista, el asesinato del candidato presidencial Luis Donaldo Colosio, la devaluación del peso y la firma del Tratado de Libre Comercio de América del Norte. Localmente empezábamos también con nuestro alboroto privado. Estábamos por iniciarnos en el aprendizaje del verdadero significado de la violencia y el crimen. De igual forma estábamos por experimentar comunitariamente las implicaciones de otros términos como impunidad, injusticia, impotencia, prejuicio, holocausto y horror. Para mí y para muchas otras mujeres menos privilegiadas que yo, la violencia comenzó tiempo antes de que Ciudad Juárez fuese clasificada como "la ciudad más violenta del mundo". En junio de 1993 nos despertamos con unas noticias terribles. Algo inexplicable, increíble había sucedido: Los cuerpos de seis jovencitas habían aparecido en las inmediaciones de Juárez. Todas ellas al parecer bajo la mano de un asesino serial. Estábamos estupefactas pues en la historia criminal del México contemporáneo había pocos casos de actos de tal naturaleza y envergadura. Estaba Goyo Cárdenas, un asesino serial durante los cincuenta en México, D.F., Delfina y María de Jesús González, "Las Poquianchis" en los sesenta en Guanajuato y Adolfo de Jesús Constanzo y sus seguidores, "los narcosatánicos" en Matamoros, Tamaulipas, a finales de la década de los años ochenta. Sin embargo, nada como esto había sucedido en Ciudad Juárez y la ciudad estaba pasmada con los crímenes. Nunca nos habíamos sentido tan amenazadas porque en nuestra mente ese tipo de criminales estaba muy lejos de nosotras, en algún lugar distante del sur de México o en los Estados Unidos, pero nunca en nuestra casa, nunca en nuestras calles, nunca tan cerca de nuestra frontera. Ese mismo año otras dos mujeres fueron asesinadas aparentemente por conocidos y ésos fueron los únicos casos que se resolvieron: ninguno de los dos apuntaba a un asesino serial. A la fecha a nadie se le ha culpado por esos seis asesinatos. Empezábamos apenas a entender el significado de violencia y crimen.

Cinco restos de mujeres fueron localizados en los límites de la ciudad en 1994. Todo indicaba que el asesino serial había atacado de nuevo. Ese mismo año otras dos mujeres fueron descubiertas inmoladas además de los presuntos cinco asesinatos seriales y, una vez más, los únicos crímenes resueltos fueron los que no tenían muestras de un crimen serial. Hasta este momento nadie ha sido culpado por estos otros crímenes.

Indudablemente no estábamos preparadas para un acontecimiento como éste. No estábamos preparadas ni como sociedad, ni como familias, ni como mujeres, ni como feministas. Ni siquiera la policía sabía cómo reaccionar ante el problema. Desafortunadamente reaccionó no cumpliendo con la ley. Al principio, las autoridades mencionaron que estaban investigando, pero cuando no pudieron presentar a ningún culpable estigmatizaron a las víctimas a través de "campañas de prevención"; luego crearon chivos expiatorios, destruyeron evidencia, solicitaron a los forenses crear o sembrar pruebas; nos mintieron (y continúan mintiéndonos). Es sabido que los asesinatos seriales de estas mujeres pobres persisten sin resolverse, a pesar de que doce hombres hayan sido sentenciados por esos crímenes no tenemos certeza que fueran ellos ya que las investigaciones no son confiables. No existe ninguna evidencia irrefutable que legitime el encarcelamiento de esos hombres. Algunos murieron en prisión y no hay consenso de que hayan sido los verdaderos asesinos.

Cuando digo que nosotras, como juarenses, feministas y activistas no estábamos listas para un caso semejante, lo digo porque vivíamos en una ciudad relativamente pacífica donde los índices de violencia y crimen eran los esperados para una ciudad como Juárez; además no presentaban esas características de brutalidad, ni los asesinatos eran hacia una población específica. Algunas de nosotras regresábamos a Juárez para escribir o hacer la investigación de nuestras tesis doctorales y de pronto nos sentimos impotentes ante esa atroz tragedia. Unas eran científicas sociales y tenían más entendimiento teórico sobre el problema; pero yo había estudiado literatura y no sabía exactamente cómo responder, excepto salir a protestar con otras activistas. Me encontraba tratando de llevar a cabo mi investigación y a la vez reconocer la importancia de asuntos más reales y urgentes como el reclamo de justicia para aquellas mujeres pobres y sus familias. Como académicas no estábamos preparadas porque no habíamos logrado una masa crítica ni podíamos conceptualizar los sucesos del todo; ni nuestro entrenamiento académico ni nuestras áreas de investigación nos habían preparado para confrontar el tema. Tampoco teníamos un liderazgo académico ni social. Los estudios de género eran incipientes en las universidades locales y en los centros de investigación y ninguna tenía el suficiente entrenamiento para tomar el liderazgo. Sin embargo, a pesar de nuestras deficientes credenciales académicas referentes al problema, así como la falta de un marco teórico sobre el feminicidio, estuvimos listas para apoyar a quienes asumieron liderar la batalla y para articular discursos subversivos. Tratábamos de comprender, develar y desafiar los nuevos significados de la violencia y el crimen en nuestra ciudad.

Para 1995 treinta y dos mujeres habían sido brutalmente asesinadas; veintiséis de ellas aparentemente a manos de un(os) asesino(s) serial(es). De los treinta y dos asesinatos sólo un hombre fue encontrado culpable de un crimen no relacionado con los seriales. 1995 fue un año importante no solamente porque el número de mujeres asesinadas se había duplicado, sino porque también estábamos ejercitando nuestra agencia. Organizaciones no gubernamentales, grupos independientes de mujeres, académicas y personas autónomas nos reunimos a pedir justicia. Todas desafiamos las campañas de prevención publicadas por el gobierno municipal perteneciente al Partido Acción Nacional (PAN), entonces partido en el poder. Las campañas estigmatizaban a las víctimas y las culpaban de sus propias muertes porque la mayoría de las mujeres asesinadas en aquel momento eran trabajadoras sexuales y obreras de maquiladora y ambas ocupaciones ya sobrellevaban un estigma social. Dentro de sus "cuestionables" quehaceres las autoridades encontraron el chivo expiatorio perfecto para justificar la violencia y los crímenes sin resolver y para reivindicar su inhabilidad o falta de voluntad política para hacer algo al respecto.

Como académicas y activistas escribimos editoriales en los periódicos, nos manifestamos en las calles, hicimos presentaciones públicas de los hechos, organizamos seminarios y ofrecimos talleres sobre el tema; hasta presionamos a los gobernantes de tal forma que el gobierno del estado de Chihuahua creó la "Fiscalía Especial de Delitos contra las Mujeres". Desgraciadamente es bien sabido y está registrado en periódicos y trabajos académicos que desde su creación la agencia ha sido liderada por hombres y mujeres negligentes, insensibles, cobardes y poco profesionales. Desde su puesto han fabricado culpables, ocultado o destruido evidencia, humillado a las víctimas y a sus familias y han puesto sus ideologías e intereses personales sobre la ley y sobre su responsabilidad como servidoras/es públicas/os. Han obstruido la justicia y cuestionado a las víctimas aún después de haber sido torturadas, violadas y asesinadas. En resumen, han establecido y perpetuado la impunidad en nuestra ciudad con respecto al feminicidio y esa impunidad está ligada al estado de crimen y violencia que vive la ciudad en la actualidad.

Durante una conferencia de prensa con el entonces gobernador Francisco Barrio en junio de ese año hice un letrero improvisado en una cartulina que decía: "¿Cuántas más Sr. Gobernador?" Pronto obtendría mi respuesta. En 1996 la cuenta de mujeres asesinadas llegó a diecinueve; dieciséis aparentemente a manos de un(os) asesino(s) serial(es). El horror incrementaba en vez de aminorar, incluso cuando la policía había encarcelado al presunto autor intelectual y material de los crímenes, así como a sus cómplices. Entre 1997 y 1998, treinta y dos mujeres más fueron descubiertas masacradas en diferentes sitios de Juárez. Veintiséis aparentemente por un(os) depredador(es) serial(es). Un grupo de académicas y activistas con quienes yo trabajaba empezaron a registrar la correlación que existía entre pobreza y violencia, entre pobreza e impunidad, entre crimen y corrupción. La clase media y media alta juarense habían dejado de cuestionar a las autoridades y habían dejado de tener miedo (si alguna vez lo tuvieron). Ahora ya tenían una "buena historia", un "perpetrador ideal" y un "excelente grupo de cómplices". En casi la mitad de los casos también tenían a las "víctimas perfectas": trabajadoras sexuales, bailarinas exóticas, meseras de bares y obreras de maquiladora que no habían recibido ni la compasión ni la solidaridad de la gente. Eran mujeres pobres, mujeres anónimas, mujeres estigmatizadas, mujeres diferentes, mujeres desechables que habían descubierto el *verdadero* significado corporal, genérico, etario y clasista de la violencia y el crimen.

Para principios del milenio muchas más mujeres fueron violadas, torturadas y asesinadas. La esperanza de una nueva era prometida se desvanecía frente a la fría estadística de mujeres masacradas en Ciudad Juárez. Según Julia Monárrez, académica que ha llevado a cabo la investigación más amplia y completa con respecto al feminicidio en Ciudad Juárez y con quien he trabajado, de 1993 a 2005, 150 mujeres fueron violentadas sexualmente y exterminadas; de ellas 112 presentaban muestras de haber sido asesinadas por uno o más asesinos seriales. El nuevo milenio también trajo consigo nuevas formas de desechar los cuerpos, de nulificar a vida. Hasta entonces la mayoría de los cuerpos de las mujeres habían sido encontrados a las afueras de la ciudad, en el desierto. Sin embargo, en noviembre de 2001 ocho cuerpos de mujeres fueron hallados dentro de la ciudad, en un antiguo lote algodonero abandonado, prácticamente frente al edificio de la Asociación de Maquiladoras. Este hecho se podría haber leído como un mensaje de los asesinos. Creo que lo que nos intentaban decir era que los asesinatos continuarían, que sucederían más manifiestamente, que esas mujeres pobres no valían nada, que nosotras no teníamos el poder de hacer nada y que la violencia y el crimen serían más brutales, más espectaculares y más dolorosos. Pero como sociedad no supimos leer el mensaje y permitimos al gobierno de Patricio Marínez del Partido Revolucionario Institucional (PRI) que nos presentara más chivos expiatorios para torturarlos y posiblemente para causarles la muerte como en los casos de Gustavo González Meza "La Foca" y Abdel Latif Sharif Sharif, dos presuntos asesinos que murieron en prisión bajo circunstancias misteriosas. Como sociedad estábamos reinventando la justicia como repetición y espejo de los crímenes.

Estos despiadados asesinatos de mujeres también tuvieron eco en la ciudad de Chihuahua en 2003 cuando los cuerpos de tres jovencitas se encontraron en las afueras de la ciudad con las mismas características de los casos de Ciudad Juárez. Durante diez años habíamos estado viviendo con una violencia brutal contra las mujeres, pero las autoridades de todos los niveles de gobierno (municipal, estatal y federal) habían prestado poca o ninguna atención a esta masacre; y la sociedad local había ignorado el problema porque se "había cansado" de escucharlo en las noticias locales, nacionales y extranjeras. No queríamos descubrir el verdadero significado de la violencia y el crimen y tal vez mucha gente sólo quería meter los feminicidios bajo el tapete. A las personas que estaban asesinando no eran "de nosotros" y, para 2008, los crímenes de mujeres se habían vuelto insignificantes dentro de una sociedad que aparentemente, después de quince años, se había acostumbrado a ellos.

A fin de comprender algunos significados e implicaciones de lo dicho hasta ahora, quisiera reflexionar en quiénes eran esas mujeres y qué tenían en común. Algunas trabajaban en la industria maquiladora; otras trabajaban en la zona comercial del centro de Juárez, varias eran bailarinas exóticas, trabajadoras sexuales, madres de familia y estudiantes. Todas pertenecían a la clase obrera empobrecida. Unas trabajaban turnos de noche a fin de salir de la pobreza en la que subsistían con sus familias. La mayoría vivían en áreas con escasa infraestructura y sin electricidad. No había transporte público o privado que pudiera recogerlas o regresarlas en un sitio cerca de su casa. Sus edades fluctuaban entre seis y cuarenta y dos años de edad, pero la mayoría de las mujeres violentadas sexualmente tenía diecisiete. Fueron asesinadas por uno o más asesinos seriales. Un buen número de las mujeres fueron torturadas y violadas antes de ser ultimadas. En algunos casos fueron mutiladas o desmembradas. La generalidad fue encontrada a las afueras de la ciudad, en espacios abiertos, en vastos terrenos deshabitados como "Lomas de Poleo", "Lote Bravo, "Campo Algodonero", o el "Cerro del Cristo Negro". Varios cuerpos fueron encontrados desnudos. En ocasiones sólo se recuperaron cráneos, huesos y pedazos de ropa. Algunos restos estaban ligeramente cubiertos por arbustos o arena. Otros, se hallaron expuestos cuidadosamente como si el(os) asesino(s) quisiera(n) dejar una postura, un mensaje y estampar su firma sobre las macabras tumbas desafiando a las autoridades y a la sociedad. Unas cuantas fueron arrojadas en lotes vacíos dentro de la ciudad, en vías de trenes, drenajes e incluso cerca de sus casas.

Después de sus atroces asesinatos las víctimas y sus familias tuvieron que enfrentarse con más tribulaciones: sus vidas habían sido juzgadas y estigmatizadas por las autoridades, independientemente de su filiación política. Los políticos y la policía nunca explicaron que muchas de esas mujeres iban de regreso a casa al alba o al anochecer porque iban o salían de los turnos de noche o de temprano por la mañana en las fábricas. Nadie dijo tampoco que si estaban caminando solas a esas horas era porque no tenían automóvil y los autobuses las dejaban lejos de sus casas. Las autoridades nunca dijeron que la mayoría de las víctimas fueron vistas por última vez después de trabajo o yendo a trabajar o a la escuela y no al alba o al ocaso después de salir de bailar (y si hubiera sido así . . .). No sólo proyectaron una imagen en que las víctimas fueron de alguna forma responsables de sus muertes, pero también reactivaron la vieja creencia de que el mejor sitio para la mujer es su casa, sin considerar los feminicidios íntimos. Además, les negaron a las mujeres trabajadoras el poco tiempo libre que podían tener. Distorsionaron la idea de "pasar un buen rato" y la convirtieron en "inmoralidad". Ellos las condenaron incluso por su forma de vestir. Irónicamente la mayoría de las víctimas llevaban pantalones de mezclilla, camiseta y tenis. Mientras que algunos miembros de la sociedad entienden la gravedad de la situación, muchos no han sido capaces de comprender y demostrar compasión o solidaridad por las víctimas y han escogido guardar silencio, no involucrarse, no demandar. Desafortunadamente, ese silencio ha pagado su precio. Desde enero de 2008 Juárez ha enfrentado una terrible guerra contra el crimen organizado y desorganizado que ha posicionado a la ciudad de nuevo en el radar nacional e internacional. Hay en la ciudad muchos criminales comunes (individuos o grupos) que se han aprovechado de la atmósfera creada por los cárteles del crimen organizado y han comenzado a cometer secuestros y robar autos haciendo creer a sus víctimas que son miembros de los cárteles; es decir, a río revuelto, ganancia de pescadores. De "los campos de la muerte" o "la ciudad que mata o devora a sus hijas", Ciudad Juárez se ha convertido en "la ciudad más violenta del mundo". Por ello es que creo que la violencia comenzó mucho antes que la ciudad obtuviera ese infame sobrenombre.

¿Cómo fue que llegamos a esta escalada de violencia? ¿Cómo es posible que tengamos, a veces, hasta veintidós ultimados en un solo ataque? Pero más importante aún, ¿cómo hemos permitido que los asesinatos de mujeres hayan sido invisibilizados por la violencia actual? Para responder estas preguntas es importante recordar la secuencia de eventos que nos llevaron a esta situación, ya que de pronto nos olvidamos o no queremos pensar en las conexiones entre la violencia actual y el feminicidio en la ciudad. Rafael Aguilar Guajardo, fundador del cártel de Juárez en la década de los setenta, tenía el control de la ciudad (junto con sus operadores Eduardo y Rafael Muñoz Talavera) hasta su asesinato en 1993, que al parecer fue ordenado por Amado Carrillo Fuentes, el "Señor de los cielos", quien se convirtió en el jefe del cártel desde entonces hasta su muerte "accidental" en 1997. Juárez, que fuera la plaza de los juarenses por mucho tiempo, llegó a ser territorio dominado por los mafiosos de Sinaloa. Contrario a Aguilar, a quien consideraban un "caballero", la familia Carrillo era muy conocida por su falta de escrúpulos y su crueldad. Consecuentemente, no sería muy aventurado proponer que el inicio de los asesinatos de mujeres en Ciudad Juárez y la toma del cártel de Juárez por Amado Carrillo Fuentes estén conectados de alguna manera.

Otro evento que no podemos olvidar es que a la muerte de Carrillo en 1997 se dio la lucha por la plaza entre Vicente Carrillo y Rafael Muñoz Talavera quien, hasta su muerte, buscó apoyo de la familia Arellano Félix, del cártel de Tijuana. Esta lucha provocó dos masacres en agosto del mismo año: una en el restaurante Max Fim donde seis personas fueron acribilladas y, la otra en el Bar Gerónimo's en el cual ocho personas fueron asesinadas, incluyendo dos agentes policíacos que estaban en el bar que quisieron repeler la agresión. En ambas ocasiones hombres fuertemente armados dispararon despiadadamente contra los clientes. Aparentemente el blanco era una pareja de capos de la droga que estaban cenando. Como sucedió con los casos de mujeres asesinadas, a nadie aprehendieron por esos asesinatos. En el mes de julio de 1997, catorce personas fueron ultimadas al estilo de la mafia en Juárez y sus áreas circunvecinas. También en julio capturaron a una banda de cerca de 100 secuestradores. Durante ese año se experimentó una ola de violencia que perturbó el espacio público: aparte del Max Fim y el Gerónimo's, hubo otro atentado en el restaurante King-Sui en donde cuatro personas fueron masacradas; y en la cafetería Space Burger secuestraron a cinco personas. Todos estos eventos se dieron a plena luz del día. Para añadir a esa aterradora situación se dio el secuestro y asesinato de cuatro médicos después de un ataque entre pandillas enemigas. Lo anterior trajo como consecuencia que se organizara una marcha contra la violencia el 31 de agosto liderada por el gobernador Francisco Barrio, el gobernador electo Patricio Martínez y el presidente municipal Ramón Galindo. La ironía de la marcha es que, como representantes del Estado se estaban manifestando contra una estructura paralela que seguramente les estaba ganando el poder y los estaba venciendo: era el principio de la develación del Estado fallido que se afianzaría diez años después. Durante ese año los habitantes de Juárez se encontraban atrapados en una atmósfera de psicosis: nadie quería salir, especialmente a los restaurantes. Sin embargo, pronto nos olvidamos del terror porque nos había llegado cerca, pero no *tan* cerca. Me di a la tarea de preguntarles a mis amigas y amigos con respecto a estos sucesos y siempre me respondían que era algo pasajero, que el gobierno tenía todo bajo control, que eso estaba pasando porque el gobierno y los narcos estaban negociando. Nunca estuve satisfecha con las respuestas pero sospechaba que eventualmente algo podría no salir bien. En septiembre de 1998 asesinaron a Rafael Muñoz Talavera y Vicente Carrillo creyó que finalmente tenía controlada la plaza y sería el jefe del cártel. Sin embargo, el brazo armado del cártel de Juárez conocido como "La Línea" así como las pandillas Barrio Azteca y los Artistas Asesinos había intentado ganarle el terreno a la familia Carrillo. Según rumores el Chapo Guzmán quiere ser el jefe del cártel de México y el derramamiento de sangre no se detendrá hasta que así lo sea. Otra cuestión que en ocasiones no se toma en cuenta con relación a estos hechos es la relativa a las fosas masivas descubiertas a principios de siglo y en años subsecuentes. En 1999 hubo reportes de un cementerio clandestino donde se suponía que habría doscientos cuerpos. En aquel entonces el presidente Bill Clinton declaró que Ciudad Juárez era una ciudad peligrosa. Sin embargo, las autoridades mexicanas solicitaron una disculpa pues "en vez de doscientos aparecieron siete". En 2004 se descubrieron cinco cuerpos en otro cementerio dentro de una lujosa residencia; esta vez el hallazgo se asociaba con el jefe de la policía a quien también se le ligaba con una banda de prostitución y tráfico de personas; pero, hasta la fecha, no lo han capturado ni nadie sabe de su paradero. En febrero de 2008 se descubrieron otras fosas en dos sitios de la ciudad: una con treinta y seis cuerpos y otra con nueve.

Dichos sucesos vinieron a confirmar que las autoridades en los tres niveles de gobierno no fueron efectivas en prevenir o resolver los casos y la mayoría de las y los integrantes de la sociedad éramos sólo espectadoras/es dentro de un argumento que nos involucraba profundamente como sociedad y personas. Desde 2008 nuestra ciudad se ha convertido en un campo de batalla con muchos "daños colaterales". Personas de todas edades —hombres y mujeres jóvenes, niños, bebés, adultos y ancianos— han sido asesinadas o heridas por estar "en el sitio erróneo en el momento equivocado". Otros han sido acribillados por haberlos "confundido" como fue el caso de los dieciséis jóvenes estudiantes masacrados cuando celebraban un cumpleaños en Villas de Salvárcar, cerca de Juárez en enero de 2010. También ha habido ataques "estratégicos" en varios centros de rehabilitación. Y las mujeres siguen desapareciendo y siendo asesinadas. No es, sin embargo, el alto número de asesinatos (casi 10,000 en cuatro años) el que ha llevado a nuestra ciudad a ser bautizada como "la ciudad más violenta del mundo", sino otras actividades criminales que el Estado no ha sido capaz de prevenir, como secuestros, extorsiones, robo de autos a mano armada, cobro por derecho de piso, prostitución, pornografía y explotación de menores, incendios. Algunas de estas actividades criminales pueden ser llevadas por el crimen organizado pero otras cometidas por criminales comunes quienes convirtieron también la ciudad en un botín.

En 2009 el ejército y la policía federal llegaron destacamentados a la ciudad como parte de la guerra contra las drogas de Calderón. La violencia se detuvo durante un mes y después volvió a estallar. Con el ejército y la policía federal en las calles, se violaron, ignoraron y criminalizaron los derechos humanos; mucha gente, particularmente la pobre, empezó a experimentar aún más los niveles de violencia. Antes de que la federal y el ejército llegaran, muchas de las colonias y barrios del poniente y surponiente estaban dominados por ciertas narco-pandillas y sus habitantes vivían con miedo; pero al menos sabían quién(es) era(n) el (los) enemigo(s). Sin embargo, cuando llegaron los militares y los federales, los soldados irrumpían en las casas sin ninguna orden de cateo o de aprehensión bajo la excusa de buscar armas y drogas y las saqueban impunemente. Hacían lo mismo con las personas que paraban en los retenes. Levaban a cabo revisiones corporales a los hombres y esculcaban las bolsas de las mujeres y, en ambos casos tomaban lo que les placía. En general hacían esto con la gente más vulnerable, la clase media baja y baja. Muchos creemos que estaban conectados con las bandas criminales pues en el momento en que se fueron de la ciudad la violencia descendió, especialmente los secuestros y las ejecuciones.

Ese año mi madre enfermó de gravedad. Yo acostumbraba a ir de El Paso a Juárez a visitarla después del trabajo y, algunos días a quedarme con ella pues nos turnábamos para cuidarla. Los días que no me quedaba en casa de mis papás regresaba a casa alrededor de las nueve de la noche. Me impresionaba manejar por las calles y avenidas. Sentía como si atravesara un pueblo de fantasmas el cual apenas un par de años antes estaba lleno de vida. Juárez había sido como Nueva York, una ciudad "que nunca duerme". Yo siempre había caminado o conducido por sus avenidas con mucha seguridad a sabiendas que nada podría pasarme, pero durante el año que mi madre estuvo enferma manejaba inquieta, con resquemor. Nunca tomaba el mismo camino de regreso a casa. Cuando tomaba la avenida principal y veía sólo dos o tres carros me entraba temor. En ocasiones imaginaba que las luces del auto que veía a distancia a través del espejo retrovisor y se acercaban desde ahí me dispararían. Siempre pensaba que podrían ser los federales o los soldados. Después de un par de semanas así, me convencí que nada me pasaría y que no podía vivir en constante recelo. Pensé en el dicho "cuando te toca aunque te quites y cuando no te toca, aunque te pongas". Así que con esta filosofía popular en mente y mi ángel de la guarda que es muy eficiente, continué yendo a Juárez temprano o tarde siempre cautelosa, pero sin caer en el estado de inquietud o terror de antes. Creo que eso es lo que ha venido haciendo la población hasta hoy. Además, no estamos seguros si hay escuadrones de la muerte en la ciudad o si en realidad los narcos se están matando entre ellos; pero ese no es el punto. La lucha por la plaza se ha convertido en una guerra civil en la que el Estado ha venido perdiendo poder y se lo ha entregado a capos, coyotes, lenonoes, secuestradores, depredadores, extorsionistas, ladrones, sicarios, violadores y feminicidas. Con ello el Estado ha venido legitimando a los criminales y se ha hecho cómplice de esos actos. En otras palabras, el Estado ha condenado a muerte a la ciudadanía. El Estado ha institucionalizado el crimen y la violencia contra sus mujeres y su ciudadanía.

No creo que no exista nadie en Juárez que no haya experimentado la violencia de una forma u otra. Algunos la hemos sobrellevado durante casi veinte años y hemos visto a nuestra ciudad caer y levantarse, levantarse y caer. Hemos descubierto las caras del horror y desesperación en las familias de las mujeres asesinadas, pero hemos visto y experimentado otros tipos de horror también. Yo tengo amigos y estudiantes a quienes han asaltado y secuestrado. Asimismo he consolado a una de mis amigas de la infancia primero, mientras lloraba el asesinato de su sobrino y un año después el de su hijo menor, ambos acribillados en la calle, sin compasión, como en un juicio sumario de Kafka. Mientras nos consolábamos recordábamos cuando éramos niñas y solíamos jugar en esas mismas calles. Ahora me pregunto por la infancia de hoy y su constante exposición al crimen y la violencia no sólo a través de la televisión, los videojuegos y el internet, sino a través de lo más sorprendente: la vida real, cotidiana.

Mientras la violencia del narco y otras actividades criminales se dan abiertamente en las calles de Juárez, la población civil se ha visto obligada a guarecerse en sus casas, a volver a sus lugares de origen, o a desterrarse voluntaria e involuntariamente en las ciudades norteamericanas o en Canadá. Nuestra amada ciudad otrora próspera, se ha convertido en un campo de batalla en el cual es difícil ubicar al enemigo. En un punto, las autoridades municipales negociaron con el gobierno federal y los federales invadieron nuestra ciudad a solicitud del presidente municipal. Obviamente el municipio tuvo que pagar por su hospedaje. En otro punto, agentes de la municipal y el alcalde tuvieron una reyerta porque uno de los federales mató a un municipal que era guardaespaldas del presidente. El municipio ha gastado demasiado en personal para mantener el orden (policía y ejército) sin tener éxito. Nuestra ciudad se ha tornado en un sitio cuyas calles solitarias y calladas permanecen minadas por los baches, producto del abandono de las autoridades municipales que negociaron el albergue de militares y agentes federales en detrimento de su infraestructura y sus habitantes. Se ha vuelto un lugar poblado de edificios vacíos, de letreros de "se vende" o "se renta", de casas como tiraderos de basura, de tapias derruidas, de narco-mantas, de sitios acordonados de amarillo o de rojo, de cuerpos que se amontonan en la morgue. Nuestro terruño está habitado ahora por fantasmas vivos y muertos, por una muda geografía otrora famosa por su música, baile y diversión.

Para la comunidad en general y especialmente para la clase media y media alta esta violencia finalmente ha venido a interrumpir su cotidianeidad. Esa gente que se cegó ante los asesinatos de mujeres por más de quince años y que ignoró otras señales de violencia ahora clama justicia y paz.

No sé si sea demasiado tarde para la justicia y la paz. Espero que no. Algunas veces me pregunto por qué no previmos lo que vendría. ¿Por qué no armamos el rompecabezas? ¿Por qué nos tomó tanto reaccionar? ¿Fue porque las mujeres asesinadas eran pobres? ¿Fue porque estábamos hartas/os de ver nuestra ciudad repudiada nacional e internacionalmente? ¿Fue entonces que empezamos a percibir la violencia como parte de nuestras vidas y la naturalizamos? ¿Fue porque comprendimos el verdadero significado de la violencia y el crimen? ¿Fue porque asimilamos el discurso del Estado y ahora lo tratamos de deconstruir? ¿Fue porque perdimos nuestra compasión, nuestra solidaridad, nuestra humanidad?

En noviembre de 2007 estuve en Washington, D.C. y visité el Museo del Holocausto. Vi el horror de la Alemania nazi y otros regímenes fascistas. Leí su propaganda. Entendí cómo se puede convencer a las personas para que ignoren la violencia en sus sociedades, pero también observé la preocupación de quienes se opusieron al régimen. Escuché testimonios de sobrevivientes. Caminé por pasillos con zapatos y cabellos apilados. Abordé un vagón rumbo a los campos de exterminio. Me abrumé de leer tanto nombre y tanto número. Temí la homogeneización, el racismo, el prejuicio de clase y la xenofobia. Durante mi visita por el museo no hubo ningún momento que no dejara de pensar en el baile de fantasmas de mujeres asesinadas en Juárez y en la/s injusticia/s e impunidad que han permanecido hasta la fecha debido a la violencia reciente. Años después de mi visita al Museo del Holocausto sé que he comprendido el significado de la violencia, el horror y el crimen. Y mientras reflexiono sobre su significado, continúo observando mi ciudad devastada por la delincuencia, la brutalidad y la angustia. A medida que camino por las calles de mi terruño continúo pensando en este holocausto silencioso de Juárez, en sus mujeres invisibilizadas, en sus muertos sin ser llorados y en su guerra civil ignorada . . . pero siento un hito de esperanza. Espero el día que este horror termine. Ansío el día que la justicia llegue. Anhelo el día que podamos caminar por nuestras calles sin temer al secuestro, al asalto, a la violencia, al asesinato, al feminicidio. Espero el día que podamos recuperar la ciudad y salgamos, bailemos, cantemos, juguemos en sus calles. Anhelo el día que podamos amar, reír y vivir de nuevo en Ciudad Juárez, en México.

MIRRORS, GHOSTS AND VIOLENCE IN CIUDAD JUÁREZ

María Socorro Tabuenca Córdoba

My family and I returned to the great Paso del Norte (Ciudad Juárez) eight months after the assassination of President Kennedy. We drove along a narrow two-way highway called the "Panamericana" (this was before it was expanded into a four-lane avenue that would have its name changed three times before returning to its original "Pan-American Highway"). They say that the road begins in Juárez, right after San Lorenzo's curve and ends in Tierra del Fuego at the tip of the Southern Cone. The airport at that time was a small adobe room, and between the airport and the city there was almost nothing: a few nightclubs, several homes, the *lienzo charro* Baca Gallardo, and the soon-to-be opened Tecnológico de Juárez. At that time, as children, we could play on the streets late at night and walk long distances without being afraid that something bad would happen. Certainly we knew about "*robachicos*," child-snatchers that could take us if we didn't behave well; however, we felt safe in our barrios of our city. As children we didn't know the true meaning of the words violence and crime.

During the seventies, we would organize house parties or go to our high school dances in the various dance halls in town. Juárez nightlife had always been famous for its variety. You could have exclusive nightclubs on one street and brothels around the corner, but people knew how to navigate the streets. Basking in the afterglow of *Saturday Night Fever*, the streets of Juárez regained the splendor of the nightlife of the forties. Disco halls were opened not only on the strip but in other parts of town where the city had developed. Soldiers from Fort Bliss and underage teenagers from El Paso would come to look for a night of entertainment. We could go out dancing from dusk to dawn without fear that something adverse could happen. As teenagers, we didn't know the true meaning of the words violence and crime. By this time the city had already changed its demographics and urban landscape. Many women had arrived from rural towns and poor cities of the northern states of Chihuahua, Durango, and Coahuila. They came to work in the *maquiladora* industry many years before NAFTA. Juárez's middle class had also changed the way it perceived its inhabitants. Before the arrival of the *maquila*, we could blend easily; we knew who was rich, but it was harder to distinguish between the classes of the middle-high and the middle-low. Unfortunately, the poor and the poorest of the poor, as it happens in most societies, were easily overlooked by the rest until the arrival of the *maquiladora*. The poor people suffered from a lack of basic resources and services, but not yet from the generalized social violence they face now.

Working women from the factories were almost automatically classified as "loose women" because they were earning their own money, and most of the time *they* were the ones who supported their families. What was worse was that they "dared" to exercise their right to have fun and go dancing. There were several dance halls and nightclubs where the clientele was mostly working women and that increased their stigmatization even more. Our society's bias was at once evident and strange. On one hand, as members of the middle class, our society and the city allowed us all manner of freedoms: we could walk and drive in the city, go out dancing and drinking, have fun in all kinds of ways, and no one thought twice about it. In fact, it was what was expected of the middle-class youth; however, when working women from the *maquiladoras* decided to exercise that right, they were discredited because they were poor. Even though those attitudes existed, they could still walk the city, go to work, and go dancing without being afraid that something terrible would happen. I don't think they knew the *true* meaning of violence and crime.

The *maquiladora boom* of the eighties brought other faces to Juárez's urban landscape. Men and women from other states further south and from the east coast, particularly from Veracruz, started establishing themselves in Juárez. The outskirts through the west and southwest experienced a fast and chaotic growth due to irregular settlement. The city's infrastructure was not prepared for such fast and steady increases in population, and the new neighborhoods lacked running water, paved roads, sewage systems and public transportation. Perhaps it was then when poverty became more visible than it had been before, but, at this point, the poor still had jobs and could travel throughout the city one way or the other without being afraid that something gruesome could happen.

Life in Juárez was still "normal," but a bit more hectic with more people and more traffic. This growth not only affected the city's movement but also the crossing of its residents into El Paso. For those of us who navigated both sides of the border, it became harder to go to the United States. The abduction and assassination of DEA agent Enrique Camarena Salazar in 1985 made the lines at the bridges unbearable. From one day to the next, we suffered the "revenge" of the U.S. government through I.N.S. agents. This is a common practice on the border. Every time Washington D.C. and Mexico City disagree on an issue, we, the people of the border, are the perfect target for retaliation. The lines at the bridge start being slower, the agents stop the cars and do thorough inspections, and a line of cars that usually takes twenty minutes to cross may take one or two hours. The customs inspections on the U.S. side of the border were similar to those experienced in 1969 during Nixon's "Operation Intercept" that began his war against drugs and from which, even after forty-three years, we are still suffering the cruel consequences. Back then we were not afraid, but rather outraged by the way we were treated by the officers. We were not drug traffickers; we had nothing to be afraid of. We knew so little about violence and crime.

The nineties arrived with the national news of the Zapatista revolution, the murder of the presidential candidate Luis Donaldo Colosio, the devaluation of the peso, and the signing and implementation of NAFTA. Locally, we were beginning to experience our own turmoil. We were about to learn the true meaning of violence and crime. We were also about to learn the implications of other words such as impunity, injustice, powerlessness, prejudice, holocaust and horror. For me and for many others less privileged than me, the violence began long before Juárez was classified as "the most violent city in the world."

In June of 1993, we woke up to terrible news. Something inexplicable, unbelievable had happened: the bodies of six young females were found in outskirts of Juárez. All six deaths were apparently perpetrated by an alleged serial killer. We were astonished because there had been few incidences in modern Mexico's crime history of acts of similar nature and magnitude: there had been Goyo Cárdenas, a serial killer in the 1950s, "*Las Poquianchis*" in the 1960s in Mexico City, and Adolfo de Jesús Constanzo and his followers called "*los narcosatánicos*" in Matamoros, Tamaulipas at the end of the eighties. Nothing like this had happened in Juárez, and the city was shocked by the crimes. We had never felt so threatened because, in our minds, those types of criminals were far from us, in some distant place in southern Mexico or in the United States, but never in our hometown, and never so close to our border. That same year, two other women were killed apparently by men they knew, and those were the only two cases that were solved; neither of those crime scenes pointed to a serial killer. To this day, no one has been found guilty of any of those murders. We started to understand the meanings of violence and crime.

Five more women's remains were discovered within Juárez's city limits in 1994. Everything indicated that the serial killer had struck again. That same year, two other women were found dead aside from the serial killings, and once again those were the only two cases solved. Again, neither case indicated the work of a serial killer. To this day, no one has been found guilty of any of those crimes. Undoubtedly, we were unprepared for something like this; we were unprepared as a society, as women, and as feminists. Not even the police knew how to react to a problem of such magnitude. Regrettably, they reacted by not abiding by the law. At first, the authorities mentioned they were investigating, but when they couldn't provide a culprit they stigmatized the victims in "prevention campaigns." They created scapegoats; they destroyed evidence; they wanted the forensics to create evidence; they lied (and continue lying to us). It is well-known that the serial killings of these poor women remain unsolved; even though twelve men were sentenced, those findings are dubious as the investigations were unreliable. There was no irrefutable evidence to legitimate those men being imprisoned. Some of them have died in jail, and there is no consensus that they were the true assassins.

When I say that we, as Juárez citizens, as feminists and activists, were not ready for this, I mean that we were living in a relatively peaceful city where the only violence and crime had been what would be expected in a city the size of Juárez. There were some of us who were returning to Juárez to do our doctoral dissertations research and found ourselves feeling powerless in face of this brutal tragedy. Some were social scientists and could have a more theoretical understanding of the problem, but I had studied literature and didn't quite know how to respond, except for going out to protest with other activists. I found myself trying to be a researcher but also responding to other urgent issues such as demanding justice for those poor women and their families. As academics, we were unprepared because we hadn't achieved critical mass, nor could we completely conceptualize the events. Our academic training and research areas had not prepared us to confront the topic. We did not have academic or social leadership. Studies related to gender were incipient in local universities and research centers, and no one had the training to assume leadership. However, despite our insufficient academic credentials on the problem and lacking the theoretical frame of femicide, we were ready to support those who would lead the fight and to articulate subversive discourses. We were trying to understand and challenge the new meanings of crime and violence in our city.

By 1995, thirty-two women had been brutally killed, twenty-six of them apparently at the hands of a serial killer or killers. Of the thirty-two murders, only one man was found guilty of a crime unrelated to the serial killings. 1995 was an important year not only because the number of women massacred had doubled, but also because we started to exercise our agency. Non-Governmental Organizations, independent groups of women, scholars and individuals got together and started clamoring for justice. All of us defied a prevention campaign launched by the Partido Acción Nacional (PAN), the political party that was in power. The campaign stigmatized the victims and blamed them for their own deaths because most of the murdered women were sex workers and *maquiladora* workers, and both of these professions already had a social stigma. In their "questionable" professions, the authorities found the perfect scapegoat to both justify the unresolved violence and crime and to vindicate their inability and/or unwillingness to do anything about it.

As academics and activists, we wrote editorials, demonstrated on the streets, gave lectures, organized seminars and workshops, and pressured the authorities in such a way that the state government created a "Special Prosecutor's Office for Crimes against Women." Regrettably, it is commonly known and registered in newspapers and academic work that since its origin, the organization has been led by negligent, insensible, unprofessional and cowardly men and women. In their positions, they have fabricated culprits, destroyed or covered evidence, humiliated the victims and their families, and positioned their own ideologies and self-interest above the law and their responsibility as public servants. They have obstructed justice and questioned the victims even after these victims have been raped and tortured. In short, they have established and prolonged impunity in our city with respect to femicide, and that impunity is linked to the state of crime and violence experienced in the city at present.

During a press conference with governor Francisco Barrio in June of that year, I improvised an accusation on a piece of cardboard: "*¿Cuántas más Sr. Gobernador?* [How many more (murdered women), Mr. Governor?"]. I would soon get an answer. In 1996, the count of slaughtered women was nineteen, sixteen of them apparently at the hand of a serial killer or killers. The horror was increasing instead of decreasing, even when the police had supposedly imprisoned the mastermind of the massacres and his accomplices. Between 1997 and 1998, thirty-two more women were found in different locations in Juárez, twenty-six of them killed presumably by a serial predator or predators. A group of women, academics and activists with whom I worked, started to see the correlation between poverty and violence, poverty and impunity. Juárez's middle and upper classes had stopped questioning the authorities, and had stopped being afraid (if they ever were). They already had a "good story," a "realistic perpetrator" and an "excellent group of accomplices." In nearly half of the cases, they also had the "perfect victims:" sex workers, exotic dancers, bar waitresses and *maquiladora* workers who would not receive the compassion of the people nor their solidarity. They were poor women, anonymous women, stigmatized women, disposable women who had discovered the *true* corporal, gendered, age and class meaning of crime and violence. By the turn of the millennium, many more women were raped, tortured and murdered. The hope of a new era faded away when we faced the cold number of slaughtered women in Ciudad Juárez. From 1993 to 2005, according to Julia Monárrez, the researcher who has conducted the most extensive study regarding femicide in Juárez and with whom I worked with, 150 women were sexually assaulted and killed, of whom 112 had signs of being assassinated by one or more serial killers. The new millennium also brought new ways of disposing of the bodies. Most female bodies were habitually discovered on the outskirts of town, out in the desert. However, in November 2001, eight bodies were found within the city in a large abandoned cotton field, practically across from the headquarters of the Maquiladora Association. This could have been read as a message from the killers. I think that they were telling us that the killings would continue, that they would occur more in the open, that these poor women were worthless, that we were powerless to do anything about it, and that violence and crime would be more brutal, more spectacular, and more painful. We, as a society, didn't know how to read the message and allowed the government of Patricio Martínez from the PRI to provide more scapegoats, to torture them, and to possibly cause their deaths as in the case of "*El Foca*" and Sharif, two alleged serial killers who died under mysterious circumstances in prison. As a society we were reinventing justice as repetition and mirror of the crimes.

These ruthless murders of women also resonated in Chihuahua City in 2003, when three bodies of young women were found on the outskirts of that city with the same characteristics of those from Juárez. We had been living with ten years of brutal violence against women, but the authorities at all levels of government (municipal, state and federal) had paid little or no attention to this bloodshed, and the local society had been ignoring the problem because they had grown "tired" of hearing about it in local, national and international news. We didn't want to uncover the true meaning of violence and crime, and many just wanted to sweep it under the rug. The people being killed were "not us" and, by 2008, the murders had become meaningless in a society that apparently had gotten used to them over the fifteen years since they began in 1993.

In order to grasp some meaning and implications from all of this, I reflect on who these women were and what they had in common. Some worked at the maquiladora industry, several worked in the commercial zone of downtown Juárez, a number were exotic dancers, sex-workers, mothers and students. All of them belonged to the working or impoverished class. Quite a few were working night shifts in order to pull themselves up from the poverty in which they had subsisted with their families. Most of them lived in areas with insufficient infrastructure and without electricity. There was also a general lack of transportation be it public or private, to pick them up or return them to a location close to their homes. Their ages ranged from six to forty-two years of age, but most of the attacked women were approximately seventeen years old. They were assassinated by one or more serial killers. The majority of the women were tortured and raped before being killed. Sometimes they were mutilated or dismembered. A large number of them were found in the outskirts of the city, in open areas, vast uninhabited lots such as Lomas de Poleo, Lote Bravo, Campo Algodonero, or el Cerro del Cristo Negro. In several cases their bodies were unclothed; in other cases, only skulls, bones, and pieces of clothes were recovered. Some of the remains were lightly covered by bushes and sand. Others were exposed and displayed carefully, as if the killer(s) wanted to take a stand, to leave his/their signature on the grisly graves defying authorities and society. A few were dumped in empty lots in the city, on railroad tracks, in the sewage system, or left near their homes.

After their atrocious deaths, the victims and their families have had to face more tribulations. Their lives have been misjudged and stigmatized by the authorities, regardless of their political affiliation. The authorities never explained that many of the women were returning home at night or dawn because of night or early-morning shifts at the factories. No one brought up either the fact that if they were walking alone at such times, it was because they did not have a car to drive home, and that the buses left them a long distance from their homes. The authorities never said that most of the victims were last seen in the afternoon after work, or going from work to school, and not at dusk or dawn after going dancing (and what if they were . . .). They not only left an image of victims who were somehow responsible for their own demise, but also revived the old conservative idea that the best and safest place for women is in the home, without considering the cases of intimate femicide. They also denied working women the few hours of leisure time they had. They distorted the idea of having a good time and projected it as an immorality. Authorities even condemned women by the way they were dressed. Ironically enough, most of the victims were wearing T-shirts, jeans, and sneakers. While some in Juárez understand the gravity of the situation and feel sorry for the victims, many have not been able to demonstrate their compassion or solidarity and have chosen to remain silent without getting involved or demanding justice. Unfortunately, that silence has had its price. Since January 2008, Juárez has been facing a terrible war against organized and disorganized crime that has positioned the city again on the national and international radar. There are a lot of common criminals (individuals or groups) who have been taking advantage of the atmosphere created by organized drug cartels, and have started committing kidnappings, carjackings, as if they belonged to the cartels. From "the killing fields" or "the city that kills its daughters," it has become "the most violent city in the world." This is why I mention that, for me, the violence began long before the city attained this infamous label.

How did we arrive at this escalated violence? How is it that we could have up to twenty-two people murdered in one incident? More importantly, how have we let the murder of women be overshadowed by the present violence? To answer these questions it is necessary to remember the sequence of events leading up to the current situation, because we often forget or turn a blind eye to the connections between the existing violence and the femicides. Rafael Aguilar Guajardo, founder of the Juárez Cartel in the seventies, had controlled the city (along with his operators Eduardo and Rafael Muñoz Talavera) until his death in April 1993. His death was seemingly ordered by Amado Carrillo Fuentes, the "Lord of the Skies," who became the boss of the Juárez Cartel from that time until his "accidental" death in 1997. Juárez, the long-time turf of *juarenses*, became occupied by *mafiosi* from Sinaloa. As opposed to Aguilar who was considered "a gentleman," the Carrillo family was well-known for their lack of scruples and their cruelty. Consequently, it may not be very daring to propose that the beginning of the killing of women in Juárez and the take-over of the Juárez Cartel by Amado Carrillo Fuentes are connected.

Another event we cannot forget is Carrillo's death in 1997, and the turf war for Juárez between Vicente Carrillo Fuentes and Rafael Muñoz Talavera, who sought support from the Arellano family of the Tijuana Cartel after Aguilar's death. This fight led to two massacres in August of that same year: one at the Max Fim restaurant where six people were gunned down, and the other at Geronimo's bar where eight people were killed, including two law enforcement agents who were in the bar and tried to repel the attack. On both occasions, heavily armed men ruthlessly opened fire on the patrons. Apparently their target was a couple of drug lords that were having dinner. As was the case with the murdered women, nobody was charged with the murders. In the month of July 1997, fourteen people were executed "*a la mafia*" in Juárez and the surrounding areas. Also in July, a band of nearly 100 kidnappers were arrested in Juárez. During that year Juárez experienced a wave of violence that disrupted public spaces: apart from Geronimo's and the Max Fim's, there was also the King-Sui restaurant where four people were killed, and the Space Burger restaurant where five people were kidnapped. All of these attacks were in broad daylight. Adding to the gruesome situation was the abduction and murder of four medical doctors after a shooting between enemy drug gangs. These events led to a march against the violence on August 31st, lead by governor Francisco Barrio, governor-elect Patricio Martínez, and mayor Ramón Galindo. The irony of this is that as representatives of the state, they were demonstrating against a parallel structure that was surely gaining power and beating them. It was the beginning of the failed state that would consolidate ten years later. During that year, Juárez residents were trapped in an atmosphere of psychosis: nobody wanted to go out, especially to restaurants; however, we soon forgot about the terror because it was close but not *that* close. As I asked my friends about these events, they always answered me that this was something that would end soon, that the government had everything under control, that these situations existed because drug lords and the government were negotiating. I was never satisfied with that answer because I knew that eventually something could go very wrong.

In September 1998, Rafael Muñoz Talavera was assassinated and Vicente Carrillo believed that he was finally the sole boss of the cartel and that he controlled the turf. However, the armed wing of the Juárez Cartel, known as "*la Línea*," as well as the gang members of the Barrio Azteca and the Assassin Artists, had been trying to acquire terrain from the Carrillo Family. According to rumors, Chapo Guzmán wanted to be the lord of the Mexican Cartel, and the bloodshed would not end until he was anointed as such.

Another issue that is often disregarded in relation to these events is that regarding the mass graves discovered at the turn of the century and in subsequent years. In 1999, there were reports of a clandestine cemetery where there were supposed to have been as many as 200 corpses. Back then, President Clinton claimed that Juárez was a dangerous city, but Mexican officials requested an apology because "instead of 200 bodies they only found seven." Another graveyard was discovered with five corpses in a luxurious residence in 2004; this time the discovery was tied to the chief of police (who had also been tied to a band of human traffickers and prostitution). To this day, he has not been caught and no one knows his whereabouts. In February 2008, other mass graves were discovered in two different homes within the city limits: one with thirty-six corpses and the other one with nine.

These events came to confirm that authorities at the municipal, state and federal levels were not effective in preventing or solving the crimes, and that most members of society were simple spectators in a plot that profoundly involved all of us. Since January of 2008, our city has become a battleground full of casualties. People of all ages—young men and women, children, babies, adults, and elders—have been killed or wounded simply because they were in the wrong place at the wrong time. Others have been gunned down in cases of mistaken identity, as in the case of the sixteen students who were massacred while celebrating a birthday in Villas de Salvárcar, near Juárez in January of 2010. There have also been "strategic" attacks on various rehabilitation centers. Women continue to disappear and be killed. It is not, however, the sheer number of murders (almost 9,000 in four years) that have led to our city being labeled as "the most violent in the world," but also the other criminal activities that the state has not been able to prevent such as kidnappings, extortions, carjackings, prostitution, child pornography and exploitation, and arson. Some of these criminal activities may be led by organized crime, but others are committed by common crooks who have taken advantage of the chaotic situation in Juárez.

In 2009, army troops and federal police squads were deployed to our city as part of Calderón's war against the drug cartels. Violence stopped for a month and then exploded again. With the army and the federal police in our city, basic human rights were ignored and criminalized, and many people, particularly the poor, started experiencing even higher stages of fear. Before the army and the police arrived, many of Juárez's neighborhoods in the west and southwest were drug-gang territories and its inhabitants lived in fear, but at least they knew who the enemy was. When the *federales* and the soldiers arrived, the soldiers would burst into private homes without warrants, use the excuse that they were looking for weapons and drugs, and then steal people's belongings with impunity. They would do the same thing to people at random street checkpoints. They would perform full-body searches on men and look through women's purses and take anything they pleased. In general, they would do this to the most vulnerable, the lower-middle class and the poor. Many of us believe that they were connected to the criminal gangs because as soon as they left the city, the violence decreased, especially the kidnappings and executions.

That year my mother was very ill. I used to go from El Paso to Juárez to visit her after work and some days to stay with her because we used to take turns taking care of her. The days that I didn't stay at my parents' home in Juárez, I would return home to El Paso around nine o' clock in the evening. I was struck at finding myself driving, scared, through empty avenues. I had the feeling I was driving through a ghost town where just a few years before had been full of life. Juárez had been like New York City, a city that never sleeps. I had always walked or driven through those avenues secure, knowing that nothing would happen; however, during the time my mother was sick, I experienced unrest and I never took the same path to return home. When I entered the main avenue and saw only two or three cars, I was afraid. Sometimes I imagined that the car lights I saw in the distance through the rearview mirror could be someone who could shoot me. I always thought it could be the police or the soldiers. After a couple of weeks, I convinced myself that nothing would happen, and if it did, I wasn't going to continue living in constant distress. As they say "*cuando te toca, aunque te quites; cuando no te toca, aunque te pongas*" (When it is your turn to die, it will happen even though you hide; when it is not, it will not, even though you expose yourself). So, with this popular philosophy in mind, and my guardian angel by my side, I continued going to Juárez early or late, and tried to pay attention to the possible dangers, but I did not fall in distress or panic. I guess that most people are doing that at present.

On the other hand, we are not certain if there are death squads in our city or if, in reality, the drug traffickers are killing each other, but that is not the point. The turf war has become a civil war in which the state has been losing power and has enabled drug-lords, *coyotes*, pimps, kidnappers, predators, extortionists, robbers, hit men, rapists and killers of women. By allowing this to happen, the state has been legitimizing the criminals and has been an accomplice to those acts. In other words, the state has given a death sentence to its own citizens. It has institutionalized crime and violence against its women and its citizens.

I don't think that there is anyone who lives in Juárez who hasn't experienced the violence in one way or another. Some of us have experienced it for almost twenty years and have seen our city fall and rise, rise and fall. We have seen the faces of horror and despair of the families of murdered women, but we have seen and experienced other types of terror as well. I have had friends and students kidnapped, robbed, or assaulted. I've also comforted one of my oldest friends as she wept first for her murdered nephew and then for her own son, both gunned down on the street without compassion as in Kafka's summary trial. While crying and consoling each other, we remembered when we were children and used to play on those same streets. I just wonder about today's children and their exposure to crime and violence, not just through television, films, video games, and the Internet, but more shockingly, in real life.

While drug violence and other criminal activities occur in the open on Juárez's streets, the city's population has been forced to find shelter in their homes, to migrate to their places of origin, or to go into voluntary or involuntary exile in the U.S. or Canada. Our beloved city, at one time a prosperous city, has become a battleground in which it is difficult to know who the enemy is. At one point, the municipal authorities negotiated with the federal police and the *federales* "invaded" our city under the mayor's request. Obviously, the municipal government had to pay for their room and board. At another point, the municipal police and the mayor had a big fight because the *federales* killed a municipal police officer who happened to be one of the mayor's escorts. The municipal government has spent a lot of money on law enforcement officers (police and army) that have been unsuccessful in enforcing the law.

Our city has become a place whose lonely and silent streets are full of holes due to their budgetary abandonment by the same authorities that negotiated with the federal government to house the military and the *federales* to the detriment of the city's infrastructure and inhabitants. It has become a place full of empty buildings with "for sale" or "for rent" signs, of walls and houses in ruins, like trash dumps, of narco-messages, of streets and places surrounded by yellow or red tape, and by corpses piled high in the morgue. Our homeland is inhabited by ghosts of the dead, but also of the living, by the silence of a geography that was once known for its music, dance and joy.

For the community in general, and especially for the upper and middle classes, this violence has finally come to disrupt their ordinary lives. Those people who were blind toward the killing of women for more than fifteen years, and who also ignored other signs of violence, are now clamoring for justice and peace.

I don't know if it is already too late for justice and peace. I hope not. Sometimes I wonder why we did not foresee what was coming. Why didn't we put two and two together? Why did it take us so long to react? Was it because the women murdered were poor? Was it because we were tired of seeing our city being bashed nationally and internationally? Was it because we had started to perceive violence as a part of our lives and we naturalized it? Was it because we understood the true meaning of violence and crime? Was it because we did assimilate the discourse of the state and only now are trying to deconstruct it? Was it because we had lost our compassion, our solidarity, our humanity?

In November 2007, I went Washington D.C. to visit the Holocaust Museum. I saw the horror of Nazi Germany and other fascist regimes. I read their propaganda. I understood how people could be convinced to ignore the violence of those societies, but I also saw the concern of the regime's opponents. I heard the survivors' testimonies. I walked by a pile of hair and shoes. I boarded a wagon to go to the extermination camps. I was overwhelmed by the names and numbers. I feared the homogenization, racism, class prejudice, and xenophobia. There was not a single moment in my walk through the museum that I could stop thinking of the ghost dance of the murdered women of Juárez and of the injustices and impunity that have prevailed to this day due to the recent violence. Long after these years of my visit to the Holocaust Museum, I know I have grasped the meanings of violence, horror and crime. As I reflect on those meanings, I continue to observe my city devastated by delinquency, brutality and distress. As I walk through the streets of my hometown I keep thinking of Juárez's silent holocaust, its obliterated women, its unmourned dead, and its unacknowledged civil war . . . but I hope. I hope for the day this horror stops. I hope for the day justice occurs. I hope for the day we can walk again through our streets without the fear of being kidnapped, robbed, attacked, or killed. I hope for the day we can take back the city and dance, sing, dine, and play on the streets. I hope for the day we can laugh, love, and live again in Juárez, in Mexico.

THE PERSONAL STORIES

SELLING TITA'S HOUSE

Maria Cristina Cigarroa

I walked across the Mexican saltillo tile, holiday dress on, to make my entrance into the kitchen. It was Christmas Eve of 2010, one of more than twenty Christmases I'd spent at my grandparents' tan brick home in Nuevo Laredo, Mexico. My grandmother Tita was molding dough into half-moon croissants. Familiar smells of *bacalao* arose from the silver pot on the stove. Apron on, she looked as exquisite as always, not a hair out of place, makeup already applied. It was evening, and she would soon be going to Mass before the rest of our family arrived. The way she could cook for hours and not have one food stain on her clothes, save for, maybe, a bit of flour on her apron, amazed me. Her yellow-green eyes, inherited by several of my cousins, illuminated her smile. Just as she had done when I was a five-year-old donning bright red lipstick, she took one look at me and said, "*Qué guapa te ves.*" *Luckily*, I thought to myself, as I imagined how my cousins would make fun of me now, *I am not wearing the same lipstick today.*

It was a ritual I had followed every year—making my holiday appearance in the kitchen, before the family party, to watch my grandmother cook. I marveled at the way she imbued her kitchen with vivacity as she laughed, baked bread, and stirred pots at the same time. On this particular Christmas Eve, my grandmother had not yet contemplated selling her house, her life-long project. She had not yet come to believe that her home, one she'd lived in since the seventies with my now-deceased grandfather Papo and seven children, was anything but safe. An interior designer, she was still using part of it as an office and thinking of further ways to decorate her masterpiece. A committed matriarch, she was still re-arranging photographs of children and grandchildren along tables in the living room. And as a devoted widow living alone, she was still comforted by the idea that my grandfather's memories were preserved and sanctified inside the house.

The need for my grandmother Tita to sell what had been her refuge would come in the following months. On this Christmas, she still maintained an unwavering peace. I, too, could not have foreseen that it was the last Christmas we'd spend in the house. It was, after all, the center of my family's universe, an anchor my relatives and I returned to time and again. I, who had been taught that holidays were always to be spent in Nuevo Laredo, could not imagine spending them anywhere else.

Every year since I was eight, a few days before Christmas Eve, my parents, younger sister and I drove from our home in San Antonio to my grandparents' in Mexico. Aside from the holidays, we also visited each month. Calling Nuevo Laredo a second home was easy to do, since once we arrived in Laredo, Texas, and crossed the International Bridge south, everything on the Mexican side of the border seemed the same. Narrow roads pinched my excitement at each red light when we had to stop. Vendors passing our car windows held baskets of chili-flavored *tamarindos* and plastic-wrapped chains of *cajeta* lollipops. School girls in uniforms, their hair pulled back in hairsprayed *colitas de caballo*, giggled together outside of the Montessori. Elderly women, with bags of groceries from *el otro lado*, returned home after long walks to Laredo, where certain food staples were cheaper. Piñatas lined street corners like life-size cartoons; the scents of *carne asada* and buttery *elote granizado* floated in the air and made me hungry. Square concrete homes painted green, pink, blue stood alongside each other. In a front yard, yesterday's laundry dried on a rope.

Once at the city's main boulevard, El Paseo Colón, I took joy in the familiar sights of the upscale Colonia Longoria, my grandparents' neighborhood. During the holidays, El Paseo, with its towering statue of Christopher Columbus and lit-up trees, was cheerful to me. I remembered how, as teenagers, my cousins and I would drive around it, *dando la vuelta* in our parents' trucks along with what seemed like half the youth in the city, listening to music and greeting friends through open car windows. From El Paseo, I could already glimpse the multi-colored Christmas lights adorning the homes of family friends. "La Casa Longoria," a gray mansion with a sweeping front yard, reminded me of the glitzy homes I saw in the old 1960s films. Right before turning in to my grandparents' driveway, I would see the *plazita* where my cousins and I had chased each other around as children and sipped on *chamoy raspas*. Behind the *plazita* was the white El Espíritu Santo Church where my parents had married and I had been baptized.

Finally arriving at my grandparents' home, I'd glance up at the tall palm trees that, like a tall canopy, enveloped it in safety. The sight of these gave me the feeling that summer— and time, for that matter—was drawn out in the city's sunny winters. This was the magic of our routine visits, that Nuevo Laredo seemed to me sheltered and ageless, a city I could return to time and time again and find nothing changed. It was also like a magical cloak of security, this understanding that my grandparents' house would always be there as my haven.

To friends and family in both Laredo and Nuevo Laredo, my grandparents' house was *una de las más bonitas* in the city. Inside the kitchen, blue tiles and brown wooden cabinets surrounded the high table where Tita turned out everything from apple pies to tuna dips to any number of Mexican *guisados*. High windows filled the space with sunlight during the day, and because no door separated the kitchen from the dining area and living room, the rich, intoxicating aromas wafted through the house, floating across tile floors and between brick columns and chandeliers. The absence of doors also allowed for conversations in the dining room to be heard from the home's second floor; the long, wooden dining table invited glances into the living room. With couches the color of sand and a coffee table topped with magazines about home décor, that room was a reflection of Tita's passion for interior design. It was a passion she'd acquired through her long-time career as an interior decorator in both South Texas and northern Mexico. Sliding glass doors separated the living room from the outdoors, so that it was easy to feel, still inside the house, that I was also lounging next to the pool. There was a peacefulness about the house that paused any sense of time passing, a feeling that I could lay on one of the couches and daydream to the swaying of palm trees.

"*Aquí en esta casa es puro vivir,*" my grandmother would say. Here in the house, living is pure joy. It's little wonder my grandmother held this belief, since the house had grown up along with my mother, aunts and uncles. Their bedrooms were a testament to their lives there: my mother and her twin sister's room, affectionately called the *Palma* room for its palm-tree wallpaper, remained just that, a *Palma* room. There was never any desire to change the wallpaper that dated to the seventies because to do so would destroy the room's character.

When holidays rolled around each year, my grandmother's Christmas tree, decked in decades-old ornaments, added a touch of allure and excitement to the home's serenity. My cousins and I would circle the tree, shaking presents from our grandparents and godparents, hoping to decipher what was inside. Experience had taught us that small boxes were money or jewelry. Next to the tree was a statue of the *arcángel*, a life-size angel swathed in gold that, to my child's imagination, had been as impressive as a Michelangelo sculpture. With its eyes that seemed to glance upward and sideward, I had believed the statue could see me sneaking around the presents. To this day, the memory of that giant angel makes me smile.

With each new Christmas, birthday, holiday party and wedding, the house only became further decorated, brimming with photographs of each festivity so that when I was there, I felt I was inside a living photo album containing a thousand memories. Pictures of my mother and aunts in wedding dresses took me back in time, as did the ones memorializing my grandfather, who had passed away in 2005. I have a vivid image of my mother and her friends pulling out photos of parties they'd had at the house and laughing at their Farrah Fawcett hairdos; images of *fulanita* dancing with *fulanito* the night they had turned the living room into *Saturday Night Fever*. I could imagine myself at their get-togethers easily, since my cousins and I had also toasted champagne there with our friends and danced on the same tile floors.

Each of us had a favorite event we remembered at my grandparents' house—for my parents, it was a party in the eighties that my father had crashed to meet my mother. For me, it was a Christmas in which my grandmother had given all the girls red silk pajamas. We were about twenty-five cousins and aunts hopping around the chimney in red, as Christmas *villancicos* and my grandmother's Luis Miguel albums played in the background. There was something liberating about dancing inside our house in identical pajamas, *sin pena*, knowing that we wouldn't be judged. *Era puro vivir.*

Despite its openness, the beauty of my grandparents' home was that, once inside, its high brick walls made me feel protected, enclosed. The neighborhood was also a quiet one, separated geographically from the honking cars and blasting radios of downtown. While the house was spacious, there were hardly any views of the street from within it, only views of the surrounding palm trees and pool; it was an inward-looking perspective typical of most large Mexican houses, a carry-over from Spanish haciendas. It enclosed a world that, while welcoming of friends and family, was also very private. With its gates closed at night, the sounds of cars were muted by the laughter and music of family get-togethers.

It was with this sensation of enclosed protection that I tried to understand Nuevo Laredo's drug violence, which began to grow in 2004, but, at first, only felt tangible if I read about it in a newspaper or saw it on television. Since my mother was young, there had been an understanding among residents that the drug cartels and gangs fought among themselves. Theirs was a presence that, much like gangs in the U.S., was known, yet the perception remained that nothing would happen to you if you were not already involved.

I imagined the cartels and gangs invading a corner of Nuevo Laredo that I could not see or hear. To be honest, I'd never given their presence much thought. If I heard anything remotely resembling a gunshot, in my mind, it was a New

Year's Eve firework. I never witnessed or heard any *balaceras* myself, and I felt assured that I would only have to confront these from a distance, through second-hand sources. By 2005, however, after I had turned eighteen years old, conversations during *comidas* became interspersed with the most recent news of violence: a police chief shot after being sworn to office, *El Mañana* newspaper's editorial office attacked by grenades, an emerging national security campaign to fight drugs. *Terrible*, my grandparents would say as they glimpsed the newspaper headlines.

When Mexican newspapers began to cover the violence less, my family and I no longer knew what to believe. *Allá*—over there in the United States—the news exaggerates what happens in Nuevo Laredo, my aunts and uncles would say, while over here, *las noticias no dicen nada*. How could the newspapers say much, when reporters were being kidnapped and murdered for naming cartels and suspects? For us, however, it was as if we had become stuck in a tug-of war, pulled by American news reports that warned us against crossing to Mexico, yet at the same time, pushed back by an uncertainty about what actually was happening. Somewhere in between this tug-of-war was my family's love for visiting my grandparents' house independently of which side of the rope pulled us. Ultimately, tradition was stronger than any news relayed on CNN.

It was during that summer of 2005, when news of the violence began making American headlines, that my grandfather found himself fighting terminal pancreatic cancer. Instead of heeding the warnings against going to Mexico, I went whenever I could to visit Papo. At a time when Nuevo Laredo residents had begun to tinker with the idea of moving to Texas, I appreciated my grandparents' house more than ever. My grandfather spent the majority of his last days there. During his final months, when he could barely walk without help, he would sit in a corner of the living room, silently, as if praying. His brown eyes, lit by the sunshine that seeped through the windows, reflected his pensiveness. Sometimes a tear would slip down a wrinkle on his cheek, not of suffering I think, but of love for his family and his home. I saw how he found peace in that house, in spite of the growing sense that the world around it was no longer safe. Even in a wheelchair, he was always present at family gatherings, his silver moustache tickling his smile to let my cousins and me know how much he loved being there. Despite news of the latest kidnapping or murder, those things that constituted a home for my grandfather were still unencumbered: the long *comidas*, the family visits, the photographs of the last whitetail deer he'd hunted, the naps under his own sheets and covers, the blessings from an American priest who would cross from Laredo to see him. On October 3, 2005, my grandfather died knowing that he could peacefully pass on from a place where he had experienced *pura vida*, where he had lived life to the fullest.

In this way, I came to understand the healing power of a home. It was with this lesson that I moved thousands of miles away that fall to begin at Harvard College, an accomplishment that had meant so much to my grandfather, only to return to Nuevo Laredo for his funeral. During those years, there was still a great uncertainty about what to believe, as the Mexican newspapers had continued to censor themselves. In addition, the trickle of refugees to the U.S. had begun. Among the first to leave were journalists and reporters who had been threatened for covering kidnappings and murders. Others, afraid of what could happen next, packed up their belongings and moved to Texas. Friends who had grown up in Laredo, as a general rule, were no longer allowed to cross south. Sometimes they would cross for birthdays or weddings, but for the most part, it was as if they'd left behind a part of their lives. "I haven't been back to Mexico in months," one of my cousins told me. Some Nuevo Laredo residents moved only temporarily, testing life across. They would rent apartments or hotel rooms in Laredo and spend nights there, or leave for several days when they heard of another shoot-out, another kidnapping, of things getting worse, *empeorando*. When friends and family told them things had calmed down, they would return to their Mexican homes as if nothing had changed. Several of my aunts and uncles chose this approach. How they could relocate and settle back again, over and over? For other residents who had stayed the whole time in Nuevo Laredo, the notion that *no pasa nada* remained. For some of my cousins, *la vida seguía*. Nuevo Laredo was still home.

These were the ideas I clung to every time my parents, sister and I drove back across to Mexico. It's not that I wasn't nervous. Each time we crossed now, my mother would turn off the radio and lower the windows, to be aware of anything that happened outside. Like my family, I was also fearful of not knowing what could happen, not knowing how dangerous things really were. I knew that the city was different. It was easy for me to notice the changes because now that I was in college, I only visited during the holidays. During one of my visits, in 2006, I saw the beginning of the transformation: camouflaged soldiers from the Mexican army at the city's entrance. It was unlike anything I had been used to seeing, these young men in helmets and guns who stood guard at the foot of the bridge and rode through the city's streets in green armored tanks and pick-ups. Nuevo Laredo, my cousins and I agreed, was looking more and more like an occupied city during a war. To me, it was like a vision from a movie or a dream, because I had never imagined there would be soldiers there. But the thoughts of our destination comforted me: so long as we stayed at my grandparents' home, everything would be okay. *Nada pasaría.* What could happen to my relatives and me, who were not involved in the drug trade and were only there to visit family? What could happen inside brick walls? For me, it was the safety of tradition, that love I had for returning, that sheltered me. It was that feeling of peace the house would surround me with, as if no one could invade us there.

Little by little, however, a different reality set in. Violence was inching its way in. It was no longer a distant danger, confined to one corner of Nuevo Laredo, but kept creeping closer and closer to our family and home. An abandoned house next to my grandparents' was vandalized and burned down. Friends of my cousins were stopped and kidnapped on their way to pharmacies, gas stations, relatives' homes. Some were cases of mistaken identity and were returned to their families for ransoms, but the anguish marked them forever: it was like a profound hole in the stomach that, no matter how alleviated, would not go away. Several of them preferred not to discuss what they had seen and suffered. Yet, with other families, like my grandparents' neighbors, their relatives who had been targeted for their wealth or other reasons no one fully understood were never seen again.

Smaller crimes produced the same chilling effect. Some of my own friends and family had their cars stolen. Parents began keeping their children home when they received news of nearby *balaceras*. Not only were the cartels to be feared now, but a number of smaller gangs had formed and were equally involved in murders and vandalism.

Even in the air, the city changed, and I could sense that something was amiss. On the sidewalks in my grandparents' neighborhood, fewer people were walking. In the plazita, a smaller number of joggers were running laps in the evenings.

Restaurant outings ceased, and house lunches and dinners became the norm. A peace movement emerged, and stickers with white doves and the phrase *"Paz en Nuevo Laredo,"* appeared on the bumpers of cars. El Cadillac, a legendary restaurant and bar that had opened in 1926 and where my parents and friends had gone for dinners, was now shuttered. No longer did my cousins and I go downtown, where as teenagers we had hopped into an array of bars and restaurants. The majority of those businesses had closed their doors. Like a giant broom, the growing violence was sweeping up the city's culture.

I awoke to the reality that the cartels controlled Nuevo Laredo the day I could no longer visit the family's ranch on the outskirts of the city. Two of my uncles in charge of handling ranch management still went on weekends, but I, like most of my family, was not allowed to go. By early 2010, cartels and gangs had fully taken over the highway by the ranch's entrance, and there was news they had already invaded surrounding ranches. They needed land to stake out their territories and move their goods; several ranchers, having received threats to give up their properties, abandoned them and fled. This was beginning to happen all over Tamaulipas, the one state in Mexico that American news reports were beginning to call a "failed state," where residents could no longer move about it without the potential of danger. One 77-year-old rancher named Alejo Garza, known to everyone as "Don Alejo," had not fled, choosing instead to defend his ranch near Ciudad Victoria until the end. When a group of men arrived with a final ultimatum to surrender his property within twenty-four hours, he told them he was not going anywhere. *"Allí estaré esperándolos,"* he said, according to the legend that emerged. After gathering his workers, he told them to take the next day off, that he wanted to be alone. Then, he set about stocking hunting rifles and ammunition by every door and window. A few hours later, invading gang members were caught by surprise, as they encountered the one man who did not follow their rules and did not flee. When the Mexican Marines arrived the following afternoon, they found the main house practically demolished by grenades and heavy gunfire, and the bodies of four gunmen and two more who remained unconscious and wounded. Inside the home, Don Alejo was also dead, his body riddled by bullets.

My cousins and I did not know what to make of this man who'd defended his ranch with his life. What was the honorable thing to do? Was it wise to abandon one's family and risk one's life to defend a beloved place? Or should he have done what others did, flee to save his life and his family's? Even though I struggled to answer these questions myself, I understood his position as a dedicated rancher. I understood because my grandfather, too, had loved his land more than any other place in the world.

The last time I visited the ranch was in the spring of 2010, and I didn't know it would be my last time there. While I had always equated Nuevo Laredo with my grandparents' house, the city had been a gateway to the ranch further out. Just as my grandmother's home was her life-long project, her masterpiece, the ranch was my grandfather's masterpiece: the dirt roads, the wide *caballeriza* where he would keep his horses, the mounted deer heads he kept in the living room of the main ranch house. When we were lucky, my grandfather would take my cousins and me along for rides through the property. He would sit us all in the back of his Dodge pick-up truck, and it would rattle as he drove us down the dirt roads. "*Bájense*," get down, he would warn as tree branches got in our way and scratched the top of his truck. Dust and leftover *maíz* from the last hunting trip covered the over-sized jackets we borrowed from our parents to shield us from the cold as we rumbled along. I loved those trips, because from that vantage point, I could see the ranch in all its glory: its prickly cacti, its whitetail deer, its gray rabbits hopping across shrubs, the vast expanse of trees we couldn't get in the city. At the ranch, I felt I had escaped school and the stresses of finding a professional career. When my grandfather passed away, the ranch became, for me, a piece of him left behind, his legacy. His old wool hunting jackets and shoes remained in a bedroom closet in the main house, and each time I saw them, I felt he was close to me.

During his life, my grandfather had never foreseen that the ranch would not be safe to visit one day. He'd never foreseen the camouflaged-clad soldiers sitting at its entrance, trying to protect it from invading gangs and cartels. Part of my grandfather's work had been renting the ranch out to hunters; it had not included allotting a post for the military. To him, the ranch had been his refuge, a place that he could escape to and not have to escape from.

As the year progressed, Nuevo Laredo's residents gradually let go of the notion *no pasa nada*. Little by little, they realized they needed to be home before dark. Many installed better alarm systems as my grandmother did, and only opened their doors to people they knew. By the end of 2010 and throughout 2011, it seemed all of the city had given up on the thought that nothing was happening. I noticed that hardly anybody walked on the sidewalks and that neighborhoods had grown emptier. Now, the statue of Christopher Columbus on El Paseo was used to display mutilated victims as a warning to the opposition, and dead bodies hung from bridges. *Narcomantas* left with the bodies spelled out what more could come. The same city where we'd watched bullfights at the Plaza de Toros and gone hunting for tacos after midnight was now ghostly after dark. Life in the daytime did go on—food vendors still sold *paletas de cajeta* and *tamarindos* at the city's entrance. Laundry still hung from ropes in front yards. Elderly women still walked home with grocery bags in hand. Yet there was an emptiness that, like a heavy weight, could be felt in the air; it was evident at night, when roads cleared and people locked themselves behind doors. *No pasa nada* was replaced by prayers for *Paz en Nuevo Laredo*. Any noise now was presumed to be a *balazo*. One night, my mother and grandmother, hearing what they thought were gunshots, called up the only two other residents still living on the block to ask them what they knew; later they learned the noises had been fireworks at a wedding. Such uncertainty for me was proof that the Nuevo Laredo I had known had disappeared, substituted by a world wracked by kidnappings, murders, and the apprehension of not knowing what could or would happen next.

In my grandmother's neighborhood, beautiful homes of brick and stucco stood quiet and still. Their owners, mostly Mexican residents who'd been born in the States and could travel back and forth, had found safety in Laredo. Where I had seen houses lit up, now I only saw darkness from their windows. Where I had heard the echo of music and laughter coming from inside their walls, now there was a deafening silence. No longer did cars line the blocks on weekend nights; there were no parties anymore. Sometimes these homes, worth millions when built, sold at a fraction of their worth, as no one wanted to move to Nuevo Laredo. Other times, their owners said what they hoped were temporary goodbyes, knowing well that furniture and other cherished possessions might be stolen, but hoping the violence would dissipate someday. Several of these owners had been threatened with death or kidnappings and were forced to leave Nuevo Laredo in haste, without loo-king back. They became part of a new exodus to the United States, thousands of upper and middle class residents searching for safety. Did it matter that these residents' homes were, like my grandmother's, life-long projects, built to enshrine lives and memories? For most of those who left, it did matter. As my grandmother told me, *"Antes no se vendían las casas."* Houses were not meant to be sold. That was the difference between life in the United States and Mexico: Over there, people upro-oted from house to house, but here, your home was forever.

That's how it was supposed to be, anyway. Now life had changed and even the strongest wills seemed powerless to change it back. Ironically, it was the beauty and extravagance of my grandmother's home that made her vulnerable and expo-sed. More and more, my family was hearing that gangs and car-tels were scoping out specific homes to vandalize and loot. The uncertainty of who could be watching and who might be next was too much for anyone to bear, but it was especially difficult for a widow living on her own. Loneliness also became a factor. By the fall of 2011, my grandmother realized how solitary she felt in a neighborhood where many of its residents had already left, in a home meant for a big family. It cost thousands of dollars to keep the lights on and the heat running, yet the majority of her children and grandchildren now lived in Texas. While the home would always remain a symbol of peace for her, there was no denying that a refuge, even a beautiful one, could become the very catalyst for leaving. That September, she made the decision to put it up for sale.

In selling her house, my grandmother would be selling a part of her: a home, a lifestyle, a memory—countless memo-ries. Yet, as she would later tell me, her understanding that she had already lived a great life there comforted her. She also felt relieved that she'd no longer be alone and would be closer to family by moving to Laredo, and we still had the ranch. Even if we might not be able to go back for years, she was happy that a part of my grandfather remained ours. So maybe homes could be sold—but not land, *la tierra no se vende.* What else could Tita do but remain positive, even when deep inside she would have given anything to stay in her house? To not have to box her belongings and hand her keys to a new owner? I thought of how difficult it would be to pull herself away from her home, to strip it of its carefully selected and arranged furniture, to choose what to keep and what to sell, and to realize, in the midst of boxes and "for sale" signs, that memories indeed were all that would remain.

An American born in Laredo, my grandmother, if given the choice, would not have left Mexico. Like the seventeen families who had founded Nuevo Laredo after the Mexican War ended, Laredo, Texas became part of the United States, she and her friends had treasured the rich subtleties of life as it was lived on the southern back of the Rio Grande. As one of her neighbors would tell me, "I moved from Nuevo Laredo, but I will always hold it dear in my heart. The ways that we lived and related together in Nuevo Laredo, *esas convivencias,* those cannot exist in just any part of the world." But the exodus for peace and security was uneven. How hard it must have been for my grandmother to say goodbye to housekeepers and helpers who'd stayed by her side and become like family but did not have the papers to cross with her now. Others simply refused to give up. One of my cousins who stayed told me, "No one will know the Nuevo Laredo I got to know, the good and the bad."

After learning my grandmother's home would be sold, I, along with my grandmother and twenty of my cousins, aunts, and uncles decided we would deal with the sadness by holding one last party inside its walls. When we arrived, the *arcángel* statue was enveloped in bubble wrap, surrounded by chairs and lamps marked by "sold" tags. The Christmas tree, bare without lights, stood besieged by moving boxes. The dining room table, no longer dressed with tablemats and plates, now served as a storing shelf for bags of old photographs. Curtains and sheets hung from the second floor balcony, prices taped onto banisters. The *Palma* room was empty, save for the palm tree wallpaper that had decorated it since the seventies. The walls had been stripped of the pictures of my mother and aunts in wedding dresses. At the bottom of the stairs, a table that had memorialized my grandfather was gone.

Gathered around the house's bar, we laughed as we had with all family gatherings, telling stories throughout the night and sharing pictures in between glasses of wine. *Chismes* went around the circular table as we ate *ceviche* and fried fish. At times, I managed to forget. But when I sat on a sold gold couch that in my childhood had been a favorite spot, I remembered. I felt the farewell when I glimpsed my uncle outside by the pool, standing alone by a palm tree, looking up and down at the home's brick columns. I sensed it when a cousin remarked that, no matter what the new owners did to the house, our family's face, *su rostro*, would never be erased from the walls. I knew it when another cousin who still lived in Nuevo Laredo asked herself if any of us would still have reason to visit the city. As I lay down to sleep in my grandmother's bed at the end of the night, I, too, wondered if I would ever come back.

ACROSS THE RIVER

Sarah Cortez

Beginning in the decade of the fifties, we used these three words, "Across the River," as an epithet for all that lay beyond the broad, sandy expanse of the Rio Grande at the cement crossing called "The Bridge" in Laredo, Texas. At least once, and often several times, during each of our frequent visits to see my father's Laredo kin, we would go "across the River"— sometimes for my dad's annual bottle of golden tequila; sometimes to eat; sometimes for the unadulterated pleasure of walking in the hot sun amid the tables of colorful trinkets.

There were several distinct and powerful cultures at odds with our "American-ness" in the dusty, rock-filled cities of the U.S. and Mexican sides of Laredo. And they were unrelenting in the ways they assailed us, even though we too were "Hispanic," as was said in those days, and both my parents' first language had been Spanish. With childhood's vibrancy of memories and the adult's fondness for recollection, I remember those forays into cultures so inherently different from the manicured lawns of St. Augustine grass in our beloved Houston.

Perhaps the foremost of these strange cultures was the welter of family dynamics surrounding my paternal grandfather, the bulk of a man my father insisted on seeing often and for whom he willingly drove the long, boring hours over mostly desolate roads. Decades previous, while my father was barely a teenager, my grandfather had taken a second wife after the death of my dad's mother, and they produced millions of children, or so it seemed to my innocent but wary young eyes. Handsome uncles and talkative but beautiful wives and aunts, often a third or half generation younger than my father, lived in Laredo—mostly on grandfather's property or in close proximity. The nucleus was grandfather, and his spreading *ranchito* in Calton Gardens was a bewildering beehive of crying babies, slamming doors, mesquite scrub and exterior walls of painted wood in the purest white. There was even a clay tennis court, already beginning its journey into oblivion, which my grandfather had had constructed for my sinewy younger uncles' recreation.

There were two locations of marvelous beauty, I thought, on his *rancho*. The intricate Saltillo tile covering the long front porch where grandfather sat on a metal Sears lawn chair watching the road. The two-story high wall of always-blooming, magenta bougainvillea, spreading across one side of his expansive front yard. But everything else associated with the place, I distrusted—the sharp-tongued grandmother, the Spanish I couldn't (and didn't wish) to speak, the screened windows through which I was sure *bandidos* from Mexico would crawl inside during the night to murder us, after hearing my grandfather tell gripping tales of these bandits who killed and ate their enemies. Sometimes I couldn't sleep after seeing the black-and-white ten o'clock Laredo news, with car accident victims strewn and mangled on bloody pavement, flies already alight on frozen features.

The other culture that possessed a less aggressive strange-ness—but retained its own peculiar air of unreality—was the face of Laredo on the Texas side. Here, Daddy had to drive our Oldsmobile very slowly over the fist-sized rocks blooming in every dirt street so as not to harm our car's underbelly. No one walking in the streets looked prosperous. Dusty curs ran every-where, collarless, ownerless. The Air Force base the only prop-erty that gleamed with Anglo briskness.

One aunt, whose husband was prominent and successful, would drive mom and me through expensive neighborhoods and point out the homes of her girlfriends, whose husbands' income supported it all—it didn't even need to be said. The only attributes a daughter might need would be a small waist-line and a refined face; a son could inherit his father's business, and often did.

In these demarked areas, homes were accented by lovely ironwork, painted white, curving to the sky, and the rectilin-ear architecture of the "ranch-style" sixties homes was soft-ened by elegant landscaping. Although, no one played in the yards. My aunt would brag about these married ladies—trips to Europe, private schools for the children, designer wardrobes purchased on shopping trips to New York City or Paris, debu-tante daughters who married rich heirs from France or Mexi-co City—as if she wasn't one of them herself.

And underneath all of this, perhaps the aspect mom and I found the oddest—the full-time maids. Everyone, even those few struggling to lead middle-class lives, had a maid. Almost no one cooked her own meals or dressed her own (presumably, treasured) small children. A huge, almost faceless, army of women crossed The River every morning to take care of households on the other side. And when they went back to Mexico? My aunts provided horrifying details: the maids smuggling food back across The River when they walked home at day's end—a supermarket fryer hung between human legs. Stolen teaspoons, pilfered closets, missing sheets, table-cloths, monogrammed hand towels. No, we didn't want a maid like that in our home, in our cherished refuge, where every large purchase was considered carefully, budgeted, then rarely duplicated.

But, lastly and finally, the greatest culture shock of all—Across the River. A place both exotic and dirty, a place alternatively colorful and drab, beckoning and inhospitable, beautiful and ugly—a place where the rules we'd come to believe were "normal" didn't hold, for better and for worse. An immense sandbox with almost everything gaily painted, but hazy, with the unremitting, blowing dust.

One of the most vivid memories from those walks into Nuevo Laredo is an erstwhile by-product of my father's love for eating fresh *cabrito*, the flesh of a young goat called a "kid." In their glass fronts, narrow restaurants would display the small kids, splayed and still-spitted on blackened, heavy metal skewers, fresh from the fire. My fascinated but horrified child's eyes were compelled into a consideration of the blackened eye sockets. The burned bone protruding over each indentation a reminder of my own skull and my barely believable or discernable—at least, to me—mortality. Dad would usher us into a cool restaurant. While he devoured his treat, Mom and I would eat something safe, something that didn't resemble a small, charred dog. Water would cascade into sun-lit fountains of glistening tile. The beautiful façade. The looming eye sockets. The crunching of bones.

On other portions of our border town walks, we would go to the *mercado*, a ponderous, beige brick, two-story building with a central, covered atrium. Here, we strolled, admiring the handiwork in straw, leather or stone. We looked and bought carefully, for as you surely have noticed, we were, above all, a *careful* family. Carved gourds fashioned into maracas, stiff, golden straw plaited into brushes or masks, intricately-painted tiles—we admired, appreciated, seldom bought. Would this lovely, exotic stuff fit into our calm, clean, jade-green-walled house in Houston? Hardly. Maybe, one or two pieces to show dad's business associates from the Midwest, to whom even our idealized Houston smacked of "the foreign."

And the most telling memory of the *mercado*? The butcher stalls. The stiff, red sides of hanging beef not a surprise, since our own neighborhood grocery still swung out beef halves on metal hooks from the large cold locker for shoppers; but here, in Mexico, the beef didn't emerge from or return to a cold locker. It simply hung amid flies: the stench unavoidable. The bloody miasma, choking. A memory not fully exorcised until a recent trip to Mexico where I forced myself into a slow stroll through another butchering section in an open-air market. Determined to gain an adult's perspective on the scent of animal death, I kept walking and kept breathing it all in. Perhaps, another considered step toward my own mortality, now discernible.

It wasn't that we ignored the glories offered by this Laredo culture of dad's relatives. We participated in the exuberance of the wedding receptions for dad's raft of half-brothers where they and their shimmering wives were fêted at long dinner dances. The acres of red carpet leading through the hotel lobby, up the wide staircase, and into the ballroom were proof positive of Laredo's munificence in sharing her beauty and love of drama. The hotel itself would make such a lasting impression on me that I remain to this day unconvinced by scores of later wedding receptions held on beige linoleum floors of gymnasium-minded church halls and in insipid, humid backyards. Where's the unending walkway of plush, strident red evoking the magic? Where's the magic?

So, the three of us—my father, the son of an elegant Castilian beauty whose fishing family entered the U.S. at the port of entry at Galveston, my mother, the daughter of a respected Mexican-American town leader several generations beyond his own Spanish relatives' arrival in Texas, and me, the shy child happily growing up in an Anglo neighborhood—we were happy to go back home to Houston. The border wasn't ours except by default, and its rich but troublesome dynamics—familial and otherwise—were something we didn't wish to inhabit permanently.

And now? Now, the urgent sadness of Mexico's inability and unwillingness to control illegal violence—both random and planned—has pulled me back to the Border. I, who never glorified the Border's ambience—on either side of the Rio Grande—find myself drawn into a deeper relationship with this place for two primary reasons.

The first is more individual and intimate than the second, and, frankly, could be interpreted as a bit self-indulgent, despite the grim reality that is its underpinning. I feel the loss of being able to walk the sunny streets of Laredo and Nuevo Laredo with my relatives as I did in happier times. My *primas* and I can no longer ogle the scores of inexpensive, silver and mother-of-pearl bracelets and earrings. Gone are the days of buying homemade candies in the soft, brown paper sacks from the last street stall on the left before reaching the bridge. Even the uncomfortable moments we experienced there as one aunt chastised an eldest daughter for spending too much money at a favorite *joyería* or as another cousin scandalized downtown by not wearing a slip under a short skirt—even these, or their era-specific equivalents, are impossible because none of us can go "across the River" any longer. The streets aren't safe; the probability leans toward death. We all feel the fear. We are all constricted and unreasonably curtailed. Although Laredo is less than four hundred miles away, the U.S. side of the town is as untouchable to us as is "Across the River." That arena of the dubious pleasure of childhood has shifted due, no doubt, at least partially to the beacon of nostalgia, informed by maturity but, now, also underscored by violence.

I'd like to think that the second reason is based on something larger than a sense of personal fear and limitation, than loss and its concomitant and complex grieving. This second reason is outrage. As I have read statistics and even the censored, down-played headlines of what the Mexican government lets the criminals do to ordinary citizens, I have become outraged. This outrage makes me, forces me, to become one with those experiencing the atrocities. For you see, I hold dear in my heart a government's moral duty to keep its citizens safe—any government, but particularly those who hold themselves out as "democratic."

Yet, through the decades of devil's bargains struck with those who profit from crime—in the beginning, mostly the trafficking of marijuana and heroin, but now, augmented by the additional commodities of cocaine, methamphetamine and extortion—the Mexican government allowed control of its own country to be usurped by a hardened criminal class. These groups of thugs, who are increasingly better armed and more sophisticated, as well as increasingly rabid in their methods and means of torture and killing, will turn to any criminal enterprise that generates phenomenal profits. It shouldn't be a surprise that they have already added extortion with its long Central American "tradition" (both as a function of kidnapping and the payment of businesses for "protection") to their array of criminal money-makers. I would expect these gangs to hone in on other profitable illegal areas, such as human trafficking and exotic pornography, in the coming years. Meantime, the death count mounts.

Thirty-five bodies dumped at a busy freeway interchange by armed, masked gunman in a major city during rush hour? Dismembered bodies of police officers dumped on city streets to be found at dawn? The young woman whose bare-breasted body, guts protruding in white coils out of her stomach, hung like a butchered pig to warn others not to complain about the cartel killings using social media? The types of people killed has reached from public servants, to journalists, to teens and children, to people only walking to work or to the false security of home after a day's labor. Would we put up with this in America? I would hope not.

So, in an unpredictable way, the absurd and terrible tragedies along the border have succeeded where familial bonds didn't. I have become part of something that is far more unpredictable than which rock will puncture the car's gas tank, more insidious than the maid who steals, something far more bloody and sad than the slaughtered beeves hanging from heavy hooks amid crooning flies. That something is those who stand against the wholesale execution of decent human beings by thugs for illegal gain, sanctioned by a government too weak or too dirty to act. Yes, there's magic in Mexico now, but it wouldn't be hard to classify it as evil. The wide staircase runs red, no longer with carpeting, no longer at celebrations of conjugal promise but with human blood, that of the innocent and that of those who will stop at nothing to profit from illegal activities.

THERE'S ALWAYS MUSIC

Celestino Fernández and Jessie K. Finch

A warm breeze wafts through the open restaurant, causing the strings of lights to sway and cast long shadows on empty tables. Where lively crowds once stood, now only a few local patrons sit. Canned *mariachi* or *norteño* music plays over tinny loudspeakers where energetic musicians used to honor the unending requests of smiling tourists enjoying a margarita or a cold Mexican beer with chips and salsa, or other traditional dishes, like *enchiladas, tacos* or *carne asada*.

This desolate scene, quite common now in many towns along the 2,000-mile stretch of the U.S.-Mexico border, is the product of two things: fear and the recession economy—but, mostly fear. Over the past fifteen years, I've watched things change. The tourist attractions, including the culture and music of northern Mexico, particularly along the border, have faded as drug-trafficking, cartels and murder have taken over print, electronic and television headlines. While exaggerated by the American media, the violence along the border is real and has caused not only concern for local residents, but has also created a panic robbing the towns on the Mexican side of the border of one of their most valuable resources, and for many, their means of survival: *turistas* along with casual visits from local residents north of the border.

The typical American tourist (including Mexican Americans) to Mexican border towns of years past had no passport; it wasn't needed. They often did not plan ahead. People walked or drove across the border at El Paso/Ciudad Juárez, San Diego/Tijuana and, in my case, Nogales/Nogales (known locally as *"ambos Nogales"*), and found a vibrant restaurant with delicious food and even better music. This happenstance border crossing allowed for adventures and exploring for the day; my family strolled in no particular direction without any planned destination. Children really enjoyed this type of walking, people-watching, visiting curio shops that sold colorful paper flowers, pottery, copperware, sandals, clothes and many other curious items like dogs with bobbing heads for car dashboards. We particularly enjoyed eating *paletas* and other Mexican treats *en la calle*. The live music was everywhere. Those times are gone and it makes us sad; and who knows if they'll ever come back. We all have to be so cautious now and many of the attractions, like restaurants and curio shops are closed, gone out of business.

Previously, there were countless hotels, rental apartments, and beach houses where, at the spur of the moment, a tourist could choose to visit Mexico for the weekend. Our family did that regularly, mostly to Puerto Peñasco, Sonora. Only an hour south of the U.S.-Mexico border, we could run on the beach and enjoy chasing the waves in and out of the sparkling ocean.

La Roca—a restaurant operating in Nogales, Sonora, since 1972 and built into the rock cliff just across the border—provided one of the finest displays of *trío, mariachi,* and *conjunto* music in the world, along with a beautiful setting and delicious food. I would park on the American side of the border and walk a block or so to the border gate where, if on duty, a Mexican immigration or customs officials would say: "*Buenas tardes. Bienvenidos.*" Another couple of blocks from the gate and up a hill, I'd be at a traditional, round, multi-layered Mexican fountain, the entrance to La Roca. I knew I was going to have a fun time, especially because of the music.

For tourists, including myself, the music was an essential part of the mystique of both Nogales and other border towns. Hearing music outdoors always brings memories of my growing up in Santa Ines, Michoacán, where music was always heard out in the open: music at the plaza, the singing of someone walking by the house, music at our picnics, the music of a distant radio in someone else's home, music everywhere, and it seemed like all the time.

Along the border, musicians looking for tips from passersby would play everywhere, in the street, wandering into shops and restaurants; this is part of why I was attracted to Nogales. Today, most of these musicians are gone; *casacareando* is no longer a stable way to make a living or even to make a little extra cash.

When visitors came to Tucson, we'd get on I-19 and head south to Nogales, Sonora, to see the shops, to visit with locals, to eat and, of course, to enjoy great live music. There was always music wherever you went, but that's no longer the case. People are afraid to go to Nogales; they've heard the State Department warnings not to travel to Mexico. Nogales, despite being only an hour's drive from Tucson, has become a much less popular destination to visit than the air-conditioned shopping malls of Phoenix, Tucson's neighbor to the north.

A group of my relatives who came from Kansas just this year were initially too frightened to visit the family beach house in Puerto Peñasco, on the Sea of Cortez. The mother and her daughter who visited had been told by their Kansas friends to avoid the "beheaded bodies" and "drug-riddled streets" in Mexico that they had heard about and seen on television. Only through the continued prodding of another local family member could these women be convinced to go to what they then found to be "a delightful, peaceful beach town" to which they hope to return.

By "great live music" I do not mean to imply highly polished or professional musicians. On the contrary, these street musicians often were anything but that. Sometimes they were off-key, unsynchronized, forgot the words to a particular request, and seldom dressed the same or in the traditional *traje*, but they were damn good and, most of all, they were authentic. They did not play a fixed set, they took requests and they made conversation with us. They were like us, *gente del pueblo*. For me, and for many others who enjoy street musicians anywhere in the world, the foremost attraction of these musicians is their authenticity.

Street musicians connect one-on-one with the audience. They stand close to me, we make eye contact, we share a smile; I join in the singing. Most of all, when occasionally they let tears well up during a sad song, a song tugging at the heart, as tears well in my eyes too, this tells me that they know life as I do, that they feel the music as I do, with the same passion. These musicians are real, they love their music as they love their own lives, as I love my own life.

Where once word-of-mouth was sufficient advertisement to fill the streets, restaurants, and hotels of Nogales, now there are specific marketing campaigns directed at emphasizing the safety of this and other Mexican border towns. The market for vacation homes in Puerto Peñasco, for example, has plummeted, allowing once million-dollar mansions to sell for a quarter of their price. There used to be busloads of University of Arizona undergraduates flocking to the beach for the weekend or to Nogales for the evening, but now every holiday, particularly for spring break, there is only a university-wide warning not to travel to Mexico, including the border communities.

Now, the musicians, who used to wander the beach and through the restaurants to play for families and students, are hard-pressed to find an audience. Some of these musicians are no longer playing; others still come around looking for the occasional tourist. Although I still go to Puerto Peñasco regularly, I miss the lively, joyous experiences of times past when more Americans also visited and everyone enjoyed the music. (Even if I had to listen to "La Bamba" several times, the most frequently requested song by Americans, played with gusto each time by musicians who would later confide to me how tired they were of repeating it.)

One of the things that I, and others who live along the border, have experienced is the changing definition of what is considered to be "the border." Over the years, the border had expanded from a political line separating the United States and Mexico to a wider cultural area uniting or joining both countries, a "border band," roughly a sixty-mile expanse both north and south of the actual border line. The policies enforced—or, rather, unenforced—reflected this tourist and local resident lifestyle and a free exchange of culture. There was easy crossing in both urban and rural areas. I, and countless others, did it regularly. One needed neither a visa nor car permit to travel to Puerto Peñasco or to many other parts of northern Mexico. Even companies such as car insurance providers used to recognize this fuzzy border band. Several years ago, for example, when my 1996 white Toyota pick-up was stolen while visiting Puerto Peñasco, this matter was easily resolved by a call to the U.S.-based insurance company who assured me that while the theft had occurred in Mexico, the U.S. coverage extended 100 kilometers across the border. Indeed, I received a check in the mail covering the Blue Book value of the truck.

For me, and for most local residents, permits and passage across the border used to be a simple, permeable entrance/exit process. This was part of the reason we crossed so frequently. Although thousands of people still cross the U.S.-Mexico border daily, the process of coming into the U.S. is now long and arduous; for most of us, it's become too much of a hassle. The automobile lines are very long—an hour is a short wait. In fact, one time we waited eight hours to get back. For U.S. Customs and Immigration officials, everyone seems to be a suspect. In contrast, going into Mexico takes only minutes.

What caused the radical change from a somewhat open border and a cultural exchange attitude to this strict perimeter mentality? The official response, of course, is that it's due to the tragic events of September 11, 2001. Although none of the terrorists entered the United States through the U.S.-Mexico Border, the consequences for those of us who live here are clear: the border has been reduced to miles of vertical fences and walls. No longer just a gate in town, miles of barriers extend out into the desert. It's no fun to cross the border anymore to enjoy what's on the other side.

The Tucson International Mariachi Conference, with which I have been intimately involved almost since its founding thirty years ago, is known as the mother of all mariachi conferences and festivals because it's the longest running such event in the world. Even representatives of Guadalajara (the birthplace of mariachi) came to Tucson to learn how we organized and operated this conference before they started a similar event. The Conference used to draw both young mariachis who participated in the workshops and a large audience for the concerts from northern Sonora but this, too, has changed with the difficulties of crossing the border. Although the Conference continues to draw many mariachis for the workshops and large audiences from the U.S. side of the border, people from Sonora are not attending because it's become such a hassle to cross the border. As a result, the Conference now lacks some of the previous international and cultural diversity.

The mining town of Cananea—made famous by the *corrido* (and later the film) *La Carcel De Cananea* (The Jail of Cananea)—lies halfway between Nogales and Aqua Prieta, Sonora. This small town used to be a lure to a variety of American tourists, but is now rarely visited. Many Americans made the trip from Nogales to Agua Prieta to tour some of the old Catholic missions founded by the Spaniards who traveled through and settled in this area. The tiny jail for which the song is named—once just a little building—was later a profitable and thriving museum. As one enters the building today, enshrined for all to see on a large wooden plaque are the lyrics to the *corrido*:

La Carcel de Cananea	**The Jail of Cananea**
(*versión breve*)	(short version)
Voy a hacer un pormenor de	I am going to detail
lo que a mí me ha pasado.	what happened to me
Que me han agarrado preso	that they have taken me prisoner
siendo un gallo tan jugado.	even though I should have known better
Me fui para el Agua Prieta	I went to Agua Prieta
a ver si me conocían.	to see if I had a reputation there.
Y a las once de la noche	And at 11:00 at night
me aprehendió la polecía.	the police apprehended me.

Me aprehendieron los cherifes	They arrested me
al estilo americano.	in the American style.
Como era hombre de delito	Since I was a criminal
todos con pistola en mano.	all of them with pistols in hand.
La cárcel de Cananea	The jail of Cananea
tá situada en una mesa.	is on top of a plateau.
En ella fui procesado	And in it I was processed
por causa de mi torpeza.	for my own foolishness.
Despedida no les doy	I give you no farewell
porque no la traigo aquí.	for I don't have it here.
Se la dejé al Santo Niño	I left it to the Holy child
y al Señor de Mapimí.	and the Lord of Mapimi.

Those of us living along the border have witnessed, as the rest of the world has been informed, that drug violence has increased rapidly since the late eighties, particularly in the larger cities, such as Tijuana and Ciudad Juárez. In the last decade, however, the narco-violence soared throughout Mexico, became more gruesome, and moved into the smaller, rural communities on the border that had previously been immune to such violence, scaring people from visiting any border town. This violence is evident in the Sonora region. On Feb. 27, 2007, Agua Prieta Police Chief Ramón Tacho Verdugo was killed. On Nov. 3, 2008, several gunmen ambushed and killed the director of Sonora's state police, Juan Manuel Pavón Félix, with guns and grenades as he entered his hotel in central Nogales alongside his bodyguard and other law-enforcement officials. The assistant police chief, Adalberto Padilla Molina, in Nogales, Sonora, and his bodyguard, Iván Sepúlveda Espino, were killed March 25, 2010, in a barrage of gunfire. The Nogales, Sonora, deputy police chief, Raúl Suárez Gabriel, and a Sonoran state police officer, Faustino Gil Castelowere, were also killed on September 11, 2011. Meanwhile, the once highly popular Elvira's Restaurant one block from the downtown port of entry in Nogales, where upon sitting for lunch or dinner we were served a small shot of tequila and where we could always enjoy a delicious meal and live music, has gone out of business after 40 years, only to re-open on the U.S. side of the border, in Tubac, Arizona, a small community on I-19, 23 miles north of the border. I haven't been there since.

There is a saying in Mexico: "If the U.S. sneezes, Mexico catches a cold"—a way of acknowledging the interrelatedness of the two countries, particularly the dependency of the Mexican economy on the U.S. Thus, the U.S. economic recession that started in 2008 and continues today has certainly cost the business, food, music and other cultural industries of the co-dependent border region dearly. I have witnessed it. Puerto Peñasco, for example, has many fewer restaurants and many fewer musicians now that Americans are not there to sustain the tourism industry. Talking with the street performers, we hear that they can no longer work as musicians for their earnings, but must also work in taco stands, as construction workers, or at any other odd job available.

Jesús, an older gentleman whom we've seen playing (various instruments, including violin, guitar and *guitarrón*) and singing for many years, commented: "*No, ya no se puede. Ya ven Uds.* [and glances around an almost empty restaurant], *no hay gente como antes. Los gringos ya no vienen. Muchos de los músicos se fueron del pueblo o trabajan en lo que se pueda. Muchos de ellos ya no salen [a cascarear].*" ("No, it can't be done anymore. You can see for yourselves, there are no people as before. The Americans don't come anymore. Many of the musicians left the town or work in what they can. Many of them don't play street music anymore.")

Manuel, a younger solo musician who plays guitar and sings, said: "*Yo tengo que salir a cantar, haber que sale. Todo ayuda. Tengo trabajo pero no alcanza para la familia. Estos últimos tres años han sido muy duros; ya no viene gente del otro lado.*" ("I have to go out and sing, and see what I get. Everything helps. I have work, but it's not enough for my family. These last three years have been very hard; people from the other side of the border don't come anymore.") While these musicians were never 100% "professional"—that is, they were not on stages or in recording studios—they had been able to survive off their craft alone in times past.

In Puerto Peñasco, La Casa Del Capitán restaurant overlooks the ocean and is a complete and most enjoyable outdoor experience. Everyone who visits this port town goes there to watch the magnificent sunsets. The acoustics are not made for stage musicians, but the outdoor atmosphere allowed the never-too-polished performers the time to chat with the clientele and take requests. Prior to 9/11, the drugs, and the economic downturn, there was always a wait, often at least thirty minutes to get a seat in this restaurant. This year, on a Saturday night at 7:00 P.M. only two couples were in the entire restaurant. A couple of musicians peeked in the door and left. The only way the owner, Christina, is able to stay afloat is because she owns the restaurant and the property, and also lives above the restaurant.

Beyond the location and manner in which musicians perform, the content of music has been influenced by the changing factors of drugs and violence on the border. To appreciate these changes, it's important to understand a bit of the history of Mexican music.

Two quite famous Mexican musical genres of the last 100 years have been *corridos* and *música norteña* (of course, *mariachi* music may be the most well-known). The labels of both *norteña* (meaning "north") and *conjunto* show how the border is built right into the musical culture of Mexico. *Conjunto* (meaning "group" broadly) refers specifically to the music that emerged in south Texas with the introduction of the button accordion. This foundational instrument of the *conjunto/ norteña* genre was introduced by German settlers in the late 1800s and later adopted by Mexican musicians (that's why this type of music often sounds like the polka). In Mexico, *conjunto* generally refers to *norteño* music.

Corridos, the songs of the people, the ballads of Mexican music, have a long history of focusing on the border—usually on its activities and characters. For example, "El Moro de Cumpas" documents the famous horse race that took place in Agua Prieta, Sonora, between El Moro (from Cumpas, Sonora) and El Saino (from Agua Prieta). "El Corrido de Gregorio Cortez" (both the song and the film) documents the heroic events of a Wild West "outlaw" near the Texas-Mexico border. "El Corrido de Joaquín Murrieta" explores the life of a man known as the Robin Hood of Mexicans in Southern California. There are many more examples of what have come to be known as "border *corridos*."

However, since *corridos* have always centered on themes important to the mass public, they have been deeply affected by the changing atmosphere of the border. So prevalent has the theme of drug violence become, that it has spurred the creation of a special category of *corridos*: the *narcocorrido*. Two of the most famous *norteño* bands, Los Tucanes de Tijuana and Los Tigres del Norte regularly focus on drug-related themes in their music. Since the mid-1970s, Los Tigres have rarely released a new CD without including at least one *narcocorrido*, and they even recorded an entire album devoted solely to these songs.

The rising popularity of the *narcocorrido* is because one portion of the listening and buying sector, Mexican and

Mexican-American male youth, demand this type of music. Even though some cities, including Tijuana, have banned the playing of *narcocorridos*, these *corridos* have become popular on radio, at live concerts and in films. Comparing two *corridos*— the early border *corrido* "El Corrido de Gregorio Cortez" and the narcocorrido "Contrabando and Traición"—demonstrates this transition well. The first celebrates a border hero and the second glorifies drug violence.

El Corrido de Gregorio Cortez	The Ballad of Gregorio Cortez
En el condado de El Carmen	In the county of El Carmen
tal desgracia sucedió,	such a tragedy took place:
murió el Cherife Mayor,	the Major Sheriff is dead;
no saben quien lo mató.	no one knows who killed him.
Se anduvieron informando	They went around asking
como media hora después,	questions about half an hour
	afterward:
supieron que el malhechor	they found out that the wrongdoer
era Gregorio Cortez.	had been Gregorio Cortez.
Ya insortaron a Cortez	Now they have outlawed Cortez
por toditito el estado,	throughout the whole of the state;
que vivo o muerto se aprehenda	let him be taken, dead or alive,
porque a varios ha matado.	for he has killed several men.
Decía Gregorio Cortez	Then said Gregorio Cortez,
con su pistola en la mano:	with his pistol in his hand,
—No siento haberlo matado,	"I don't regret having killed him;
lo que siento es a mi hermano.	what I regret is my brother's death."

Venían los americanos
más blancos que una amapola,
de miedo que le tenían
a Cortez con su pistola.

The Americans were coming;
they were whiter than a poppy
from the fear that they had
of Cortez and his pistol.

Soltaron los perros jaunes
pa'que siguieron la huella,
pero alcanzar a Cortez
era seguir a una estrella.

They let loose the bloodhounds
so they could follow the trail;
but trying to overtake Cortez
was like following a star.

Se fue de Belmont al rancho,
lo alcanzaron a rodear,

From Belmont he went to the ranch,
where they succeeded in
    surrounding him,

poquitos más de trescientos,
y allí le brincó el corral.

a few more than three hundred,
but he jumped out of their corral.

Cuando les brincó el corral,
según lo que aquí se dice,
se agarraron a balazos
y les mató otro cherife.

When he jumped out of their corral,
according to what is said here,
they got into a gunfight,
and he killed another sheriff.

Decía Gregorio Cortez
con su pistola en la mano:
—No corran, rinches cobardes,
con un solo mexicano.

Then said Gregorio Cortez,
with his pistol in his hand,
"Don't run, you cowardly rinches,
From a single Mexican."

Y se encontró a un mexicano,
le dice con altivez:
—Platícame qué hay de nuevo,
yo soy Gregorio Cortez.

Now he has encountered a Mexican;
he says to him haughtily,
"Tell me the news;
I am Gregorio Cortez.

—Dicen que por culpa mía
han matado mucha gente,
pues ya me voy a entregar
porque eso no es conveniente.

They say that because of me
many people have been killed;
so now I will surrender,
because such things are not right."

Venían todos los rinches,	All the rinches were coming,
venían que hasta volaban,	so fast that they almost flew,
porque se iban a ganar	because they were going to get
diez mil pesos que les daban.	the ten thousand-dollar bounty.
Cuando rodearon la casa	When they surrounded the house
Cortez se les presentó:	Cortez appeared before them:
—Por la buena sí me llevan	"You will take me if I'm willing
porque de otro modo no.	But no other way."
Decía el Cherife Mayor	Then said he Major Sheriff
como queriendo llorar:	as if he were going to cry,
—Cortez, entrega tus armas,	"Cortez, hand over your weapons;
no te vamos a matar.	We are not going to kill you."
Decía Gregorio Cortez,	Then said Gregorio Cortez,
Les gritaba en alta voz:	Shouting to them in a loud voice,
—Mis armas no las entrego	"I won't surrender my weapons
hasta estar en calaboz.	Until I'm in a cell."

Contrabando y Traición	**Contraband and Betrayal**
(El Corrido de	**(The Ballad of**
Camelia la Tejana)	**Camelia the Texan)**
Salieron de San Isidro	They left San Isidro
procedentes de Tijuana	coming from Tijuana,
traían la llanta del carro	they had their car tires
repleta de hierba mala	full of "bad grass" (marijuana)
eran Emilio Barela y	they were Emilio Barrera and
Camelia la tejana.	Camelia the Texan.

Pasaron por San Clemente
los paró la emigración
les pidió sus documentos
les dijo de dónde son
ella era de San Antonio
una hembra de corazón.

Passing through San Clemente
they were stopped by immigration.
He asked for their documents,
he said, "Where are you from?"
She was from San Antonio,
a real woman of passion.

Una hembra si quiere un hombre
por él puede dar la vida
pero hay que tener cuidado
si esa hembra se siente herida
la traición y el contrabando
son cosas incompartidas.

If a woman truly loves a man,
she can give her life for him
but watch out if that woman
feels wounded,
betrayal and smuggling
do not mix.

A Los Ángeles llegaron
a Hollywood se pasaron
en un callejón obscuro
las cuatro llantas cambiaron
ahí entregaron la hierba
y ahí también les pagaron.

They arrived in Los Angeles,
and continued to Hollywood.
In a dark alley,
they changed the four tires.
There they delivered the weed,
and there they were also paid.

Emilio dice a Camelia
—hoy te das por despedida
con la parte que te toca
tú puedes rehacer tu vida
yo me voy 'pa San Francisco
con la dueña de mi vida.

Emilio says to Camelia,
"Now you can disappear
with your share,
you can make a new life.
I'm going to San Francisco
to be with my true love."

Sonaron siete balazos
Camelia a Emilio mataba
la policía sólo halló
una pistola tirada
del dinero y de Camelia
nunca más se supo nada.

Seven shots rang out,
Camelia killed Emilio.
The police only found
a discarded pistol.
Of the money and Camelia,
nothing more was ever known.

More recent *corridos* on the subject of the border have documented the dangers of immigration. "El Corrido de Esequiel Hernández" records the story of the 1997 killing of a goat herder boy by a Marine. Another tragedy memorialized in song is "El Vagón de la Muerte" ("The Boxcar of Death") which speaks of a boxcar full of would-be immigrants who all suffocated on their journey north after being locked into the train car. Indeed, with immigrants being funneled into the Arizona desert, an increasing death toll prompted me to write the *corrido* "Peligro en el Desierto" ("Danger in the Desert") to inform would-be crossers of the desert's dangers. The U.S. Border Patrol has even officially attempted to use *corridos* as a deterrent to Mexican undocumented immigrants, passing out free CDs called *Migracorridos* in a 2009 campaign, that included airplay on radio in various Mexican locations, including Michoacán, a historical immigrant "sending" state in central Mexico.

As I reflect on the changes that the border has undergone as a result of drug violence, I am saddened by the fact that border residents on the U.S. side have been scared into not entering Mexico. Even I do not cross the border freely and without specific plans, as I did before to enjoy the food, music, and other aspects of border culture. I am saddened, as well, by the fact that the content of a significant segment of *corridos* emphasizes and glorifies drug-trafficking and violence, and that this aspect of Mexican culture has become the most prominent theme for *corridistas*. I am saddened, furthermore, by the fact that narco-violence has become the face of Mexico to the U.S. media and, as a result, to most Americans (and, perhaps, the world).

It seems to me that international borders should serve as connections—meeting points of two or more cultures—where ideas, culture and people can flow as easily as free trade goods and produce, and where there is always music. That was the border I enjoyed. It seems so long ago.

MY TIJUANA LOST

Richard Mora

From its earliest days, Tijuana has been a gritty, welcoming city. The prohibition of alcohol in the U.S. in 1920 turned Tijuana into a party town, with dollar-wielding businessmen, politicians and Hollywood personalities driving the expansion of colorful bars, social clubs and brothels. Up through the nineties, a thriving tourist industry comprised mostly of day-time curio shoppers and nighttime revelers filled Avenida Revolución, the main strip in the heart of Tijuana. It was there that my cousins and I overheard tourists speak languages unknown to any us, purchased fireworks as children, and hung out late into summer nights as energetic teens.

Over the past decade, Avenida Revolución has been ren-ovated with wider sidewalks and yet it has little foot traffic most days. During my visits, I stroll down the sunlit street without having to maneuver my way through throngs of for-eign tourists like I did years ago. Most of the street vendors, including many of the Mixtec women and children offering handmade crafts every few yards, have moved on.

Gone, too, are the festive nights that brought my cousins, friends, and me down from the *Colonia Mexico* hill to *La Revu*—nights when thousands of young partygoers from throughout the city and from across the border swarmed the bars and clubs, filling them beyond capacity. Young men and women dancing, flirting, laughing, and drinking. Not a big partier myself, I was constantly entertained by the many drunkards. Groups of young women stumbling into each other as they sang along and yelled in celebration of life, if of nothing else. Some dancing feverishly to beats only they could hear, looking more sweaty and clumsy than sexy in their form-fitting outfits.

There were also the occasional fistfights between groups of rowdy young men that typically ended with bouncers manhandling those involved or with the shrill of sirens followed by arrests. The one fight I was involved in was a disagreement that came to blows when words and reason failed. A group of Chicanos from San Diego took my cousin nodding at them as a sign of disrespect rather than what it was—a gesture of acknowledgement common among Tijuana's youth. Out of consideration for the establishment's manager, my cousin took the verbal exchange out onto the sidewalk. I interjected in English and explained to the Chicanos that, though they outnumbered us, they were out matched because we were known on *La Revu* and *Tijuanenses* do not care for loud, brash Chicanos; they ignored my take on the situation and kept running their mouths. Then, to my right, punches were thrown and a small melee ensued. A couple of my cousin's friends who were passing by saw him and immediately joined our faction, evening the odds. When someone from the crowd of onlookers yelled out, "*la placa!*" my cousin, a friend, and I slipped out of the gathering crowd. With our hearts racing and adrenaline still surging through us, we stripped down to our white undershirts and disappeared into the shadows of a side street. An hour later we returned to *La Revu* and learned that the police had rounded up one of my cousin's friends and all of our adversaries. A few days later, my cousin's friend told him that once behind bars, inmates he knew took it upon themselves to add to the Chicano's misery by taking their jewelry, jeans, and pricey sneakers. A night in jail was about as bad as the consequences got for fighting. Today, *narco juniors* at clubs and bars react to the most minor of transgressions—whether real or imagined—with pistols, rather than with clenched fists. So, verbal tangles with strangers carry the possibility of the ultimate penalty—death.

To hear a few of the remaining vendors comment on it, the Avenida Revolución of my childhood and youth is lost forever. International news reports of the cartel atrocities and the subsequent travel advisories put out by foreign governments scared the tourists away. Given that negative reputations can take on a life of their own, it is hard to know when, if ever, the tourist economy on the strip will completely rebound.

Over the past two decades, I have seen a gradual shift in Tijuana's collective psyche. It took many *tijuanenses* this amount of time to accept that drug wars endangered them. During the early nineties, when the Tijuana-based Arellano Félix cartel was at its most powerful and unleashed brutal violence, the reaction of most was a reassuring, *He who doesn't owe, doesn't fear.* The proverb seemed an apt assessment. Mexican law enforcement agencies regularly described drug-related violence as the fallout of rival drug dealers settling scores. The situation is different now, and such explanations no longer hold much, if any, sway with most *tijuanenses*. Consecutive years of indiscriminate gun violence committed by feuding cartels have resulted in a growing tally of innocent victims—from folks driving to work to folks out shopping—who were killed in the merciless crossfire. The ongoing violence reiterates a hard truth that I, like those around the world that find themselves living among murderous bands, know full well: *Bullets have no names.*

There is one incident in particular that made it clear that my mesmerizing Tijuana, the city at the center of many of my childhood memories, would turn bloody. On November 22, 1997, heavily armed hitmen carried out a daring, daytime attempt on the life of Jesús Blancornelas, a founding editor of *Zeta*, a widely read Tijuana newspaper. The hired guns ambushed and shot up Blancornelas' car as it moved down a busy Tijuana street. The assault left Blancornelas with four gunshot wounds and a bullet lodged in his spine; and Luis Valero, his driver and bodyguard, dead. Within days, it came to light that the attack was in response to *Zeta* publishing the photograph of Ramón Arellano Félix, a leading figure of the Arellano Félix cartel which controlled drug trafficking routes throughout Baja California. I understood then that with their deadly retribution, the cartel was attempting to impose its vicious codes not just within the *narco* underworld, but throughout society as a whole. The brazen attack sent a straightforward message—*do not meddle in cartel business or your blood will run.*

Admirably, *Zeta* responded by living up to its motto, "Free like the Wind." It continued to investigate and report on drug traffickers, especially the dealings of the Arellano Félix cartel. Even after co-editor Francisco Ortiz Franco was murdered in front of his two young children in 2004 and Blancornelas died of cancer in 2007, the pages of *Zeta* regularly feature exposés on the key players in the drug trafficking world and the Mexican military's anti-narco operations in Tijuana. I read them studiously, whether online or in print.

Largely as a result of sensational reports like those in *Zeta*, President Felipe Calderón has dispatched the army to drug violence hotspots throughout the country, including Tijuana. The unannounced army checkpoints set up throughout the city are little more than theatrics, rarely resulting in major arrests or drug seizures. When not standing around, soldiers ride, heavily armed with assault rifles, in big camouflaged 4x4 pickup trucks, their faces hidden behind black masks. However commonplace these days, the sight of military vehicles filled with faceless young men trained to kill by placing the weight of their index fingers on crescent triggers still unnerves me. Government officials claim that soldiers opt to hide their faces to protect against cartel henchmen who threaten soldiers and police officers with offers of *silver or lead*—complicity or death. Human rights activists in Baja California counter that anonymity has resulted in greater impunity and abuses of the innocent. Multiple truths abound and so I am left to craft my own truth from the media accounts—the hooded soldiers, like the little green plastic soldiers I once kept in a cardboard shoe box, are heroes or villains, victims or victimizers, depending on the hour of the day.

During my childhood and adolescence, from the early eighties to the mid-nineties, much of the fight against drugs in Tijuana was composed of operations against addicts, low-level drug pushers, and young men loitering on the streets. White police trucks filled with young, black-clad, athletic officers of the tactical units sped into working class *colonias* looking to round up everyone who fit the description of a drug user or a drug peddler—young, male and idle. These police sweeps regularly resulted in foot chases, with police officers yelling out a mix of curse-laden orders and threats to the dehydrated, under-nourished addicts and the unemployed young men who scurried between hillside homes to evade capture. Watching these impromptu track meets, I always rooted for the under-dogs. That is, I always sided with locals, with young men known to me; a few who bought me ice cream cones, one who had held me as an infant, and one that had tried patiently to teach me how to spin a wooden top on a coin.

Those who got caught typically received forceful hair tugs, blows and slaps to their heads and kicks to their legs. Police officers emptied their pockets, checked suspected *tecatos* for needle tracks on their arms in the fading ink lines of their crudely-drawn tattoos, and studied the pupils of suspected marijuana and crystal meth users. The young men were loaded onto the bed of the truck and handcuffed to a bar; the cuffs tightened enough to bruise. We, the onlookers, shouted words of encouragement to the apprehended and accused the police officers of being inhumane brutes. The young, cocksure offi-cers met our protests with scowling stares or simply ignored us. The more blatant the disregard for human dignity, the greater our ridicule and disdain for law enforcement agents who failed to snatch their prey.

Along with others, I championed the addicts with a knack for escaping the cruel grasp of uniformed tormentors and turned them into ephemeral legends. I praised their exploits, dispensing with most facts and adding such absurdly comical details with each retelling that some accounts became install-ments of an ongoing series. One ran fast and got away, only to be arrested outside the police station where he stopped to catch his breath. Another collected so many recyclable glass bottles on each of his runs down the hill that he made enough to quench his thirst with a cup of shaved ice drenched in dif-ferent flavored syrup after each escape. The stories added lev-ity to a reality that included frequent brutishness by men and women tasked with protecting the citizenry.

By the time I was an adolescent, I had learned that if I wanted to avoid being harassed by the police I had to keep an eye out for their marked and unmarked cars. So, I did, especially during moments when my mind could have easily wandered—while my friends and I played handball or sat around on the concrete remnants of an old water tank and ate chips drenched in hot sauce. With the sound of screeching tires turning the corner and yells of *la placa*, I was off, running scared down one of the escape routes my friends and I had devised or learned from watching *tecatos* and *marijuanos*.

Every time I visited my family, I saw the walking wounded—fiends and recovering addicts. Among their ranks were people I hold dear. People I remember still. One summer, I ran into Ratón, a man from my grandmother's *colonia*, at the U.S.-Mexico border. I was in the passenger seat of an air-conditioned car, with the heat and exhaust of hundreds of vehicles inching toward California, pushing the temperature outside above the 100-degree mark. Ratón was hustling between cars carrying a plastic bucket filled with melted ice water and soda cans on his shoulder, as sweat dripped from his thin, pointy face and made his white cotton T-shirt nearly translucent. He saw me through the windshield, smiled and came over. I rolled down the window and we greeted one another with handshakes. In the course of our conversation, I told him I was heading home to Los Angeles and flying back to college soon. Ratón, who I had known my entire life, said he was proud of me for sticking with my studies and shared that his drug rehabilitation center had him working under the hot sun to sweat out the crystal meth toxins. I told him that kicking his habit was a good thing. He smiled, we shook hands, and he got back to hawking cold beverages.

I saw Ratón again five months later, during the holiday season. He was not well. We greeted one another with smiles and a hug. Ratón, like the other addicts in my grandmother's neighborhood, asked me for a dollar to medicate himself. I handed him one of the bills I carried in my pocket for these sorts of interactions, and he walked on.

During that same Christmas visit, I checked in on a childhood friend who was in the throes of a crystal meth addiction. I found him in the ramshackle small bedroom added on to his older sister's house. The folded, burnt aluminum on the small nightstand next to his bed explained his gaunt face and distant demeanor. We talked briefly, about what I no longer remember. Perhaps it was about the subterranean club house we had dug thirty yards from where we sat. Or perhaps we recalled the times when young men in their twenties shared dirty puns and jokes with us as we carefully peeled the thin foil off the paper gum wrappers for them; thin paper that they would later use to roll marijuana joints. During the first awkward lull in our conversation, he stood up and stepped outside. I heard him fidgeting with the padlock and then the distinct click of the arched shackle locking. I knew even before I tried the doorknob that I was locked in. It wouldn't be long before he returned. I was certain of it. He'd soon want a hit off his makeshift pipe on the nightstand. Sure enough, minutes later the door creaked open. He looked at me with a quizzical look and asked, "What are you doing in here?" "I am waiting for you," I told him. He nodded and looked around. It was time for me to go. I got up, shook hands with him in our distinct style, and left, even more determined to keep my word to my grandfather by steering clear of all this drug shit.

Of all the people I saw with addictions, the one that pains me most is that of the woman with whom I shared my first kiss. She was a cute twelve-year-old at the time and chose to share a kiss with me, a boy two years her junior, instead of one of the teenage boys constantly flirting with her. I am sure she opted to spend time with me because I was safe—my hands didn't wander. At ten, I gave no thought to venturing beyond her mouth. That was new and special to me. That was enough. A few years later, she stopped attending school and started dating an older guy who had her sneak out of her grandparent's house at all hours of the night to party and do drugs with him and his friends. Eight years after our kiss, the sensory memory of our lips touching was undone when we greeted one another and hugged. Her meth addiction had left her bony to the touch, with cracked, dried lips, nothing like the beautifully shaped mouth in my memories. While in her embrace, I was engulfed in the putrid chemical smell emanating from her aged flesh and long shabby hair. I held my breath and felt for her, but more for her two little children growing with druggies for parents.

The cartels have found a steady stream of clients in Tijuana for products—(black tar) heroin and crystal methamphetamine—they mostly export clandestinely to the U.S. Now, more than ever before, venomous drugs are ravaging the lives and dreams of *tijuanenses*. Sketchy drug rehabilitation centers continue to spring up and business is brisk with junkies returning to give sobriety yet another go. The concrete banks of the Río de Tijuana are dotted with homeless drug addicts crouching like gargoyles on a treacherous ledge.

Aware that the Sinaloa cartel is battling the remnants of the Arellano Félix cartel for control of Baja California, I approach Tijuana somewhat suspicious and guarded, upon my returns. I fear the stillness of the ordinary will be imploded by cartel assassins indiscriminately unleashing death with bursts of bullets. So, I take note of slow-moving vehicles, especially the window-tinted SUVs favored by *narcos*, and of anything that strikes me as odd. Once, with the survival skills I learned in the barrios of northeast Los Angeles, I keyed in on the waist-level bulges under the leather coats of four young men who sauntered into a taco establishment with the vibe of *narco juniors*. I quickly rounded up my female cousins and we left the taco establishment, with me still craving *tacos de suadero*. My cousins did not fault me for being cautious and wanting to avoid the moments of mayhem that have left thousands dead.

When in Tijuana, though, I mostly go about my days mundanely. I take my cues from *tijuanenses*, who continue to live their lives. Work. School. Shopping. Outings to the movies. Daily life in Tijuana goes on. As it must.

I return to my tormented city when I can. As *I* must.

THE BRIDGE TO AN ALIEN NATION

Paul Pedroza

When I was seventeen, I crossed over the bridge into Ciudad Juárez on foot for the first time. It was 1998, and it was also the first time I'd visited that mysterious city in over a decade. My oldest brother George was with me—he was the one who convinced me to come over with him into the famous strip. The air was golden with the rays of the setting sun when we locked the doors of my mom's Grand Am in the parking lot beneath the bridge. The dying sunlight reflected off the thin strip of the Rio Grande and burned my eyes as we began our trek over the Santa Fe Bridge.

My head was on a swivel as we climbed. Behind me, the sights of downtown El Paso and the Franklin Mountains could only elicit a quick establishing glance over my shoulder— there they were, right where I'd left them, right where I'd need them to be to help me find my way back. What lay ahead of me was what really captured my attention. My heart raced as we climbed toward the thin, cracked yellow line that marks the point where two countries meet. I was nervous. Hell, I was almost a wreck of nerves and emotion, downright scared of what I might come across once I paid my quarter and stepped off the bridge.

I could see nothing clearly given the distance and pollution, and the squat sprawl of the blocks and blocks of near-century-old buildings seemed more familiar at a greater distance. George chatted casually, "Dude, when was the last time you've been over? Have you *ever* been over?" He laughed, and I could tell he felt proud of himself, like he was creating one of those minute experiences that, when piled together, add up to something like adulthood. This would be the closest I'd come to the strip since the last time I came over, and I didn't remember too much from those days anyway. The city rose like jagged teeth from a maddening mist, and the closer we came, I could see that the buildings couldn't hide the abuse they took from the elements and the sun, despite the lack of humidity or inclement weather.

We'd reached the peak of the bridge, and George stopped for a smoke. I could tell by the way he leaned against the chain link fence, its lip curled toward us to discourage climbers, and the way he lit up, that this was a ritual for him. He crossed over all the time to meet his girlfriend for a night out. Sometimes they'd just hit the strip, but often she'd pick him up at the foot of the bridge, and they'd head out for a movie or dinner or both. I guessed that that moment was his last alone for the night, and he always looked forward to it. He never seemed concerned about being mugged or even just harassed, but he was always prepared for it either way.

I always had the impression that the way he shaved his hair down to the scalp and his love of heavy metal T-shirts lent him a "don't mess with me" aura. He and I stood out either way, as tall and as pale as we are, so it seemed necessary to take it further with our black clothing and boots. Those were the days when standing out like that in the streets didn't quite make you a target. He also wore the thickest wallet chain I'd ever seen, and he would elaborate on the ways he'd use it as a weapon, if necessary. I mostly tried to let my hair hang in my eyes and let my natural scowl be my shield from any threat, real or perceived.

The thin yellow line distracted me, and I wanted to study it since we had a few minutes. It extended the width of the bridge, and I extended it beyond and split the river in two. Thousands of miles of yellow streaked east and west into the borderlands of my mind. I called out to George and told him to watch as I jumped back and forth from one country to the other. "I'm an American now," I said and then jumped. "Now *soy* Mexicano, *güey*," in my cracked Spanish. I usually threw in a curse word I'd practiced over and over on the kids at school just to reassure myself that I had the right to bend the language on my tongue and in my mind. As I jumped and jumped, the declarations became more concise: "American," jump, "Mexicano," jump. George stood there, chuckled a little, then said, "Come on, man. It's getting dark." He flicked his cigarette butt into the river and started walking, hands buried in his pockets. Afraid to go on, I'd jumped to try and entertain and distract him, but once he mentioned the dark coming in, I stopped. He was right. It was getting dark fast, never mind that it was still early fall. I didn't want to stay there longer than I had to, and so I ran to catch up.

And yet, I was curious. I wanted to see things I'd never seen before. I'd worked at Taco Bell earlier in the year, and I'd walked along Dyer to get there and passed old, ratty motels and stared at a few prostitutes from afar, curious about their very existence. But this was different. I wanted to see "real" prostitutes, and the only place I knew I could find them was . . . Still, I only wanted to see them from afar, and with something like a fence or a bright, pedestrian-heavy block between us. I wanted to see the aggressive cabbies and boisterous brothels, the aggressive cigarette vendors with their duty-free smokes, the aggressive doormen calling innocent ones like me into their bars and strip clubs. I realize now how much I'd wanted to see all of these people in as close a manner to a television documentary as I could possibly have them, but in the moment I lied to myself and said anything would be fine. Standing on top of that tremendous bridge, I felt just as big in spirit.

We walked on, and once we handed over those quarters to the man in the booth at the foot of the bridge, we were in. Twenty-five cents paid entry into a new, exotic world. My brother led, of course, and I trusted him. Since he was dating a woman from Juárez at the time, he really knew his way around. George, never unsure and never having to stop and ask where to go, still couldn't assuage my anxiety with his strong sense of direction. It may seem like a strange thing since Juárez is so close to El Paso, but few people in my family crossed over regularly. It was the sort of place one made an effort to visit once in a great while, but I only fell into this tradition due to age at the time. Yet, it wasn't my first time being in Juárez. I'd spent my entire life up to that point living chin to nape with the city.

When I was a kid, every once in a while, my grandpa would fire up the old Ford Elite and take me along to a neighborhood grocery just beyond the river and the barbed-wire-crowned fences. We would head through south El Paso and cross the bridge in mere minutes, and when we got there I couldn't tell the difference between that neighborhood and the one we drove through to get there, but the drive from my grandparents' neighborhood was always memorable because of the way the surroundings would slowly grow older and more run-down.

As we got out of the car, he would share the rules of the visit: don't get lost, don't even leave my side, don't touch anything unless I let you, and so on.

It was my first experiences in a grocery so unlike the chain stores that we usually patronized. It had a different feel, something more improvised and organic. In the chain stores, I was always afraid to touch anything because the products were always stacked and sorted perfectly. If I did, I imagined I would cause trouble for the employees who had to come around and fix what I'd done. This grocery, however, seemed to invite the customer to grab and smell and restack in creative ways, almost as if every customer helped lend it this unique feel. It had different smells: less antiseptic soap, more of the natural, musky aromas of fruit and vegetables just beginning to over-ripe. There were flies but no other bugs that I could see, and they didn't seem to bother anyone, so I made sure to learn to not let it bother me either. The stuff that needed a cover was covered, and the rest should be washed at home anyway.

The people interested me more than the store. At those chain groceries, no one—not customer or employee—acknowledged anyone else unless absolutely necessary. The food was the focus and everything else was tuned out. Here was a crowd of friends, though, and the air buzzed with more than just the wings of flies. People chatted, haggled and compared purchases. Some, upset at the cut the butcher handed over when compared with that of others, stormed back to the counter and demanded something better, often yelling at the top of their lungs. No one seemed genuinely angry, though. Their meat replaced, the customer fell into a pacified contentment, a vague smile on their lips as they headed to the checkout lanes.

My grandpa spent more time saying hello and chatting than he did shopping. We'd leave with little more than a single bag half full, more often than not with a cut of meat my grandma would cook up for dinner that night. I wonder whether the meat department really could boast of the best tasting, most generous cuts in the area that could warrant such a trip, but I know that the charms of the place had a bit to do with it, despite my grandpa's frugal ways.

My oldest memories of crossing over, then, are quite pleasant: friendly people, delicious natural food, etc. These, however, didn't come to mind as I walked over with George, and I wonder now why that is. What I've figured out has a lot to do with not only the ill-defined, sinister shadow that has become associated with the Mexican side of the border by the media and the horrendous stereotypes, but also the way in which the people of the region craft and sort these ideas themselves. The situation has only gotten worse since 2008, when drug-related violence spiked and murder became a part of daily life. It's not only the responsibility of the media. The way we, the border dwellers, look out over Juárez and how we react to what we see are just as important in the creation of the cultural heritage that future generations will have to manage.

When we began walking around the strip, the streets were bustling. We walked tall and scowled just like the other men. George made short trips into liquor shops just to let me know how good a deal he could get on Presidente and Crown Royal, cracking his knuckles and sharing stories of the parties he'd been to in Juárez with Sandra. Vendors sold Popsicles to the thirsty pedestrians. There were puddles of sour-smelling funk, but I was the only one that seemed to notice them, so I tried to stop noticing as I jumped over them. When my brother stopped one of those aggressive cigarette vendors to buy a few packs of Marlboro Lights, I was excited. The man, whose clothes were as darkened by grime as his teeth, offered some to me, as well. "Cheap, no tax, *rebajas para todos, joven*." I declined, but I also began to relax and almost feel like I belonged, so long as the sunlight held out. I began to wonder whether I was in fear of vampires and smiled.

George took his time. He walked down one street as he lit another cigarette, hung a left, and then headed down another. He'd promised to be quick about his business, which still wasn't clear to me. When we were about a block away from a large, orange single-story building, he told me he'd come to place some bets on college football games at the OTB. The place was clean and bright, and there were a lot of people with money to burn inside. The air in the room buzzed with conversation, but it wasn't like the grocery I'd visited with my grandpa. The buzz was greedy, of a darker kind of hope, and I waited against the wall and avoided eye contact while my brother did his business.

Afterward, I assumed we would head back to El Paso, but George needed to see a friend who worked at a bar only a few blocks away. The sun had set in the meantime. We'd spent nearly an hour at the bookie, mostly waiting in line as the mostly American crowd argued over betting lines. The sunlight bled away, and the neon lights buzzed grotesquely. Traffic snarled significantly with night having fallen. Avenida Juárez was choked with cars waiting to enter the United States. We headed west, in single file. I stood up straight and reinvigorated my scowl but kept my eyes on the concrete.

The bar was about three blocks away from the OTB, and the side street it sat on played host to numerous establishments. The ones with the signs were typically bars, clubs and strip joints. The ones that weren't so obvious usually operated out of narrow doorways and joints in the façades of certain buildings, and they were mostly and obviously brothels, even to someone as green as me. My brother found his bar, and I waited by the door, astounded to come across one of the few places that actually didn't allow anyone under eighteen inside. He and his friend chatted. I acted like it was only natural that I be there for what felt like hours. When they finished up, we left the way we had come.

When you're in survival mode, you fool yourself when you believe that you mature with every step you take into what you believe to be foreign territory. Sometimes you think you've mastered an area just because you once walked through it in a single direction. That was how I felt as I let the bar's door close behind me. I'd walked it before and nothing happened, so it stood to reason that I could do it again and expect the same. We walked. We got about halfway back to Avenida Juárez when someone grabbed me by my upper arm. The hand's strength was tremendous. I looked deep into the shadows from which it emerged and saw nothing, but I could hear a voice aching to feign feminine tenderness. When her face emerged from the shadows, I couldn't help but stare at the stray hairs on her lip that her tweezers had passed over and at the Adam's apple that bobbed with her attempts to tantalize. She was almost as tall as I, and I stood over six-feet-tall back then. To this day, due to my heart attempting to climb out of my mouth, I cannot recall verbatim what it was that the transsexual prostitute said, but I understood enough to know what she was offering me. George laughed nervously a little, probably imagining the kind of trouble I was going to give him later when I'd swear off of Juárez for the rest of my life. I struggled against the hand and couldn't find my words. She cooed and cajoled, and I fought against my monkey mind to find something to say that would free me, and what finally came out shamed me in a certain way then, and shames me more so now in a completely different way. "*Que estás fea!*" I yelled as I loosened my arm and practically ran. It shamed me then because of my weak grasp of the language, my ill attempt at seeming hard. Now, I truly wish I could have expressed my feelings in the moment in a much more eloquent and inoffensive manner, but you go with what gets you by, I guess. It shames me now because I'm afraid of what my words may have done to her, although, unfortunately, I suspect she was used to such abuse.

Either way, I was free and happy to be so. The walk to the bridge was a cakewalk then. I did all the talking about what had happened, trying to justify myself. Maybe George felt sorry for me, I don't know. I watched for his reaction on his face and admired the way the neon lights changed his features. He only smiled whenever I brought it up, and I brought it up at least a half dozen times between then and the moment we parked in the driveway at home. Even the pass through the checkpoint on the U.S. side of the bridge was stress-free, although I feared that I wouldn't be able to pronounce the word "American" in the proper tone, volume or inflection. But I did. And we went home, and my first experience of our sister city first-hand, bared to the bone, came to the end.

I crossed over on foot maybe six times more after that day, until George's interest in betting on college football waned, which happened once he figured he wasn't going to be able to bank on it like he thought he would. Juárez still had its allures for me though, and there was many a time I crossed over in a car with George and Sandra to see a movie or hang out at her parents' place. All it took was what some might call exposure therapy, and much of what I had to endure really felt like emotional crises to me, afraid as I was of shadows and suggestions that others had instilled in me. This is nothing new, nor is it unique. It's not even a thing of the past, and if anything, there are real and even more sinister reasons not to cross over these days, thanks to cartel violence and intimidation. Most people, even those who used to cross over on a daily basis for reasons business-related and otherwise, feel it's best not to bother anymore. It's not worth it, they say. And they may be right, but this is nothing new. People have been saying it's not worth it for many decades. Mexico doesn't seem to exist in the majority of U.S. citizens' minds except for strange, seeming self-sustaining pockets of tourist-hounded areas like Cancún, Puerto Peñasco, etc. There's a marked difference in the amount of working knowledge and interest in the average border dweller, but it's common for even these to reject Mexico as an interesting, vibrant place to visit and settle in. The food, the music, and a few other cultural items, like style or *macho bravado*, are considered safe and are typically integrated in some degree in the greater American cultural tapestry, and yet, Mexico itself looms in the shadows of our darkest fears. I speak from experience as I've spent many years since the days of these visits not crossing over. When 9/11 happened and the strictest measurements of border crossing ever seen were implemented, many people breathed sighs of relief. It's too much work to cross over now, they say. Nothing changed for me. As soon as George married Sandra, and she moved to El Paso for good, my trips into Juárez—save for a disastrous night spent stranded at Sandra's parents' house thanks to a tremendous rainstorm and subsequent flooding—ended seemingly for good.

I have no excuses, but I do have reasons. I've always told myself, echoing what I've heard many a friend and relative say, that all that I want and need I can find here, on "our" side. It takes a great deal of effort to forget the markets and swap meets where I used to find interesting trinkets and elaborate, gaudy bedspreads that I'd run my eyes over appreciatively without buying. The smells of cheese and chile and lime, as foods boiled away in ancient, crusted pots, are recalled instantaneously and yet shuffled away without hesitation. We're conditioned to promote an almost caste-like system in which we, the citizens of the United States, are invariably at the top. We use this as a weapon against an entire nation, dealing with any guilt arising through denial. When the bullets started flying, we found our foundational condemnation, and now we build all sorts of walls to make it forever.

Of course, we, the everyday people, don't consciously think this way. The everyday people view these issues with more gray than the zealots and fundamentalists. With every day that passes, when more bodies pile up and fewer people cross over, it becomes more difficult to heal, to close the rift and find common ground again. Those market days long ago were the days, not of blissful childish ignorance, but of open-minded inclusiveness. I was open to Juárez and her charms and her wonderful people, but now these are merely intellectualized constructs in my mind. I cannot justify them anymore with face-to-face experiences, drawn on the narrow streets where lives are lived under the same desert sun. This is the true lost world of the border. This is a world long gone. One cannot be fully "bicultural" in such a climate, and what results is a faction state: you're either with us or with them, and what determines the "we" that one represents differs among starkly convoluted lines. "They" are drug runners and *sicarios* and poor people mind-addled by cheap smack and coke, because life's so dense with violence and get-rich-quick schemes that it cannot be faced with a clear eye.

"They" is a concept well-defined. Not "us." It's not uncommon to meet people of Mexican descent who disavow any connection to that entire culture, who are ashamed of their physical characteristics, who scour any hint of accent from their English, and vice versa. One of the distinguishing characteristics of the former frame of mind involves Juárez and her reputation, which sometimes hinges on grotesque exaggerations. This is what afflicted me that evening I crossed over with my brother back in 1998, roughly a decade before the cartel violence gripped the city. All of the good that my grandpa instilled in me, quite purposely, couldn't compare to the raw buzzing energy I felt then. I chose to believe the worst about the "other side" of my homeland instead of working to recognize all of the good. It takes that sort of exposure therapy to disabuse one's self of such glaring misunderstandings. Even today, in the midst of the violence and disregard for human life, there are millions of people who desire nothing more than a chance to raise a family and live as comfortably as possible. We hear this all the time from people who support human rights and want nothing but the best for Juárez, but even they stay away, and for good reason. The land is lost to everyone, although the good at heart hope it's only temporary.

I visited home again this past summer, and one simmering evening, George and my little brother Hilario and I headed towards Yarbrough along the Border Highway. The ill-famed border wall stretched along the right, and Juárez, dark as night for hundreds of yards beyond the security lights, sank its claws into my gut. What if stray bullets hit our truck? Worse yet, what if the *sicarios*, bored with the slow burn of the early night, chose our vehicle for moving target practice? What if we were to witness a shootout right along the river? I felt my body tense, my eyes shot back and forth over the land looking for signs. The search for detail made me dizzy, and so I relaxed my eyes and tried to take in the whole city. What I saw was what I always saw growing up: the sprawl beneath a deepening azure sky, the street lights flickering faintly, everything seeming to nestle in for the night. I couldn't see what I told myself I wasn't looking for beyond the police station, although I'm certain more than a few people died that night like most others recently. I mourned quietly as I held onto a bit of hope for

Juárez, a weak hope that's growing minutely stronger every day.

An absurd urge to turn the truck around and pass over the bridge shook me as we pulled ever closer to my partner Carol's grandma's house, an urge to visit the places that everyone says they miss, many of which I've never had the privilege to enjoy: those iconic bars at which I've never had the pleasure of a drink with friends, La Feria and its wonderfully terrifying rides and cheap food, the Chupacabras 100 Kilometers. Instead, we kept on driving east, and eventually we turned left and headed north, headed away from the smelly waste processing facility just across the river, away from the ominously open gate, a lone green and white van sitting in the growing darkness. By the time we passed Shawver Park, Juárez was out of mind once again, just like any other moment of the day, until we headed back and there she was. Always waiting. Always patient, ever ready to make peace and invite us back into her open arms.

SUCKING THE SWEET

José Antonio Rodríguez

The year is 2009; the month is November. The wind at night sidles up against my window. I hole up in my apartment packing for the trip down to Texas to visit family for the Thanksgiving break. This space is a bit of a dump really, but it's cheap enough that it leaves me a little extra to fly home. A third-floor attic with a ceiling so low I can touch it easily even though I'm only 5'8". Two tiny bedrooms for my roommate and me. Old peanut-butter colored carpet with black stains bulging on uneven floorboards. The rusty furnace at one end heats only a five-foot radius around it, not good for upstate New York where it's already snowed. Not good for someone from south Texas who's only been here a couple of winters, whose blood hasn't thickened yet, as the locals say. The lights are dull yellow like those of my childhood homes, meek lights that force you to squint to read. My room barely fits a twin bed and a 2 ft. x 4 ft. foldout table from Staples that acts as a desk. But I relish every freezing second of it—every wind shear against my face, every ritual of layering, every shake and rattle of my bony frame—because I'm actually here on a university

233

fellowship to study, teach and write. To write. Amazing, really, that I settled in this cold quiet city to find my stories, that it seems the stories themselves brought me here.

And when I think of those stories, I think of sweltering heat. The city of McAllen, where I grew up, sits right on the border with Mexico, an hour inland from the Gulf, close enough to breathe heavy with humidity, but too far to get any significant rain. So distant from the arctic winds, that you never feel even a hint of snow. The temperature rises to the nineties around April and hovers in that vicinity until October, except for the summer months when it boils past a hundred. Then the daily news talks of people dying of heat exhaustion. The anchors sit behind desks in their perfectly tailored suits, ties tight against collars, and recommend fans. And you sweat. Then you rush to the grocery store on an errand, smell the bustling traffic, the concrete and rubber and exhaust from rickety pick-up trucks, and you sweat some more. Then you come back, sleep cramped in beds like suckling piglets, where the sheets stick slick to your body, where you sweat more than you thought was possible. Then in the morning you walk to the air-conditioned grade school, and you feel blessed because you don't sweat, because you can almost forget you ever sweated, almost for the entire day.

Then you come home to your Catholic mother, married at seventeen, with ten children by age thirty-four, her fire-red hair and scintillating hazel eyes dimmed by that dazed look —motionless, sitting at the dining table in a nightgown, her arms plump, her hands on her lap swollen from scrubbing cloth against washboard. *¿Cómo te fue?* she asks but doesn't wait for an answer. It's alright, though, because every time you bring home your report card, she smiles at your good grades, the best grades, and you know that makes her proud. She has said it time and again: do good in school and you can escape this life. So you sit at the table and start your homework. Then your father comes home from working a twelve-hour shift as a field hand for some citrus farm at the edge of town, his job prospects limited by his third-grade education and complete inability to learn a word of English.

I ask the boss how to say something in English but the minute I turn around, I forget, he says, chuckling . . . in Spanish.

Only in his forties, he moves like an old man, and his dark skin and blue-black hair sigh gray with dust. He sits on a deflated couch, groans for help removing his cowboy boots, and you kneel before him, pull them one at a time. First, a quick jerk to loosen the heel. Then gently. In his socks he shuffles out to the front porch.

In this part of town, all the mothers are leaning in kitchens thinking of new shapes in which to cut potatoes for dinner, all the fathers are smoking in rusty lawn chairs in the front porches of withering frame houses. All of them slanted, weathered, the concrete blocks under floorboards sinking in the sandy soil. The nicest houses with giant refrigerators, tall beds, climate-control, reliable cars, and manicured lawns, are far away in the north part of town. But you never see those houses because the only time you leave these streets is on weekends, when you pile into the *cucaracha* and drive south to Mexico. Everyone fights for the window seat, a chance at some hot breeze lapping a face.

An hour's drive over shimmering hot highways, past orange and grapefruit orchards and sugarcane fields, across a bridge straddling a slow mossy river, through dusty shops and people selling trinkets from pushcarts, past all that clatter, puttering along on a lonely bumpy road with clouds of dust like curtains closing behind you, you finally reach the Mexican village where you were born, where you spent your first years. The one with a one-room Catholic church and no health clinic, the one with small bleak houses like sheds leaning against fields of corn and sorghum, the one with roosters to call you back to life every morning. You're visiting relatives. Elders talk about the farm land, the tiny plot that used to be more but became only seven hectares when a road and a ditch were drawn through it many years ago, the plot your father passed over to his sister when your family left Mexico. The plot that your mother, when pressed, says just didn't yield enough anymore.

You can't help but notice the absence of 7-11s, concrete, traffic, toilets. Do you miss them already? A stone's throw away is the little shack with a corrugated tin roof that says abandoned, the one where you were pushed out into a world far away from any doctor, any sterilized white linens, any weight scale, any clocks and their corrosive counting of time. The one where you and your family attempted sleep every night.

The evening's falling over every living thing, the dark descending like a great fog. Barely a drop of electric light hums through some neighbor's window. Brush and mesquite move like they're dancing with shadows. A goat gnaws on something in the shade. The dirt road's pocked with animal shit.

While you're saying your good-byes, getting ready to pile back into the car, the wind kicks up dirt that grinds in your teeth. Then every sparkling lesson you've been taught about that land of promise called the United States comes to you as an elixir, and you marvel at your good fortune that you left, that every day you leave, move further and further away from this dark corner, becoming something mighty and tall with all that is right, becoming something you don't know, yet you hope will render you almost unrecognizable to what you are now, becoming one of them, becoming American.

Amá sits in the front seat because of her car sickness with their pet Chihuahua Blackie and Apá sits in the backseat with their other mixed-breed Pantera because Apá, now past seventy years of age, would rather someone else drive instead of him. We're in a snazzy 2008 Mazda 6—the newest car my parents have ever had—that my sister Alba bought for them, driving down to McAllen from San Antonio, from my sister Myrna's home. Down to the border for a few days before I fly back to upstate New York. No more patched-up, overheating cars for Apá and Amá. No more heat, no more gusts of wind crashing against your temple. Just sit back and be lulled by engine's soft rumble, the plush seats, the cool whir of the air conditioner.

I haven't told my parents yet, but I've been writing a memoir—if only for myself, an exercise in self-reflection. Some attempt to make sense of a life lived transgressing borders, or better put, a life transgressed by borders. The story starts in that Mexican village, the one I was taught to forget, to discount as some backward way of life. The one I was supposed to leave behind to become something new, better. The one I can't forget because it comes to me in dreams, waking dreams. The one that I now see held something else besides cramped beds and sweat, something I feel an urge to rescue from that place where willfully forgotten things go—denied, negated, no longer honored through memory, or tradition, or ritual. That place where they die a kind of protracted death.

I asked a therapist in Binghamton once why, despite all the years and the miles traveled, that place loomed so large and vivid in my mind and my imagination. "It was the place where you acquired consciousness. How could it not be significant?" he responded serenely. And I thought of who we are as children before we are taught flags, pledges of allegiance, names of countries, their margins on a map, and the armed men who guard them.

The memoir is almost finished, and I think ending it on a trip back to that village would be a fitting end. I think it would be satisfying to the reader for the narrator to return to the place where it all began because this holds the potential to articulate a measure of resolution, a kind of stasis for both reader and narrator. Having begun to settle so many conflicts of identity within, having begun to find a way to live them inside me, I feel a great urge to return. But I haven't been there in a long time, and I don't want to go alone because I'm apprehensive about driving in Mexico where driving rules aren't as strictly followed. I'm so American that way, about driving rules. I ask Apá in the backseat if he'd like to go with me:

No, he says.

¿Por qué?

Drogas.

¿Qué?

Traficantes.

And I ask again and he tells me what few details he's gathered from visiting with relatives: drug traffickers now organized into paramilitary groups have infiltrated the village. Fleeing the towns where they get into skirmishes with military forces, they've moved their operations to the rural areas. I imagine stealth. I imagine them keeping a low profile, lying, if not completely successfully, to the few residents about why they're there. I imagine them laboring in the dark hours. But it turns out, they've established armed checkpoints at the two entrances to the village. So no, they're not hiding, not at all. Rather, they keep watch over the residents, intimidate them, subdue them. Yes, the village is less populated than it used to be; many have found it necessary to leave it, their home, come to this side through the bridge or through the shallow parts of the river, looking for we already know what. Only a few families remain, but the grade school is still open, still calling the children. And they must surely come to it.

I've read about the "drug war" in American newspapers over and over—the ubiquity of high-caliber weapons, the brutal conflict, the innocent bystanders—violence like a hurricane that's always only incoming. Though of course this is different, isn't it? The violence I read about in *The New York Times* was in distant places I'd never been to and, perhaps, never would, places like Ciudad Juárez or Mexico City, or the Guatemala/Mexico border. The journalist's voice in my head as I read the article—clinical, detached, like the rendering of pure statistics. The violence I'd hear about in the local news, in the local American and Mexican channels, while visiting my family in McAllen was shocking, yes, and painful but tempered somewhat by the sheen of the television screen, regardless of the language. Change the channel before they go from talking about drug-related crime in the city of Reynosa to showing its plaza through which I've strolled, the architecture of the Catholic church with its bell tower, the market where Amá would buy tortillas and detergent because they were cheaper than in the U. S. Change the channel before they go from talking about torture to showing the remains of the tortured, because they will show them. I've seen the images— humans slaughtered like beasts, headless bodies sharing that elemental resemblance in death and dismemberment. Change the channel. The violence my parents' neighbors with family and friends south of the border spoke about, their assertion that the local news was not reporting everything, that what we heard was only a fraction of what was happening, was distressing but . . . It hadn't happened to people I knew. Not that I knew of. Maybe I just didn't want to think about the vastness of that enterprise threatening so many so indiscriminately. Maybe I wanted to believe that at least my first home, even if only it remains surrounded by withered swaying mesquites, was safe from much of this splintered and hostile world— tucked away from paved roads and duplicitous politicians, from garish store-display windows and middle-class tourist shoppers, from scrutinized drug markets and modern weapons of warfare.

Now all that enterprise has come to nest there, precisely there—that place where I ran barefoot on dirt roads, where Amá made tortillas from the corn Apá harvested, where Apá improvised scarecrows, where the night glowed soft and quiet with the songs of moths around a kerosene lamp, where I walked out into that star-crushed night when I couldn't sleep, the neighbor's horse eyeing me, our bodies silvered with moonlight, my back to the road, to the world, innocent of that kind of violence.

And I, driving along this straight and wide Texas highway, cannot help but conjure them in my mind: Mexican boys angry and scared with mean stares, perhaps in pseudo army fatigues, long sleeves rolled up to the elbow, AK-47s strapped to their shoulders and dwarfing them. Maybe they'd like my father's car. Maybe they'd like it enough to yank us out of it. What are you here for? they'd ask my father and me, leaning in, resting their glistening forearms on the lip of the window, like the officers at the international bridge. My father would speak for both of us, say we're visiting relatives. See, we're not outsiders exactly. I wouldn't tell them I've come to visit this place where I was born for a book I'm writing. I wouldn't tell them my stories. I'd just look out in front of me at the low trees, the dusty winding road. And they'd notice my nervousness, the way I grow quiet, the way my face becomes blank so that others may read whatever they want to read on it and move on. And so one of them would come to my window, the passenger side, and look in. I'd have to turn my eyes to him, look straight at him, as if nothing stands outside of the ordinary; otherwise, I'd raise suspicions. I'd pretend I was okay with what he did, whatever that would be, with who he was, whoever he would be.

Would I be up to the task? Looking into him?

What would I see in his eyes? Some glimpse of what he's lived pulsing out from their dark center? What deaths? What fears? What home?

And what would he see in mine?

I ask Apá if their presence is temporary, if he thinks they'll leave. No, he says, *siempre regresan*. They always return.

I can't go back, I think. The images of oppressive violence, the kind that imposes a silence over those who have no choice but to endure it, have invaded my memories of the place where I learned my name, the place where I became, and I fear they will never be the same—the memories now unsettled, un-homed. What will my waking dreams be now that those men have come?

I thought an abandoned, rotting home alone and bereft of even one witness was sad, perhaps the saddest thing, and despite the resources of my imagination, I couldn't envision anything worse. But I was wrong. I don't know what to say, what to tell myself, because a great and heavy hollow in my chest has temporarily displaced language. I think it is the weight of loss, but I'm not certain. I'm not certain of so many things.

I keep driving, and for a long time nobody speaks.

With the light diminishing, our outlines become less defined, our bodies more breaths in the dark. The narrator's last scene cannot be now. The memoir must find a new end.

I turn to my mother sitting next to me and past her is the window and past the window is the sun settling just beneath the horizon, straight as the most sublime of mathematical equations. The sky begins in gold and moves through shades of orange, lavender and blue, aglitter with budding stars. I swear, for the briefest of moments, I am four years old again in that village, and black flakes descend over everything. I open my palm that is now small, the small palm of a boy, his palm, my hand, his hand. He stretches out his hand and feels the flakes that seem larger because his hands are small, the burnt sugarcane that floats away above the fields and then falls like the confetti of *piñatas*.

The boy and his mother sit on upturned buckets under the doorway that faces the sun slowly settling beyond the cornfield. In his mother's hands is a short cut of sugarcane, not flakes but raw solid sugarcane like thick bamboo. He has never seen this before. *Ten*, she says, hands it to him so that he may suck the sweetness until it is nothing but flax, then she shaves off the flax with a pocket knife and sucks the sweetness brought to the surface, and this goes on back and forth, this sharing of sweetness at the threshold of a house surrounded by the early flitter of translucent wings. The sugarcane has a brown spot further down that looks like a bruise, and he fears this may mean that spot may be no good, may hold no sweetness. He fears it may be bitter. *No*, she says, *esto es lo más dulce*. And she is right—when he takes it to his lips, it is the sweetest.

Soon the small cut of sugarcane is reduced to nothing. And he doesn't know what is more, what is heavier: the memory of the sweetness on his tongue or the mourning of her empty hand. *Tienes sueño*, she tells him, as she caresses his face, brushes the gnats and flies away, the ones frantic around his eyes like they want to touch all that he sees, the ones around his lips and chin where some of the sweetness lingers. Sometimes he wishes he were a fly to taste the last of the sweet when he can't taste it anymore. With her apron, she scrubs some of the dirt and sweat—shapes like the winding borders of countries—from his face. *Mapas*, she says softly, because his skin is grimy, marked by the debris that has settled on his body.

The boy runs off through cornfield stalks through the tilled earth because it's all he can do with the sweet memory on his tongue. He lets himself fall on all fours, clods of dirt crumbling under his hands, his hands and feet sinking into the cool like a blessed drowning of limbs, until the earth feels like the softest bed. Falling is like sleeping. Everything is beautiful then. The black flakes fall. He doesn't have to look up at the warm-hued sky because it has come down to him, falls around him, making everything glow soft pink. The sky is with him now. That distant place that he dreamt of reaching one day, that place where the sky kisses the ground, where sky and ground are one—it was here all along.

THE SICARIO IN THE SALON

José Skinner

A student in my undergraduate creative writing workshop at University of Texas-Pan American in the Lower Río Grande Valley bursts into tears. We've been critiquing a story she's written about her breakup with her boyfriend, and another student has called it "banal." I, delighted to hear an undergrad use such a word, have the students look it up on their laptops. "Drearily commonplace and often predictable," says *American Heritage*.

I assume the weeping student considers all this a prolonged attack on her piece. I curse myself for my insensitivity, born of eagerness to exploit a "teachable moment," and attempt to apologize.

"No, no, it's not that," she says. She's upset, she tells us, because the week before, her grandfather, a rancher a few miles to our south in the Mexican state of Tamaulipas, was "picked up" by men in a late-model SUV and held for ransom. Everyone of means in the extended family on both sides of the border pitched in, but this was not enough for the kidnappers. They looked over his ranch, liked what they saw, and had his wife bring them titles and deeds. A bill of sale was prepared and signed by a crooked notary, and, voilà, now her grandfather's ranch was theirs.

The story is mind-boggling. A country's juridical system so broken that kidnappers, far from having to skulk away with their loot, are able to boldly move into their victims' very homes? Or have their victims pay their ransom on the installment plan, as another student tells about someone she knows in Nuevo León—released with a down payment, the balance of the ransom to be paid monthly, with death as the penalty for default? This kind of thing is happening with increasing frequency in Tamaulipas, Nuevo León, Chihuahua and other border states.

"It's becoming banal," says another student.

I might have asked: What else is it? That's right: Kafkaesque. If Kafka were writing these stories, he might have the grandmother and grandfather continue living at the ranch, guests in their own home; or have the victims write their kidnappers into their wills, notarized by the same crooked notary; or have the tax man levy taxes on the victims for running the business of their own kidnapping.

We've also been studying Orwell, and it's hard not to notice the Orwellian euphemisms that attach, in the news media and in everyday conversation, to events involving the narco wars: kidnappings are *"levantones"* (pickups), shootouts are *"fiestas,"* criminals are *"mañosos"* (tricky guys), and when they end up killing you, you're affectionately known as a *"muertito"* (a little dead one). Depending on where and how their bodies are found, *muertitos* can be broken down into *ecobijados* (wrapped in blankets), *encajuelados* (found in car trunks), *encintados* (gagged and tied with duct tape), or *entambados* (stuffed into 55-gallon drums, often with their severed heads placed decoratively on top). It's all part of *"la situación social de excep-*

ción"—the "exceptional social situation," as the Reynosa daily newspaper *El Mañana* sometimes calls it, that arose after president Felipe Calderón declared war on the narcos in 2006.

That's when people talk about *la situación* at all. Discretion is the better part of valor, at least in Mexico proper, as illustrated by a story from a student in another class, which she titles "One Crazy Day." She—I'll call her Jasmín—and her mother were in a beauty salon in Matamoros, Tamaulipas, waiting to get their hair done. The wait was long; the stylist was taking her time on the hair of the young man before them. Another waiting woman started bad-mouthing the narcos: "Killing innocent people, they are. I wish a guerrilla army would rise up and kill all the mafiosos." Jasmín and her mother squirmed. One doesn't speak in public in Mexico of *la situación*. The woman went on: "I don't know why these men don't go back to their countries and stop harassing us. All we've sacrificed for, and they just come and take it."

The man's haircut over, he stood, brushed off his shoulders, paid the stylist fifty pesos, and calmly waited for the woman to take the chair. Then the man—whom Jasmín described as "average-looking" and dressed in "average clothes"—brandished a pistol and told the stylist, "shave this *vieja*, because if you don't, I'll kill her on her way out."

Too afraid to leave, the student and her mother watched the woman get shorn down to what Jasmín called her "rosy scalp." The man—whom Jasmín termed a "*sicario*," a henchman and hit man for the narcos—watched too, gun in hand, before leaving. As she got her own hair done, Jasmín observed the shaved woman buying a hat at a store across the street.

"A person's looks can be deceiving," Jasmín wrote. "You don't know who they are or where they come from. . . if you're at a beauty salon with random strangers, just shut your mouth."

"Who am I to judge these men?" Jasmín went on about the likes of the *sicario* in the salon. "They are not doing the correct things, but these are matters which are out of their hands. They are being threatened by killing [sic] their families, or even tortured."

Jasmín seemed to share the opinion of many, which is that the *sicarios* are coerced into serving the narcos, as much victims of *la situación* as those they kidnap, extort, or kill. Some take this to its logical limit, asserting that even the top narcos, the *jefes*, are victims of the whole nightmarish scenario, as afraid for their lives as anybody. The shorn woman seemed to believe the *sicarios* came from "other countries," presumably Central America, in accordance with the theory that young Central American men trying to make their way to the U.S. via Mexico are captured by the narcos, most often the group known as the Zetas, and pressed into service ("*la leva*"). This theory would have it that the seventy-two Central Americans massacred in 2010 in Tamaulipas refused such service or were somehow deemed unfit. (Another theory has it that they were killed merely to keep them from joining the ranks of rival cartels, and yet another that it was to punish the coyotes, or human smugglers, some of whom had failed to pay the $500 "tax" the Zetas levy for each man smuggled into the U.S.) The 183 young men taken at gunpoint from the Omnibuses de México as those buses passed through San Fernando, Tamaulipas, in March 2011, met the same fate, and were buried in a common grave, or "*narcofosa*."

A student I'll call Pablo, whose father was a narco in the much more civilized and orderly eighties—when the ruling PRI national party supposedly made sure the various smuggling outfits stuck to their respective "*plazas*" or turfs—finds these theories ridiculous. Those young men were killed because everybody knows they carry cash on them to pay the coyotes. So why take them off and kill them? Why not just rob them? Well, so they can't identify the robbers. Then why didn't they kill all the passengers, and the driver? Pablo doesn't have an answer for that, except to say the Zetas, arguably the most violent of the new gangs, and the one controlling San Fernando—are psychotically bloodthirsty, unlike the narcos in his dad's day.

The truth is, those young men would have never reported such a robbery to the authorities, because the police, many of whom work for the cartels, would at best have done nothing. Even the bus drivers, limping into Reynosa with the few passengers they had left, kept mum. And the bus companies kept sending buses through San Fernando.

A student whom I shall call Ricardo, whose mother is a dentist in Reynosa, believes the ranks of the narcos and their *sicarios* began to swell after 9/11. In the wake of that event, cross-border visits by U.S. citizens dropped sharply and never fully recovered, leading to increased unemployment in Reynosa and other border cities. At the same time, the U.S. increased border security, making it harder for young men on the Mexican side to cross over to the U.S. to work. The result was a backup of "ni-nis"—those who neither work nor study (*ni trabajan ni estudian*), and many ni-nis are tempted to become *sicarios* for the cartels. According to the *Centro Nacional de Evaluación para la Educación Superior*, there are 150,000 "ni-nis" in the state of Tamaulipas.

But as a visiting anthropologist told a friend of mine after a tour of Mexican border schools, young people don't even have to be in the second "ni" (*ni estudian*) to be tempted to work for the cartels. When he asked *secundaria* (high school) students what they hoped to become in life, half of them said: *sicarios*. One might think they were pulling his leg, if not for the fact that legitimate work is hard to come by, and the narco lifestyle, glorified in *narcocorrido* ballads, exerts a strong romantic pull. Even if they were to find work, either on the U.S. side of the border or in Mexico, it would be the work of *bueyes* (oxen), and, as the narcos like to say, "*mejor vivir cinco años como rey que cincuenta como buey*" (better to live five years as a king than fifty as an ox). Never mind that few lowly *sicarios* or *chiquinarcos* (child narcos) ever reach the higher ranks; this still seems more likely to them than being an undocumented dishwasher at Denny's and going on to own the franchise.

I have my students look up the etymology of *sicario*. Originally, the *sicarii* were members of a Jewish sect who used daggers (sicae) to murder Romans and their supporters. One student finds that the "Iscariot" in Judas Iscariot may well be a Hellenized version of the word. Another student ventures that maybe this is the reason the *Policía Judicial* are called in street slang "judas"—they are tempted to betray their duty and become *sicarios* for the narcos.

As in all stressful situations, black humor arises. When Valley public schools received an advisory from the State of Texas warning them to beware of narco-related gangs trying to recruit students (Governor Rick Perry, hankering to further militarize the border, is ever-eager to promote exaggerated claims that the violence is "spilling over" from Mexico into Texas), one of my students in the MFA creative writing program, a teacher in a Valley middle school, told her pupils to study hard for the Texas Assessment of Knowledge and Skills tests: "The cartels want an educated *sicario*, you know!" Her principal didn't think it was funny and sent her a memo saying so.

Another MFA student, on entering our classroom one evening—the previous class had apparently had a party, and the wastebaskets were overflowing with tamale husks and pizza crusts—exclaimed, "it's like a *secuestradero* in here!" A *secuestradero* is a room or house where multiple kidnap victims are held, and from a socio-linguistic perspective it's interesting to note how this term has replaced *"chiquero"* or *"pocilga"* (pigsty).

"The *secuestrados* don't get to eat this well," someone else said seriously. A discussion ensued on the horrors of being held for weeks or months in a hot, fetid room or box, not knowing if you were going to live or die.

I steered the conversation to what we'd started discussing in the previous class: the importance of choosing good names for fictional characters. We had to admit the narcos had some pretty good nicknames. *La Barbie* came to mind, as did *El Ingeniero* (The Engineer) and *El Muletas* (Crutches) and *Piolín* (Tweety Bird).

"I know they call him *La Barbie* because he's blond, but he actually looks more like Chucky," someone said.

"I think there's already an El Chucky," someone else said. "That name's already taken."

"*El Mochaorejas* and *El Cochiloco*," said Pablo. "Ear Lopper and Crazy Pig. Those were guys in my dad's day." I remembered Pablo's golden-toothed dad laughing about those men one sweltering afternoon at a barbeque by the Río Grande as he reminisced about the good old days.

"The narcos in México have more imagination than our *cholo* gangs here in the States," Pablo added. "If Sad Girl, Sleepy and L'il Puppet are already taken, the *cholos* don't know what to call the new jump-ins."

"I like the alliteration and assonance in Tony Tormenta," said the middle school teacher. "And that *tormenta* means storm. You guys know he was killed, right?"

Tony Tormenta, the Number Two in the *Cártel del Golfo*, had recently been spotted in public in Reynosa and Matamoros, ringed by his corrupt municipal and state police. Such flagrant public appearances are considered bad form, but Tony was reputed to be hitting the *perico* (cocaine) hard and *le valía madre* (he couldn't give a shit). The military had enough of the in-your-face, and one fine Friday morning in November they descended on him in the streets of Matamoros. At least a hundred were killed in the two-hour firefight, including a reporter. I had been invited to the annual *Congreso Binacional "Letras en el Estuario"* readings in Matamoros for the following weekend, but one of the organizers called me to tell me all events were being moved to Brownsville, which seemed to me a wise decision. "You should've heard it," he said. "This was war. This was Baghdad. Worse." Quite a fiesta, in other words.

"You could think of his men, those corrupt cops and all, as the arms of a hurricane, and he was at the center, like the eye," the middle-school teacher continued, on a roll. "Also, you could say he was tormented within, if he was doing so many drugs. So the name works on that level too."

"Except the eye of the hurricane is calm, and if he was all coked up he wasn't calm, so there's a contradiction," someone pointed out.

"Not to change the subject, but you know what's great about Reynosa and Matamoros now?" another student said. "The drivers are a lot more polite. After you, sir. No, no, please, after you. And less honking. You don't want to honk at the wrong guy."

"Yeah, but it's creepy the way the taxi drivers call on their cell phones when you cross the bridge, reporting to the *mañosos*. '*Fresa* chick with mom, black Escalade, Texas plates, Hidalgo County issue.'"

"How do they know she's your mom?"

"And you drive a *black Escalade* over there? That's what the *maña* drive. No wonder they follow you."

"Actually, we don't go over there any more. I'm just saying."

"Those guys calling stuff in, they call them *halcones*. What's it in English?"

"Falcons."

"Falcons, right. Those are the spies. *Narcoespías*. They're everywhere."

A student challenges the others to come up with as many compound words with the prefix "narco" as they can think of. Narcoterrorism. *Narcoataque*. *Narcocorridos*. *Narcobloqueos* (roadblocks thrown up by narcos). *Narcomenudeo* (dealing in small quantities of drugs). *Narconovelas* (soap operas about narcos). *Narcosatánicos* (devil-worshipping narcos). *Narcomantas* (banners hung by narcos in public places, to urge soldiers and police to join their prosperous ranks, to warn other gangs to stay out of their way, to ask the public to stay inside on a given day because of a planned battle, etc.). *Narcomensajes* (messages directed at enemies, hung on or near dead bodies).

"I think the *narcomensajes* are funny," says the middle-school teacher. "I mean, sort of. Sometimes." She brings an example to the next class. It's a photograph of a sign on the side of a *tambo* wherein a body is stuffed. The *tambos* (there are three in the picture) are lined up on a sidewalk where street food is sold (lettering on the fence behind advertises *aguas frescas*). The sign on the tambo reads, "This is what's going to happen to The Engineer and all of those with him. We're going to make *posole* out of them." (*Posole* is a dish made of hominy and pork.)

"Okay, they don't know how to spell," she concedes. (The sign reads "*Los bamos aser posole*" instead of "*Los vamos a hacer posole*.") "But the main thing is that they're *writing*. Isn't that what you say to do, Professor? *Just write*."

The exceptional social situation in Mexico fed the imagination of one undergraduate student who, after coming to my office to announce that he had renounced Christ and was now

"OK with the Devil," wondered if I'd like to travel with him around Tamaulipas so we could witness the works of his new-found deity and visit shrines to La Santa Muerte and Jesús Malverde. "We'll be fine, sir," he said, his eyes shining too brightly. "The Devil and me, we're OK now." I was about to report him to the Dean of Students, something we're strongly encouraged to after the massacre at Virginia Tech perpetrated by a disturbed creative-writing student, when I came across his girlfriend, who told me, stricken, that his parents had taken him to a mental hospital and notified the university. This was not the first student I'd observed descend into what is known by the catch-all term "schizophrenia," which commonly strikes in late adolescence and early adulthood, but he was the first to correlate his madness with the insanity taking place in Mexico.

The student was correct in claiming that shrines to La Santa Muerte and Jesús Malverde, which the Catholic Church has condemned as devil-worshipping, have popped up in many Mexican border states, and that altars for these figures have been often erected at sites of drug busts. (Sometimes the Mexican military destroys the shrines after a bust, even though many soldiers believe it's bad luck to do so.) A rogue church known as the *Iglesia Católica Tradicional Mexico-Estados Unidos* plans to build a multi-million dollar temple in Mexico City to the Señora Blanca, as La Santa Muerte is also known. On the U.S. side of the border, sales of candles and other items dedicated to her are brisk. In Mexico City, thousands in the poor barrio of Tepito attend a rosary for her, with marijuana smoke instead of incense used as purifying smoke. Like the folk saint Jesús Malverde (malverde translates as "badgreen"), a Robin Hood figure and a favorite of outlaws and those living on the edge of the law, she is an "angel of the poor." She is also the unofficial Virgin of the Incarcerated.

In thinking about poverty and criminality in Mexico, and criminality as rebellion against poverty, I go back to a class I taught some years ago on the literature of Central America. In studying the revolutions and civil wars of the eighties in that part of the world, we came across a quote from a high official in the Reagan administration regarding the leftist guerrillas: "If we can't beat them, we can at least reduce them to banditry." That's precisely what happened. After pouring millions into the coffers of right-wing military regimes and their death squads, the U.S. broke the backs of the guerrilla armies in El Salvador, Guatemala and Honduras. Now impoverished young men don't join, say, the Guerrilla Army of the Poor, but become Mara Salvatrucha gangsters or runners for the Zetas in those countries. Those countries remain oligarchies with an astounding gap between rich and poor, with the added bonus of enjoying some of the world's highest violent crime rates— Honduras has the highest murder rate in the world.

I go back to what the woman in Jasmín's hair salon said about the narcos ("I wish a guerrilla army would rise up and kill all the mafiosos.") Certainly there is nothing like a good revolution to squelch crime. The Cuban revolution cleaned out the mafia in that country once and for all, and I personally remember how safe Managua was in the aftermath of the Sandinista revolution. She'd better hope such an army doesn't get sucked in to the "situation" and become what the guerrillas of the *Fuerzas Armadas Revolucionarias Colombianas* have become (and here we come to the last word in today's lesson, *chicos*): *narcoguerrillas.*

A WORLD BETWEEN TWO WORLDS

Sergio Troncoso

One conceit of the living, and perhaps the young, is to believe that what will be is progress, and what was is only the past, best left behind. What if, in your lifetime, you witness a culture and a way of life that has been lost? What if you are the self-critical sort, so that you assure yourself that nostalgia has little to do with this remembrance of what has been lost? What if you know this past was *better* than the current state of affairs? Moreover, what if your cultural memory of the border matters only to those who were and are open-minded enough to care about living in a unique bicultural, bi-national existence? Your loss could be forgotten in the United States of Amnesiacs, and the current, murderous state of affairs could easily become the norm. How many in the self-obsessed capitals of Washington, D.C. and Mexico, D.F. have understood or appreciated the border as you do?

Yes, I grew up in El Paso and Juárez. My house on San Lorenzo Avenue in the neighborhood of Ysleta was less than a mile from the Zaragoza International Bridge. After my parents had met in a plaza in the fifties, and they had been married at the downtown cathedral in Juárez, they had crossed the border for better opportunities. My mother insisted on living in the United States with her parents—Don José and Doña Dolores Rivero, my *abuelitos*—and my father did not want to lose my mother, and they were young and in love . . . the reasons for their border crossing were endless and intertwined. In an adobe house they built together, with kerosene lamps for the dark desert nights and a spooky outhouse in the backyard, the life they began in Ysleta was never far from Juárez. Here was the start of my life as a young *mocoso* who 'blossomed' into a teenager, too hotheaded and stubborn to avoid feuds with teachers and principals. We crisscrossed the border every week to visit *familia* in Mexico, we lugged groceries from Waterfil (the hamlet in Mexico just across the bridge from Ysleta), we attended weddings and funerals on both sides, we ate Sunday dinners at my parents' favorite Mexican restaurants—all of that life was lost when Juárez descended into the bloody chaos of today. Instead of a border of bridges, it has become a border of walls.

Instead of the promise and confusion and intrigue of a foreign and not-so-foreign country within arm's reach, the 'other side' was transformed into a no-man's land of two dozen murders on many weekends, Mexican soldiers patrolling the streets with submachine guns, decapitations, mass graves and entire neighborhoods and businesses abandoned. For too many in El Paso, the border ceased to be an opportunity or an adventure, and metamorphosed into a fearful liability. Yes, the border as a world between two worlds, this breathing living entity has been lost. Perhaps, in understanding and appreciating what we have lost, we can also steel ourselves for the fight for a 'progress' that hearkens back to this better past.

In Ysleta, my father always missed Mexico more than my mother, even though both were *mexicanos*, both preferred Spanish to English, and both had *familia* in Chihuahua. My mother adopted the United States enthusiastically, from voting at the elementary school at Mount Carmel on every Election Day, to exercising with 'la Denise Austin,' to avidly reading *The El Paso Times* for news and politics. But my father often reminisced about what he had left behind. He recounted his university days at La Escuela Superior de Agricultura Hermanos Escobar, where he studied agronomy, and rhapsodically told the story about meeting his future bride at El Monumento a Benito Juárez, near Avenida Vicente Guerrero and Constitucíon.

On this plaza in the mid-fifties, teenage boys were arrayed in stiff white shirts rolled up to the elbow and cuffed khaki pants with razor-sharp creases, their polished shoes brilliant if worn. They strolled purposely in one direction, while teenage girls in wavy, ankle-length cotton dresses, white socks, and black pumps strolled in the other, a wheel within a wheel around whitewashed cottonwoods and green wooden benches. From car radios wafted the sounds of Pérez Prado's "Cerezo Rosa" and Los Panchos's "Bésame Mucho," alongside Elvis Presley's "I Want You, I Need You, I Love You" and Frankie Lymon and the Teenagers' "Why Do Fools Fall in Love?" My mother was a saleswoman at a Juárez department store, occasionally modeled clothes at local fashion shows, and (I kid you not) resembled Jane Russell. My father was a poor university student whose mother had died of a brain aneurysm when he had been ten years old.

In part to remember those days, but also to make Sunday a special family day, my parents often drove us to Juárez in our Ford pickup for an early dinner, to Ciros Taquería near the cathedral, or to Tortas Nico in front of El Mercado Juárez. I had no choice but to wear a buttoned shirt or at least a polo shirt, and was not allowed to wear what I loved on the dusty streets of Ysleta—my Led Zeppelin, Boston or Dallas Cowboys T-shirts. I had to ditch my white Converse sneakers under my bed, and polish my tight black shoes. I combed my thick, Donny-Osmond black hair, which my parents re-combed to their satisfaction, as they did with my brothers Rudy and Oscar. My sister, Diana, the oldest, was for the most part left alone since she enjoyed dressing up on Sundays, even as a teenager. Why this formality in Juárez? On these trips, we often visited relatives in Juárez. My godmother, Doña Romita, owned a *puesto*, or stall, at El Mercado Juárez, and on my birthday she gave me *trompos*, Cantinflas marionettes, and onyx and marble chess sets. But it was more than just these visits to the relatives before or after our Sunday dinners in Mexico that prompted my parents to get decked out, even though we were still a poor, but rising young Mexican family from Ysleta. My parents were proud *mexicanos*, and over there in Juárez, this pride mattered.

Why? As we strolled the stores near the Juárez cathedral, my sister losing herself in another colorful embroidered Mexican blouse with my mother by her side, I was especially surprised by how friendly my father would be. In El Paso, he wasn't exactly surly, but more taciturn. Yet on the other side, my father constantly ran into old friends from La Agricultura, or older brothers of younger classmates, or favorite teachers. I rolled my eyes whenever my mother waved and flashed her smile at girlfriends from her childhood, and beckoned me forward to shake their hands politely. In Juárez, my parents had been popular in a way they never were in Ysleta. In Juárez, also, my father would strike up casual conversations with street vendors and store salesmen in a way he rarely did in El Paso. I got the sense that he felt he belonged in Juárez: he knew the language and relished that his jokes and clever allusions would be perfectly understood. Of course, most everybody in our neighborhood in Ysleta also spoke Spanish, but my father's casual confidence all but disappeared on the American side of the border. Part of it was that many *mexicanos* in El Paso were not *mexicanos* anymore, but *americanos* trying to make that leap to becoming American. Their Spanish might be perfect, but the values they possessed were different from *los compadres* from Juárez, Delicias or Chihuahua City. "Everybody over here," my father must have repeated to me a thousand times in El Paso, "worries too much about money. It's all about money." Yet, he also worried about money, but after a certain point, he didn't. To worry too much about money was a sickness, he thought. In his own way, Rodolfo Troncoso cared more deeply about *amistad, familia, tradición* and *respeto*. The English words friendship, family, tradition and respect would not possess the same meanings to him, nor to me. It was about belonging to a culture and a place, belonging in your bones, belonging in a way that was left unsaid, in a way that was understood between people without uttering a word.

At Los Hermanos Mesa, a barbershop on Avenida Vicente Guererro near Calle Uruguay, where my father had his hair cut for forty years, this milieu and this culture that was so important to him, and to me, flourished. I must have gotten my hair cut at Los Hermanos Mesa for about a decade throughout grade school. The barbershop was managed by three brothers, Nati (short for Natividad), who was the real boss; Enrique the unrelenting punster; and Eduardo the quiet one, who had difficulty speaking. (I myself had stuttered in early grade school.) Nati had inherited the barbershop from his father, and so Los Hermanos Mesa had been a family business for two generations. My brothers Rudy, Oscar and I would join my father as we drove from downtown El Paso to Juárez across one of the international bridges. At Los Hermanos Mesa, Nati greeted the children with a solemn handshake and a wink. He was tall and thin, with a mustache, and usually wore a white apron or smock. At the entrance of the shop, in front of the wall-to-wall window, Nati's barbershop chair was a curvy contraption of chrome and white. The top of the chair was an adjustable, cushioned headrest for when his clients were tipped horizontally for a shave with a straight razor. At its base was a moveable footrest that never seemed to get dirty. A row of similar chairs followed in a line in front of wall-to-wall mirrors, one brother behind each chair. The last two or three chairs were often empty, or were occupied by a client of Nati's older sons, or by one of Enrique's buddies arguing or laughing. In my mind, the pecking order was always clear. When he spotted my father, Enrique, short and fat, would announce with a happy growl, "*¡Troncoso! ¿Cómo estás, hombre?*" It took me aback how my father was not an imposing authority figure in this barbershop, but a buddy from the old days, still everybody's shy kid brother.

The windows of Los Hermanos Mesa overlooked the traffic and passersby on Vicente Guerrero, and the sunlight streamed into the storefront. As I waited my turn for Nati, the bustle, camaraderie, and the light always transformed this place. Years later I would think of Ernest Hemingway's short short story, "A Clean, Well-Lighted Place." Both were places with rituals that created a space to feel comfortable in a hectic world. As my father would say, it was a barbershop where people were like family, or as he would put it, "*de confianza,*" where you could be who you were, where they knew you, where you could relax and catch up on the news of the old neighborhood, where you could teach your children to be respectful and polite. I know my father thought Nati was an exemplar of the good man, in the way he treated every single person who walked into Los Hermanos Mesa. Nati greeted them by name, if he knew them, and conversed with them in this gentle but serious manner. Even if his brother Enrique guffawed at another joke, and Nati found it funny, I never saw the older brother lose his composure, in a fit of laughter, or in a fit of anger. Perhaps, by himself, Nati would have made the place too quiet, but you also wanted to hear what Nati had to say, because you knew that whatever he said he had thought about carefully, perhaps over many days or weeks, and what he said was invariably wise. There were people in this world who knew how to treat other people, who valued you. Even as a child, I got the sense that they were this way by how they talked to you. That's one of the reasons I always reminded my father, as we inched across the international bridge in our Ford pickup, that I wanted Nati, not Enrique, for my haircut. Rudy and Oscar did not care who cut their hair. But for me, it was Nati, or I would not go to Juárez at all.

The memories of places like Los Hermanos Mesa only beckon to what has been lost. Here are the stories of two 'cousins' from the Juárez of today, this nightmare of the past four years, the capital of violence, the city on the border that exemplifies how the breakdown of civil society has become the strange norm. These 'cousins' have visited my house, and we have visited theirs, scores of times. They are part of my family.

Pepe grew up in Juárez, and had graduated, like his sister, from the Instituto Technológico de Ciudad Juárez with an accounting degree. I had always known him as a *pelón* who was good at baseball, the son of a rancher's caretaker. Yet Pepe was also good at math, and had landed a coveted job in Juárez for a commercial enterprise that helped banks and individuals transfer money to different parts of Mexico and the United

States. His mother and father had been even poorer than my parents, but recently, to make matters worse, Pepe's father had died and his mother refused to leave her dilapidated house on the outskirts of Juárez. When I had visited them years ago as a child, I remember it felt like stepping back in time. Inside their home, the adobe was exposed, and the dirt would crumble into your hands if you rubbed your palms against the walls. Spiders crawled over the roof beams in the weak, yellowish light. The sharp, musty smell of kerosene permeated their kitchen. I never told Pepe this, but I sometimes imagined his mother was a witch. Not because she was mean or ugly or capable of magic, but because when Jovita leaned heavily over her ramshackle stove in the semi-darkness, the flickering light of the fire and kerosene lamps cast her silhouette into an eerie dance on the walls. Whenever she handed me steamy *atole* to drink, I closed my eyes and imagined I would open them as a frog or a horse or a plump chicken. I was always mildly disappointed when I opened my eyes and I was still the quiet boy I had always been.

As an adult, my cousin Pepe was ambitious. Not only did he work at his accounting job in Juárez, but he also started a fast-food chicken restaurant in El Paso. Pepe also possessed a coveted Green Card, and could work legally in the United States. He wanted to better himself; he struggled to pull himself up from the poorest of the poor, just as I had desperately fought in the strange world of the Ivy League. Pepe wanted to help his family survive, and thrive, on the border. So Pepe was overworked, but he was doing just fine, juggling a life between two jobs in a commute back and forth across the international boundaries. After his father died, Pepe vowed to help his mother. Her shack next to a ranch, which is how I would describe it, was near the Central Camionera southeast of the city center, on the edge of the edge of the world.

One night in 2009, Pepe returned to visit his mother and give her money and groceries for the week. As he left his mother's house in the darkness, Pepe was attacked by a gang of four men. They beat him, and stole his money and his truck. After he regained consciousness—had they walked away out of boredom? had being knocked out saved Pepe's life?—he staggered back into his mother's house. That had not been his first taste of violence, but that incident had been the worst in the neighborhood he had grown up as a child. Pepe knew friends who had been carjacked, and a good friend whose father had been kidnapped, but nothing that serious had ever happened to him. Was the attack on Pepe related to the drug wars? Or was it simply the latest coda in a milieu where casual and brutal violence was becoming the norm? Before the year was out, Pepe would leave his business in El Paso, and give notice at his accounting job in Juárez. He abandoned the border for Monterrey, but was that a better choice? His sister and her husband also left for Puebla to escape the increasing violence in Juárez. They begged their mother to join them, but Jovita refused, preferring to hide in her imagined anonymity with the hope that the *narcos* would see no reason to bother a poor old woman. Yet for her children, the violence had hit too close to home.

Another cousin, I'll call him Chavita, also lived in Juárez, while his mother and sister lived in Guadalajara. I had known Chavita's mother as a teenager in Ysleta. Two years ago, at the Guadalajara Book Festival, La Feria Internacional del Libro, I would marvel at how 'Doña Luli' had metamorphosed into the owner and manager of a specialty tortilla factory that produced succulent, innovative creations for high-end restaurants and special events.

Chavita, however, returned to the border his mother had left behind. A U.S. citizen who had grown up in Guadalajara,

Chavita had studied architecture and landed a job in El Paso with a construction company, designing everything from shopping malls to office towers to military housing. In his 20s, Chavita lived in Juárez, worked in El Paso and loved music and dancing. As he attended fiestas in Juárez and a few scattered concerts, he noticed how rich the Juárez culture and night scene were, yet also how infrequent and badly organized were the events when he compared them to those in Guadalajara. At the Feria Internacíonal del Libro, Chavita had often visited the hundreds of booths and exhibits, and loved other mega-cultural events that attracted thousands to discuss and debate everything from books to movies, and provide venues for dancing and cafés for mingling. "There was nothing like that in Juárez, not regularly, and I didn't see any reason why we couldn't have it here, too. This city was teeming with young people who love music, who read, who want to meet each other, who love to dance. I wanted to do something about it."

Chavita began to organize fiestas in Juárez. He contracted rock bands from both sides of the border, and soon purchased a Juárez bar that featured live music. Every weekend his multi-level bar organized three or four events that attracted up to 800 people. An opportunity then arose when a bigger place came up for sale, and Chavita and his wife expanded. This place, I'll call it Café Miro, had somewhat of a sentimental meaning for them: it was where they had met one night, and the rest, as they say, was history.

Just like his mother, Chavita, the young entrepreneur, was making it happen. He was also living in between two worlds, two cultures. He arrived at his job as an architect in El Paso at 6:30 a.m., worked until 4 p.m., then drove across an international bridge to Juárez to manage Café Miro with his wife until 10 p.m. Then he would do it again the next day. "The lines at the bridges started getting longer after 9/11, so I had to purchase two trucks. I'd drive to a parking lot near the Juárez side of the bridge, park my truck and hop on my bike. I'd bike across the bridge, flash my passport, and bike into El Paso to another parking lot on the American side, throw my bike into the back of the truck, and drive to work. My life was divided in two, between El Paso and Juárez. So many people were doing exactly the same thing, day in and day out. You got to know them. I also knew most of the federal guys at the bridge, by first name, and they knew me too. It was crazy, but it worked."

Chavita imagined bigger and better things, and he had a knack with people and for convincing them to support his dreams. He had gained experience organizing events at his first bar. Café Miro was an even bigger success, although he was overworked and literally on the move all the time. He remembered the Guadalajara mega-events that had originally prompted him to organize his first dance party years ago, and he expanded again. First at Carta Blanca Park and then at the Hipodromo Park in Juárez, he and a partner organized a music festival that attracted such bands as Los Bunkers, Utopia, Molotov, Los Amigos Invisibles, Sr. Bikini, Plastilina Mosh, División Minuscula, Quiero Club and Kinky. The first year, 2,500 people attended their arts festival. Chavita and his partner published a music magazine and a website to promote their festival, to feature their bands and to allow fans to submit favorite photos and clips. Chavita was an avid user of Facebook and understood the power of social media. The second year, 4,500 young people showed up, and not only was their festival filled with great live music, but also art exhibits, high-end coffee and great beer. "You wouldn't imagine how much time we spent selecting the right coffee. We wanted things to be high-class, high-end. Everything had to be just right. We wanted young people to have fun, to come together, for music, for dancing, for the arts. People began waiting for our festivals to happen." The third year, 7,500 people danced the night away at another of Chavita's events. No obstacle was too big to stop him for too long. Bad luck would not get in his way. One day, he jumped in his Ford Explorer to buy medicines at a pharmacy, suddenly a car with tinted windows blocked his way at an intersection, and several men in masks jumped out and pointed 9mm guns at his head. One simply said: "*Nomás dame la llave y vete*. Just give me the key and go now." Chavita walked away from his truck, and survived. He loved Juárez. Although the incident spooked him, he never thought of leaving the city. In 2009, on the fourth anniversary of their festival, the drug-war violence broadened and deepened, but still 5,000 people "demanded rock music" for a few nights in Juárez.

A few phone calls portended the beginning of the end. Strangers asked to talk to the owners of the music festival, and when they got Chavita on the phone they demanded a percentage of the profits for "security services." These strangers were clueless as to how much money the festival made each year, they did not know or care who Chavita was, and they laughed when he protested about his years of work and sacrifice to get to this point. For a few days, Chavita ignored these calls. One day, as he sat drinking coffee at Café Miro, an older man wearing a cheap dark suit approached the manager, talked to him in low and insistent growls and brazenly began to inspect the place. Chavita had never seen this man in his life. The older man handed the manager a letter and told him to deliver it to the owner. To his great credit, the manager did not point to Chavita and say, "He's right there. The guy with the laptop." The letter went into details about the offer of "security services," and what would happen to the owners if they did not comply. It was nasty stuff.

Chavita called the phone number in the letter, and this was more or less what they said: "We know where you live. We know where you bank. We know what cars you drive. We know about the bar and we know about the festivals. This is what your payment will be every week. If you don't have a liquor license, or if you need a permit for anything, or if you have problems with inspectors, we'll get you the licenses and the permits, we'll solve those problems with inspectors. We are the government now. We'll provide you with drugs to sell at your events. This is how much you will sell." As Chavita said, it was very businesslike in a certain way, and in another way it was very graphic about what would happen to him and his family, and his partner and his partner's family, if they did not comply.

Two days after that call, Chavita closed down Café Miro, dismissed all his employees, and ripped the place apart for anything valuable he could take with him or store in a warehouse. In those same two days, he packed everything he could from his home, and abandoned Juárez for El Paso. "It's not about you anymore. It's about your family. I have two kids, four and eight years old. I had to leave. In a way, I walked away just in time. Before anything horrible happened to me. I don't hate Juárez. On the contrary. But if anything worse had happened to me, if anything had happened to my family, I would probably think differently. I just believe Juárez has so much potential and I would like to go back. I still go back two or three times a month, to talk to my ex-employees, for my birthday party, but perhaps I shouldn't do that anymore. People don't understand that unlike Tijuana or some of these other border cities, El Paso and Juárez are a community intertwined, one city, not two, more so than any other place along the border."

Recently I was talking to a friend about my history with Juárez. This friend is a *mexicano* who has written some gritty, brilliant reportage on the drug violence for years. His work helps you to understand the Machiavellian politics among and between the cartels and the government that are revealed by gruesome, yet targeted slaughter, cryptic communiqués and assaults on entire towns. I mentioned to him a fact few know: my grandfather, Santiago Troncoso, has an avenue named after him in Juárez. On a bronze statue of a paperboy in front of a building that has long been newspaper offices—El Papelero, a monument to the freedom of expression in Mexico—my grandfather's name is one of three on a plaque at the base of the statue. Santiago Troncoso was editor and publisher of *El Día*, one of the first dailies in Juárez in the late twenties. He was arrested dozens of times and his print shop mysteriously burned to the ground thrice, each time after he penned another critical article against government corruption or the powers-that-be. In life, the political puppet masters hated his guts, but after he retired, they erected a statue in his honor. That's Mexico. Eventually Santiago Troncoso became a naturalized American citizen. In the fifties, on this side of the border, the McCarthyites also pursued him, grilling him at the U.S. federal courthouse for once being head of the Mexican printers' union and a potential communist! I knew him in high school as the cranky *abuelo* who warned me against a career in journalism: "It is too hard a life and if you tell the truth they will hate you forever."

After I told him the story about my grandfather, my writer friend stared at me and solemnly said, "You know what they did to that statue not long ago?" In hushed tones, he described a scene, but left many details out, which unnerved me. I swallowed hard as his few words permeated my mind, and I imagined the images my friend had left unsaid to spare me. A hazy morning. The light revealing something next to, or draped over, El Papelero. Only up close would the images become clear: a human being had been disemboweled and beheaded. A horrifying mix of meat and metal. A warning to all journalists. Don't fuck with the *narcos*. To hell with the freedom of expression. What power does an inert statue have against such brutality? What power do reminiscences of Los Hermanos Mesa— and what Juárez used to be—have against submachine guns? What power resides in the small ambitions for a better life of someone like Pepe, or in the dreams of a city with music and arts of Chavita? How can even these words counteract decapitations, dismemberments, and the dollars, billions and billions of dollars, which reward the most brutal for servicing the United States and its drug habits? If you pitted an individual with great ideas against another one with a machete—a cage match featuring a philosopher against a foot soldier, so to speak—I would think the latter would always have the upper hand. Yet, it must be possible to overcome this brutality when we face it in our communities, otherwise killers without a conscience would always win, and every city, not only in Mexico but also across the globe, would become another Juárez.

I think the answer is that people don't want to live in a society where violence is normal. People cannot achieve what they want, they cannot strive for what most fulfills them, in the kind of city Juárez has become. They cannot raise their children as they want, and they cannot dream of crossing to the other side for a better life, and they cannot live in peace even if they are poor. On this side, we cannot anymore imagine Juárez as an adventure or a possibility, as the place to shop for groceries, or as a destination where our children could open their minds to discover another way of life and culture. The Juárez/El Paso metropolis before the drug violence erupted on Avenida Santiago Troncoso, and all the other streets and byways on the other side, was anything but ideal. Too often the citizens of each city used each other. El Paso, richer than its twin to the south, took advantage of the cheap labor on the other side, what once were cheap groceries, gas, and medicines. I also remember how cheaply you could get away with behavior in J-town that would be illegal in the United States. So the Juárez/El Paso area before the recent drug violence was not a bilingual, bi-national, bicultural Zion, but it was one world. One entity. One place. One city where you could live in between worlds, and have the hope of creating something new. A third way to be, not along the border, but *on the border*.

That is what the violence has destroyed, that unity, however tenuous it ever was. It has destroyed the idea of that unity and the reality of living so uniquely astride an international border. This 'real idea' was always a work-in-progress, and for the moment it is lost. Yet that real idea of unity had great value. It had value for my father who left his country of Mexico, for good reasons, for better opportunities for himself and his family, yet who did not feel the need to abandon 'everything Mexico,' and certainly not the love of family, a deep respect for hard work, nor the joys of a simple life. Before the violence, my father could live here, and he could return there, the best of both worlds. This real idea of unity also had value to those like Pepe and Chavita who literally lived in between El Paso and Juárez, making the most of their abilities and creativity. They learned to jump from one language to another, from one side of the international bridge to the other, and from one set of rules and conventions to another. Their ways of doing border business fostered adaptable, innovative individuals. The border opened up who they could be, and they were flourishing.

In this manner, I identify the most with my 'cousins' Pepe and Chavita, because this border mentality became ingrained in the deepest part of my cells. That is, not to believe in national myths or blustery pronouncements, but to judge the person in front of you. That is, not to rely on stereotypes or seldom spoken prohibitions, but to test the waters with engagement and to find out for yourself what would work and what would not. Living on the border, in between two worlds, I believe, made me somewhat of a skeptic of both sides, but also made me find my own way, through practice. That way of thinking and questioning frightens ideologues, nationalists, and anyone who prefers to follow orders and duties. I prefer to reach conclusions and judgments by testing the water myself. I became interested in philosophy, and Aristotle in particular, because I lived on the border. I wanted to probe and question where I was and who I was, rather than just accept what others said I should be. *Los cerrados*, 'the closed ones' as I call them, those who do not approach life in this practical manner, flourish in the hinterlands of both the United States and Mexico.

That power of returning to that work-in-progress that was one city between two nations will be one day what will stop that machete from its bloody work. Enough people on both sides of the border will tire of living in violence, which is just another form of authoritarianism, and will organize themselves to defeat the brutal who now have the upper hand. Perhaps the killers will kill so much, that what will be left of Ciudad Juárez will not be much of a 'city' at all, and so they will finish destroying the prize for which they so readily slaughtered thousands. In any case, it will be the power of returning to that unique border life and whatever messy possibilities it harbored that will stop the violence. It was a better life than what we have today, and we understand that fact mostly in retrospect, as we often do, when we lose what we value before we had a chance to appreciate what it meant.

GLOSSARY OF SPANISH WORDS

¿Cómo te fue?	How did it go?
¿Por qué?	Why?
¿Qué?	What?
abuelitos	grandparents
abuelo	grandfather
allá	over there
Allí estaré esperándolos.	I will be there waiting for you.
ambos Nogales	both Nogales
americanos	Americans
amistad	friendship
Antes no se vendían las casas.	Before, houses were not meant to be sold.
Aquí en esta casa es puro vivir.	Here in this house, living is a joy.
Arcángel	archangel
atole	thick corn flour drink
Avenida	avenue (typically used in a name like Avenida Juárez)
bacalao	dried cod dish
bájense	get down
balaceras	shoot-outs
balazo	shooting

bandido (pl. -s)	bandit (pl. -s)
barrio	neighborhood
Buenas tardes. Bienvenidos.	Good afternoon. Welcome.
caballeriza	enclosed premise to house horses
cabrito	young goat
cabrones	bastards
cajeta	Mexican sweet made of carmelized milk
carne asada	grilled beef steak
casacareando	musicians playing in public for money
Central Camionera	main bus station
ceviche	seafood dish with lime and lemon juice
chamoy raspas	shaved ice flavored with fruit and chile
chiquero	pigsty
chiquinarco	child narco
chismes	gossip
cholo (colloq.)	gang member
colitas de caballo	pony-tails
colonia	poor area or neighborhood
comidas	lunches
compadres, los	godparents or close friends
confianza	reliable; trust
conjunto	Music group or style with the bajo sexto and button accordion
corridistas	writers of ballads
corrido	ballad or narrative song
cucaracha	clunker; literally means "cockroach"
dando la vuelta	driving around
drogas	drugs

El Foca	"The Seal," nickname of serial killer
el otro lado	the other side of the border (the United States)
El Río de Tijuana	The Tijuana River
elote granizad	roasted corn in a cup
empeorando	getting worse
en la calle	on the street
encajuelado	placed in a car trunk
encintando	tied with tape
encobijado	wrapped in a blanket
entambado	stuffed in a drum
era puro vivir	living life fully
esas convivencias	those ways of living together
esto es lo más dulce	this is the sweetest part
familia	family
Federales	Federal Police
fresa (colloq.)	upper-class person
fronterizos	inhabitants of the borderlands
fulanita/fulanito	persons unknown or unnamed
gente del pueblo	simple folk
guisados	stews
guitarrón	large guitar
hacienda	estate
halcón (colloq.)	narco spy or lookout
InstitutoTecnológico de Juárez	Technological Institute of Juárez
Juarenses	people from Juárez
la placa (colloq.)	law enforcement
La Revu (colloq.)	Avenida Revolución
La tierra no se vende.	Land is not meant to be sold.
La vida seguía.	Life went on.
Las noticias no dicen nada.	The news say nothing.
leva	conscription

levantón (colloq.)	kidnapping
Lienzo charro Baca Gallardo	Mexican cowboy rodeo 'Baca Gallardo'
maíz	corn
maña, la maña (colloq.)	narco (group)
mañoso (colloq.)	narco (individual); tricky person
mapas	maps
maquiladora	border assembly plant
maracas	rattle gourds
marijuanos	potheads
mercado	market
mexicanos	Mexicans
mocoso (colloq.)	brat
mordida (colloq.)	bribe; literally means 'bite'
muertito (dimin.)	dead one
Nada pasaría.	Nothing would happen.
narco junior	young narcotrafficker
narcoataque	narco attack
narcobloqueo	narco roadblock
narcocorrido	narco ballad
narcofosagrave	dug by narcos
narcoguerrilla	guerrillas at the service of narcos
narcomanta (pl. -s)	banner hung by narcos
narcomensaje	message from narcos
narcomenudeo	dealing in small quantities of drugs
narconovelas	narco soap operas
narcos	narcotraffickers
narcosatánico	devil-worshipping narcos
No pasa nada.	Nothing's wrong; it's okay.
paletas	lollipops
palma	palm tree
Panamericana	Pan American Highway

paz en Nuevo Laredo	peace in Nuevo Laredo
pelón	baldy
perico (colloq.)	cocaine
plaza	turf
plazita	plaza
pocilga	pigsty
prima (pl. -s)	female cousin
puesto	stall
pulque	alcoholic drink from maguey plant
qué guapa te ves	you look very pretty
rancherita	popular rural Mexican musical style
ranchitos	mall ranch
rancho	ranch
ratón	mouse
respeto	respect
roba chicos	kidnappers of children
San Lorenzo	Saint Lawrence Catholic Church
secuestradero	place where kidnap victims are held
secuestrado	kidnap victim
sicario	hitman
siempre regresan	they always return
sin pena	without embarrassment
su rostro	his or her countenance
taco de suadero	beef brisket taco
tamarindos	tamarind candy
tambo	55-gallon drum
tecato (colloq.)	heroin fiend
ten (imperative)	here
terrible	terrible
tienes sueño	you're sleepy

tijuanense	native or inhabitant of Tijuana
tradición	tradition
traficantes	traffickers
traje	outfit
trío musical	group of three
trompos	tops
turistas	tourists
una de las más bonitas	one of the prettiest
vieja (colloq.)	woman
villancicos	Christmas music from Mexico
Zeta	Tijuana newspaper
Zetas, Los	paramilitary group of narcotraffickers

CONTRIBUTORS

Liliana V. Blum is the author of the short story collections *Yo sé cuando expira la leche* (Instituto Municipal del Arte y la Cultura de Durango, 2011), *The Curse of Eve and Other Stories* (Host Publications, 2008) translated by Toshiya Kamei, *El libro perdido de Heinrich Böll* (Editorial Jus, 2008), *Vidas de catálogo* (Fondo Editorial Tierra Adentro, 2007), *¿En qué se nos fue la mañana?* (Instituto Tamaulipeco para la Cultura y las Artes, 2007) and *La maldición de Eva* (Voces de Barlovento, 2002). Her stories have been translated into English and Polish and published in literary magazines in the United States, England and Poland. Her work had been included in several anthologies, namely *Atrapadas en la madre* (Alfaguara, 2006), *El espejo de Beatriz* (Ficticia Editorial, 2009) and *Óyeme con los ojos: 21 escritoras mexicanas revolucionarias* (Universidad Autónoma de Nuevo León, 2010). She lives in Tampico, Tamaulipas, and is currently working on a novel and a new short story collection.

Lolita Bosch was born in Barcelona in 1970, but has lived in Albons (Baix Empordà), the United States, India, and for ten years in Mexico City, Mexico, a country she now considers her home. She has an undergraduate degree in philosophy from the University of Barcelona and a graduate degree in creative writing from the Universidad Nacional Autónoma de México, where she also completed postgraduate work in letters. She has received numerous prizes, from children's literature to adult fiction: the Lletra d'Or, the Talento FNAC, the Omnium de literatura infantil, and the Jove Narrativa. The cinematic adaptation of her novel *Elisa Kiseljak* was honored with the Premio Especial del Jurado del Festival de Cine of San Sebastián 2011. Since 2006, she directs the Colectivo FU de Literatura, with which she organizes festivals, publishes literary essays and opens quality public libraries in Latin America.

Recently she has published *Això que veus és un rostre* (CCG Edicions, 2005/Sexto Piso, 2009), *Elisa Kiseljak*, (La Campana, 2005), *Tres historias europeas* (Caballo de Troya, Debolsillo, 2006/LaButxaca, 2010), *La persona que fuimos* (Mondadori, Empúries, 2006), an anthology of Mexican literature *Hecho en México* (Mondadori, 2007), *Insólita ilusión, insólita certeza* (Mondadori, Empúries, 2007), *Una: la historia de Piiter y Py* (Almadía, 2008), *La familia de mi padre* (Mondadori, Empúries, 2008), *Japón escrito* (autoedición, Barcelona, 2009), an anthology of contemporary Catalán literature *Voces de la literatura catalana* (Empúries/Anagrama, 2010) and an anthology of literature for peace in Mexico, *Nuestra Aparente Rendición* (Grijalbo, 2011).

María Cristina Cigarroa is a native of San Antonio, Texas. She graduated from Harvard College in 2009 with a B.A. in Romance Languages and Literatures, specializing in Latin American Studies. She is currently a graduate student at the University of Texas School of Law obtaining a dual degree in Law and Latin American Studies. She has been published in the *Austin American-Statesman*.

Sarah Cortez is the author of an acclaimed poetry collection, *How to Undress a Cop*, and winner of the PEN Texas literary award in poetry. She has edited *Urban Speak: Poetry of the City* and *Windows into My World: Latino Youth Write Their Lives*, winner of the 2008 Skipping Stones Honor Award. She has also edited *Hit List: The Best of Latino Mystery* and *Indian Country Noir* (Akashic Books). In May 2011, her latest anthology entitled *You Don't Have a Clue: Latino Mystery Stories for Teens* was released by Arte Público Press. *Kirkus Reviews* has hailed the anthology as "a consistent, well crafted collection," while the starred review in *Booklist* says the book "presents stories that are notable both for their authenticity and for their language."

In 2012, Cortez was inducted into the Texas Institute for Letters. Her memoir, *Walking Home. Growing Up Hispanic in Houston*, was recently published by Texas Review Press.

Her work has appeared in *The Sun, Rattle: Poetry for the 21st Century, The Houston Chronicle, the Dallas Morning News, The Texas Review, New Texas, Louisiana Review, Blue Rock Review, Pennsylvania English, The Midwest Quarterly* and many other publications. Her work is widely anthologized in collections by Penguin, the Great Books Foundation and other international publishers.

Since 1976, **Celestino Fernández** has served as Professor of Sociology at the University of Arizona where he also has served in several administrative positions, including as the University's first Vice President for Undergraduate Education, Vice President for Academic Outreach and International Affairs and as the founding Executive Vice President and Provost of Arizona International College. Currently, Professor Fernández serves as a University-wide Faculty Fellow, and as Director of Undergraduate Studies in the Department of Sociology. He teaches courses and conducts research on various topics and issues pertaining to culture (including Mexican music and *corridos*), immigration, ethnic diversity and education. Dr. Fernández has published approximately 45 articles and book chapters on these topics. Professor Fernández received both the M.A. and Ph.D. in sociology from Stanford University. During 2000-2001, he served as an American Council on Education (ACE) Fellow at the University of Phoenix. Dr. Fernández has received wide recognition for his work. He was honored by the American Association for Higher Education for his "Distinguished Leadership in Higher Education" and by the Governor of Arizona for his commitment to "quality and excellence." He also received the "Distinguished Alumni Award" from his undergraduate alma mater, Sonoma State University. In 2007, Dr. Fernández was named University Distinguished Outreach Professor in recognition of his "exceptional service to the community, state and nation" (only one of five professors at the University of Arizona with this title).

Jessie K. Finch is a Ph.D. Candidate in Sociology at the University of Arizona. She specializes in immigration and race as well as culture, specifically popular culture and media. She has published on undocumented immigrants and Latino culture. She has an M.A. in Sociology from the University of Arizona (2011) and a B.A. in Sociology and Music from the University of Tulsa (2007). She is the recipient of a National Science Foundation Graduate Research Fellowship.

Rolando Hinojosa-Smith, the Ellen Clayton Garwood Professor of Creative Writing at the University of Texas at Austin, is the author of the Klail City Death Trip Series. He is the recipient of numerous literary awards, including the most prestigious prize in Latin American fiction, Casa de las Américas, for the best Spanish American novel in 1976. His novels include *Ask a Policeman: A Rafe Buenrostro Mystery* (1998), *The Useless Servants* (1993), *Becky and Her Friends* (1989) and *Dear Rafe / Mi querido Rafa* (2005), all published by Arte Público Press.

Nicolás Kanellos is the Brown Foundation Professor of Hispanic Literature at the University of Houston. He is founding publisher of the nation's oldest and most-esteemed Hispanic publishing house, Arte Público Press. Arte Público Press is the largest non-profit publisher of literature in the United States. His monograph, *A History of Hispanic Theater in the United States: Origins to 1940* (UT Press, 1990), received three book awards, including that of the Southwest Council on Latin American Studies. He is the author of various other award-winning books on Hispanic cultural history, including *Hispanic Literature of the United States: A Comprehensive Reference* (2005), which was named an Outstanding Academic Book by *Choice; The Encyclopedia of Latino Literature* (2009) and *Thirty Million Strong: Reclaiming the Hispanic Image in American History* (1998). Dr. Kanellos is the director of a major national research program, Recovering the U.S. Hispanic Literary Heritage of the United States, whose objective is to identify, preserve, study and make accessible tens of thousands of literary documents of those regions that have become the United States from the colonial period to 1960.

Richard Mora is an Assistant Professor of Sociology and is affiliated with the Latino/a and Latin American Studies program at Occidental College. He graduated *magna cum laude* in Sociology from Harvard College, and received a Master's in Education from the University of Michigan's School of Education and a Ph.D. in Sociology and Social Policy from Harvard University. Dr. Mora is a recipient of the Paul and Daisy Soros Fellowship for New Americans. His current academic interests include the youth cultures, education, gender, and juvenile justice. He has published in the journals, *Berkeley La Raza Law Journal*, *Journal of Inquiry and Action in Education*, and *Perspectives on Urban Education*, *ReVista: Harvard Review of Latin America*, and in the edited volumes, *The Phenomenon of Obama and the Agenda for Education: Can Hope Audaciously Trump Neoliberalism?* (Information Age Publishing, 2011), *Encyclopedia of School Crime and Violence* (Greenwood Press, 2011), *Latina / Chicana Mothering* (Demeter Press, 2011) and *Great Lives from History: Latinos* (Salem Press, 2012). In addition, his fiction is included in *Latinos in Lotus Land: An Anthology of Contemporary Southern California Literature* (Bilingual Press, 2008), under the *nom de plume* Victorio Barragán.

Diego Osorno is a journalist and writer. He is the author of five books, *Oaxaca sitiada: La primera insurrección del siglo XXI* (Grijalbo Mondadori, 2007), *El Cártel de Sinaloa: Una historia del uso político del narco* (Editorial Diana, 2009), *Nosotros somos los culpables: La tragedia de la Guardería ABC* (Grijalbo Mondadori, 2010), *País de muertos: Crónicas contra la impunidad* (Debate, 2011) and *Un vaquero cruza la frontera en silencio* (Conapred, 2011). Moreover, his work has been included in anthologies of narrative journalism in Spain, Argentina, Colombia, Cuba and the United States.

His book *El Cártel de Sinaloa* was chosen by the newspaper *Reforma* as one of the best books from Mexico in 2009. His book *Nosotros somos los culpables* was adapted for theater and performed in 2011. The magazine *Chilango* chose him as one of the eight most promising writers from Mexico in 2010 in an edition edited by Álvaro Enrigue.

In Mexico, he has covered the principal armed conflicts of the recent decade, and outside the country he has reported on conflicts in Lebanon, Syria, Bolivia, Venezuela, Cuba, the Basque region in Spain, Haiti, Honduras and Argentina.

Paul Pedroza was born and raised in El Paso, Texas. In 2010, he received his MFA in Fiction from the University of Illinois at Urbana-Champaign, where he taught narrative writing and served as a Fiction Editor for the literary magazine, *Ninth Letter*. His work has appeared in *Rattle*, *PALABRA*, *BorderSenses*, *Confluencia* and in the anthology *New Border Writing: A Still Life in Words*.

José Antonio Rodríguez is the author of the poetry collections *The Shallow End of Sleep* (Tia Chucha Press/Northwestern University Press, 2011), winner of the Bob Bush Memorial Award for Best First Book of Poetry from the Texas Institute of Letters, and *Backlit Hour*, winner of the Stephen F. Austin State University Press Poetry Award (forthcoming 2012). A former editor of the national literary journal *Harpur Palate*, he has also received the Allen Ginsberg Poetry Award and three nominations for the Pushcart Prize. Recent work has appeared or is forthcoming in *POETRY*, *The New Republic*, *New York Quarterly*, *Green Mountains Review*, *Water-Stone Review*, *Upstreet*, *Platte Valley Review* and elsewhere. He has taught writing at The University of Texas-Pan American and at SUNY-Binghamton University, where he earned a Ph.D. in English and Creative Writing.

José Skinner is author of *Flight and Other Stories* (University of Nevada, 2001), which was a Barnes & Noble Discover selection and a finalist for the Western States Book Award for Fiction. His work has been published in *Colorado Review, Bilingual Review, Witness, Other Voices, Puerto del Sol, Third Coast* and many other literary magazines. A graduate of the Iowa Writers' Workshop, he has taught at the University of Texas-Pan American on the Texas-Tamaulipas border for the last ten years, where he is an associate professor of English and director of the MFA Program in Creative Writing.

María Socorro Tabuenca Córdoba has a Ph.D. in Hispanic Literature from the State University of New York at Stony Brook. She was a researcher at El Colegio de la Frontera Norte, where she was also the director of the Juárez office and the Dean for the North West Region. At present, she is the chair of the Department of Languages and Linguistics at the University of Texas at El Paso. She is the author, co-author and co-editor of various books, including *Mujeres y fronteras. Una perspectiva de género* (Instituto Chihuahuense de la Cultura: Fondo Estatal para la Cultura y las Artes, 1998), *Border Women Writing from la Frontera*, with co-editor Debra A. Castillo, (University of Minnesota Press, 2002) and *Bordeando la violencia contra las mujeres en la frontera Norte de México*, with co-editor Julia Monárrez (El Colegio de la Frontera Norte, 2007). She has published articles on northern Mexico's border literature, Chicana/o literature and Juárez's femicide representations in film and media.

Sergio Troncoso is the author of *From This Wicked Patch of Dust* (University of Arizona Press, 2011). In a starred review, *Kirkus Reviews* said, "Troncoso is clearly adept at his craft, telling a story filled with rich language and the realities of family life. . . . With its skillful pairing of conflict over religious and familial obligations with the backdrop of a Mexican-

American family's love for one another, Troncoso's novel is an engaging literary achievement." *Southwest Books of the Year* chose the novel as a Notable Book. Troncoso also wrote *Crossing Borders: Personal Essays* (Arte Público Press, 2011), selected for the Bronze Award for Essays in *ForeWord Review's* Book of the Year Awards and praised by *The El Paso Times* as "engrossing and revealing." His novel, *The Nature of Truth* (Northwestern University Press, 2003) is a story about a Yale research student who discovers that his boss, a renowned professor, hides a Nazi past. Troncoso's first book *The Last Tortilla and Other Stories* (University of Arizona Press, 1999) won the Premio Aztlán for the best book by a new Mexican-American writer and the Southwest Book Award from the Border Regional Library Association. His stories and essays have been widely anthologized, most recently in *Nuestra Aparente Rendición* (Grijalbo, 2011) and *You Don't Have a Clue: Latino Mystery Stories for Teens* (Arte Público Press, 2011).

Troncoso was born in El Paso, Texas and now lives in New York City. After graduating from Harvard College, he was a Fulbright Scholar to Mexico and studied international relations and philosophy at Yale University. In 2012, he was inducted into the Texas Institute of Letters.

ABOUT THE EDITORS

SARAH CORTEZ is a poet, educator, and law enforcement officer. She is the author of a memoir, *Walking Home: Growing Up Hispanic in Houston* (Texas Review Press, 2010), and a poetry collection, *How to Undress a Cop* (Arte Publico Press, 2000), which won the PEN Texas Literary Award in Poetry. She is the editor of *Windows into My World: Latino Youth Write Their Lives* (Pinata Books, 2007), winner of a 2008 Skipping Stones Honor Award; *Hit List: The Best of Latino Mystery* (Arte Público Press, 2009); *You Don't Have a Clue: Latino Mystery Stories for Teens* (Piñata Books, 2011) and *Indian Country Noir* (Akashic Books, 2010). She lives and works in Houston, Texas.

SERGIO TRONCOSO is the author of *Crossing Borders: Personal Essays* (Arte Público Press, 2011), *From this Wicked Patch of Dust* (University of Arizona Press, 2011), *The Nature of Truth* (Northwestern University Press, 2003) and *The Last Tortilla and Other Stories* (University of Arizona Press, 1999), which won the Premio Aztlán and the Southwest Book Award. He received his undergraduate degree from Harvard College and two graduate degrees, in international relations and philosophy, from Yale University. He won a Fulbright scholarship to Mexico and was inducted into the Hispanic Scholarship Fund's Alumni Hall of Fame. A resident faculty member of the Yale Writers' Conference, he lives and works in New York City.